D0065474

THE PAGEANT OF JAPANESE HISTORY

THE PAGEANT OF
JAPANESE
HISTORY

BY

MARION MAY DILTS

*Illustrated by photogravures from Japanese Art
and Drawings by Toyojiro Onishi*

LONGMANS, GREEN AND CO.

NEW YORK · TORONTO

1938

DILTS

THE PAGEANT OF JAPANESE HISTORY

COPYRIGHT · 1938
BY MARION MAY DILTS

FIRST EDITION

952
D 58

PRINTED IN THE UNITED STATES OF AMERICA

To my Mother and Father
and to R. T.
This book is fondly dedicated

FOREWORD

FOR the general reader who wishes to get an intelligent view of Japanese history, and for students of senior high schools and colleges who do not intend to become Orientalists but who seek real information in palatable form, this book was written. Specialists and advanced students already have Sir George Sansom's very notable work on the cultural history of Japan, the standard political history up to 1911 by Brinkley, and the fascinating as well as monumental volumes by Murdoch which end with the Restoration of 1868. For the layman, however, there are very few books in print on this subject which are not either colored by sentimental adoration of all that seems to us quaintly exotic in Japanese civilization or designed to express the personal opinions and prejudices of their authors.

Miss Dilts during her college days at Wellesley had become interested in Japan, and after graduation, some years ago, had gone there, not as a tourist, but actually to live in a Japanese family where she might study social conditions and national characteristics without intermediaries. After her return to America and resumption of a full-time position in scientific work, she devoted practically all of her leisure hours to an intensive study of Japan. Longmans, Green and Company had heard of her, and knowing the

need of a short history that was based on thorough scholarship they asked her to write this book.

By the close of 1936 the manuscript had been completed
up to the beginning of the new phase of Japanese history
that opened in 1868, and it had been gone over for possible misstatements or mistranslations by the learned cura-
tor of the Japanese Library at Columbia University. In
order to state the events of the last seventy-five years, and
particularly of the last ten years, concisely and accurately,
Miss Dilts felt that she needed another trip to Japan and
fresh contacts with people of all strata there, the interplay
of whose ideas and idiosyncrasies with the world forces
about them was making current history. At the same time
attention had just been called to the inadequacy of material about the Orient that was available for use in the visual
education systems of American high schools, and the Rockefeller Foundation made a grant through one of the scholarly societies which enabled Miss Dilts to apply for a leave
of absence from her office and to spend the summer and
autumn of 1937 again in the land and among the people
whose history she has written.

The book embodies the results of some of the most recent researches of Japanese scholars, particularly in regard
to the origins of the race and the primitive periods, and
gives throughout a clear impression of having been written
by someone who was able to draw from a great fund of detailed information the really salient items, and to state these
concisely, clearly, intelligently, without attempting to in-
terpret them. The facts of history are one thing, the interpretation of them is another, and to those who wish to see

the pageant of Japanese history unrolled before them without controversy or comment — like some great scroll of painting — it is a pleasure to recommend a volume which seems destined to become, at least for a time, the standard one of small compass and for general readers on its special subject.

LOUIS V. LEDOUX

Cornwall-on-Hudson
February 6, 1938

ACKNOWLEDGMENTS

As I recall the many who in various ways have helped to produce this book, gratification and humility are closely mingled. The encouragement and interest shown in such concrete form by Mr. Ledoux and by friends both Japanese and American, too numerous to mention, have been deeply appreciated. The scholarship of many with whom I have been privileged to discuss divers phases of Japanese history and culture has been very inspiring, as has the work of many others, also, whom I have had the opportunity of knowing only through their writings. Though the majority of these are mentioned in the Notes which follow the text, it is a pleasure to mention especially the names of Sir George Sansom, the late Dr. Robert Karl Reischauer, Mr. Arthur Waley, Dr. Jiro Harada, Mr. S. Mihara, Mr. S. Aoki, Mr. Noritake Tsuda, Professor S. Goto, Mr. A. L. Sadler, Mr. M. Paske-Smith, Mr. Neil Skene Smith, Mr. James A. B. Scherer, Mr. Harold G. Henderson, Dr. Hugh Borton, Mr. E. Kiyooka, Mr. M. Nezu. To Mr. Bradford Smith, Mrs. M. D. Jelliffe, Miss Edna Coulson, Miss Ethel Coulson, I am indebted for criticism and help in the preparation and revision of the manuscript; to Mr. Harold F. Dodge, Mr. K. Atarashi, and Mr. M. Ishizawa for assistance in connection with maps and illustrations. I also wish to express my gratitude to the Rockefeller Foundation.

The person to whom I owe most, however, is Professor Ryusaku Tsunoda, who, being largely responsible for Columbia University's having the most complete collection of Japanese study materials anywhere outside of Japan, made possible the existence of this book. He has been my teacher, interpreter, friend and critic. Those who have been his students will find much to remind them of him in this volume, which is tangible evidence of my appreciation.

M. M. D.

CONTENTS

LIST OF ILLUSTRATIONS

TEXT ILLUSTRATIONS

MAPS AND CHARTS

THE PAGEANT OF JAPANESE HISTORY

CHAPTER I

CLUES TO THE EARLY SETTLERS
(BEFORE 400 A.D.)

IT IS hard to tell where to begin the story of Japan. Just as the real history of our country begins with the coming of ships full of adventurers from the continent of Europe, so the real history of Japan begins with the coming of progressive seafarers from the coast of Asia. But for more than a thousand years before the arrival of these people who knew how to keep records of their doings, there were tribes of primitive folk living in Japan as well as in North America. These primitive peoples, living so far from each other, were very much alike. Our Eskimos and Indians had dark skin, straight, stiff black hair, with very thin beards, and high cheek bones just as did the primitive settlers of Japan.

Both peoples lived in pits, or caves, and used implements

of finely chipped stone for cutting. Both made clay pottery and decorated it with designs resembling the rope, and baskets which they made of twisted vines. Both went fishing with bone fishhooks and hunting with stone-tipped arrows, and both performed songs and dances in order to keep in the good graces of the sun, their ancestors and various nature spirits. In short, many think that the earliest inhabitants of our country and some of the ancient ancestors of the Japanese came from the same place, the northeastern part of Asia.[1]

These primitives, however, left no written accounts of themselves, and it is only in recent years that we have come to know anything about them. While for the past half century scientists and scholars in our country have been busy searching in the ground for remains and studying the languages and traditions of the Eskimos and Indians, Japanese scientists and scholars have also been looking for information about their country's prehistoric times. It was not a simple problem to discover what kind of people were living on these islands in the Late Stone Age, where they came from, when and why, and what they did after they reached Japan. But modern Japanese found four good clues to work on.

They began studying the Japanese language in its earliest recorded forms and compared it with other languages. They looked for mention of their islands in Chinese and Korean records. They dug thousands and thousands of excavations to find ancient dwelling and burial sites as well as human skulls and bones to compare with similar remains from other parts of the world. They also began to trace the history of the various beliefs and rites which make up their native cult. All their findings in the ground thus far lead to the conclusion that through many centuries there were two great routes of migration to Japan, one from southern China via Shantung and one from Siberia and northern China via Korea.[2] Many people think there was a third route up through the islands of the South Pacific and possibly a fourth down from Saghalin, but as yet there is no concrete evidence to support these theories. One may, however, trace three different influences in early Japanese civilization : southern, northern, and central-eastern Asiatic.

These three influences are shown in the Japanese language as clearly as in archeological remains and religious customs. Though all the signs the Japanese use in writing are derived from China, the Japanese language itself is very different from Chinese. For example, in Japanese a greeting corresponding to, "How do you do?" is "Ikaga desu ka." In Chinese it is, "Nin hao." While in Chinese, verbs function rather indifferently and grammatical relations are shown only by the order of the words in the sentence, in Japanese the verb plays a most important role. With its many possible endings to indicate aspect, tense and mood, it is the key to meaning. These endings and particles make it rather like the Ural-Altaic language of the northeastern Asiatic tribes. On the other hand, it has been found that many of the Japanese names for things closely resemble words used in Malaya and the South Sea islands.

In Korean and Chinese records of the third century A.D. Japan was mentioned as "Wa." "Men of Wa," the

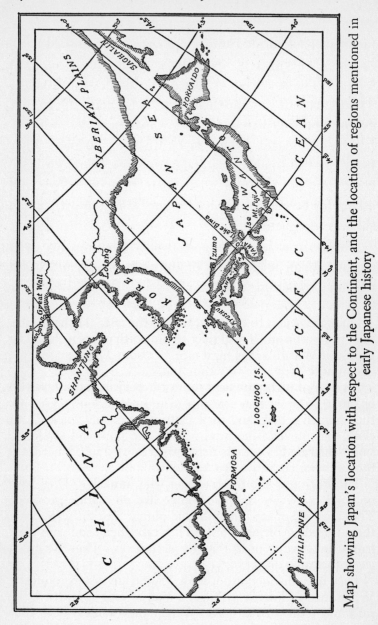

Map showing Japan's location with respect to the Continent, and the location of regions mentioned in early Japanese history

records state, "dwell in the midst of the ocean on a mountainous island divided into more than one hundred provinces. Thirty-two of these have communications with China. The sovereign of Great Wa resides in Yamato." There was civil war and anarchy among them, the records go on to say, until an unmarried woman appeared, who, by her skill in magic, gained favor with the people. They made her their queen. Several envoys are reported to have come from her to Chinese governors, bringing tribute and asking for help against a neighboring kingdom with which she was in difficulty.

Chinese travelers of almost twenty centuries ago who reached Japan made notes of things they saw and heard which go something like this : [3]

One ruler seems to be stronger than the rest. He has a vice-ruler in Kyushu and a rival ruler to the north of his realm. The people of Wa are a long-lived race. Persons who have reached one hundred years are very common.

All men of high rank have four or five wives and others two or three. The women are faithful and not jealous. They tie their hair in a bow, and their clothing is of one thickness of cloth, put on over the head. They use pink and scarlet to smear their bodies with as rice powder is used in China. It is their general custom to go barefoot.

The roads are like the tracks of wild animals. They have no good rice fields, and the people live on marine products. They are fond of catching fish, and plunge into the water after them regardless of the depth. They take their food with their hands but have wooden trays to place it on. They are much given to strong drink.

They have distinctions of rank. Some are vassals to others. When men of lower class meet a man of rank, they leave the road and retire to the grass. When they address him, they either squat or kneel with both hands to the ground. This is their way of showing respect.

There is no robbery or theft among them. The wives and children also of those who commit grave crimes are put to death.

They use only an inner, and no outer coffin. Mourning lasts ten days only. During this time members of the family fast, weep and lament while their friends come singing, dancing and making music. When the funeral is over, the whole family goes into the water to wash.

There are markets in each province where they exchange their surplus produce for other articles which they need. The people of Wa are not acquainted with the New Year or the four seasons, but reckon time by the spring cultivation of the fields and the autumn ingathering of crops.

These few sketchy descriptions contain all the information yielded by continental records. The Japanese scientists who began to dig in the ground found their labors better rewarded. The earth yielded up most valuable information about the early settlers. In certain gravel pits scientists found bones which they believe belonged to continental mammals. These seem to show that the islands were once a part of the mainland, or connected to it by strips of land over which men as well as animals may have traveled ages and ages ago. It may have been that the Sea of Japan was once a mere lake, which wanderers could cross at will, until drainage from the plateaus enlarged it to its present size. The oldest remains which have yet been found of men living in Japan seem to have belonged to tribes which had attained the culture of the Late Stone Age.

Thousands of excavations made throughout the Japanese islands have brought to light three chief types of remains :

FOUR POTTERY GRAVE FIGURES

XCAVATION OF A STONE AGE DWELLING SITE

shell mounds, dwelling sites of a transitional period, and dolmens. The shell mounds marked the dwelling places of men of the Late Stone Age. The deposits of broken pottery and stone tools, together with bronze swords and pieces of harness and sometimes big bronze bells marked the dwelling places of men who were learning the use of metal. The dolmens, or stone-lined burial places, contained clay figures of people and horses, both elaborately appareled, and iron swords and complicated armor, together with not very skillfully made bronze mirrors.

Shell mounds have been found along the coast of Asia from southern China to Siberia, and in several east and west coast states in our own country. They were made of the shells which ancient people cast away as they ate clams and oysters. Among the shells are stone axes, knives, arrowheads, bone needles, fishing hooks, bowls and cooking pots of molded clay with "combed" designs, and many other everyday conveniences of Late Stone Age families.

These people seem to have lived in rocky caves and shelters along the banks of rivers and lakes or the shores of bays. They probably spent their time hunting and fishing rather than farming. In Japanese waters they found many kinds of seaweed which they used for food, in addition to the great variety of fish and shell fish. Japanese people even now eat

shell   coin   sell   buy

much more fish and seaweed than they do meat and vegetables.

In China, the ancestral home of many of these settlers, the sign for "shell" is part of the signs for "buy," "sell," "treasure" and "coin," which seems to indicate that shells were used in those days in place of money. Perfect ones of rare shapes and lovely colors were probably valued more

poverty   wealth   treasure   greed

highly than the common ones used as cooking and eating utensils. No doubt they were often polished and worn as jewelry. Japanese people are still very fond of gathering shells and playing games with them, and Western ladies are familiar with their cultivated pearls.

But just as the American Indians thousands of years later were driven before advancing Europeans, so in the course of centuries, these early inhabitants of Japan had their land wrested from them by more civilized tribes from the Asiatic continent and were driven farther and farther to the east and north. Some of them mingled and married with the newcomers, learned their ways and became like them, but others, like many of our Indians and Tennessee "Mountain Whites," resisted stubbornly and kept to themselves. Remnants of them still exist in settlements on Hokkaido, the northernmost island of Japan. They are called Ainu.[4]

The invaders with bronze swords and bells who next

took possession of the land have been traced, by things they left behind them, to the Siberian plains. They were soon followed by others from the continent, by the dolmen builders, who knew how to use iron in addition to bronze. With this and other superior knowledge the dolmen builders were able to get control of the southwestern half of the islands. From the clay figures of men in armor, and horses in ornamental trappings which were found in their large stone tombs, from the many shaped vases, gilded bracelets, rings, and beads of jade, crystal and other semi-precious stones, it was easy to conclude that this wave of immigrants came from communities under the influence of Chinese civilization. Many of the dolmens contained finely made swords and beautifully decorated mirrors of polished bronze such as were used in the Han colony in Lolang, of which more will be told in the next chapter.

A number of these tombs have been identified from references in the Kojiki and Nihongi, the earliest histories of Japan, as belonging to certain emperors, and are held in great respect. Archeologists are not permitted to disturb them.[5] When one was damaged by a storm some years ago, however, there was an opportunity, while repairs were being made, to look inside. People were amazed to see how many objects of continental craftsmanship it contained. The ruler who is supposed to have been buried in this dolmen, according to historians, lived in the fourth century. The buried treasures were evidence of his relations with the kingdoms of the Korean peninsula.[6]

When the Japanese extended their search for origins in the study of their native cult, broadly speaking, they found that it contained two kinds of deities, the gods of their own land and the gods from elsewhere. They also found that there were three different influences apparent in their religion just as there were in their language and in the remains discovered in the ground.

There was a worship of animals, especially the fox, and a worship of bows and arrows. There was a belief that people going off in trances could, in the unconscious state, communicate with the spirit world to find out why calamities occurred and what should be done to avoid them. Ancient records tell how Empress Jingu in the third century learned in a dream of a "better land than this, a land of treasure dazzling to the eyes where are gold and silver and bright colors aplenty," [7] and went herself in command of an army and a navy to conquer it. Then, too, there were men who claimed to be able to tell from the way the bone cracked when they burned the shoulder blade of a stag, if and when journeys or voyages ought to be started. Animal cults and magic such as this were practiced by tribes on the Siberian plains, and when some of them came to Japan they kept their traditional habits.

Peoples of southern Asia worshipped the heavenly bodies ; the sun was very strong there and rather feared. In Japan, however, they could not help loving the sun for its genial warmth. They sang and danced, clapped their hands and laughed to express their joy and gratitude. They worshipped a sea god too and loved bubbling springs and fountains of crystal-clear water. Bathing was a ritual with them. It was part of their religion to be pure and clean. They thought not so much of sins as of impurities which had to be washed away. Illness and death occasioned not only great washing ceremonies, but even desertion of the house of the person who passed away and the building of a new one for his heirs. This was not as difficult or as wasteful as it sounds, for houses in those days were simply a hole in the ground, with a few poles at the corners tied together with vines and roofed over with skins or thatch. The love of cleanliness still persists in Japan. Almost everyone bathes every day as part of a personal code of conduct. In front of Shinto shrines you still will find a large stone or metal basin of water from which worshippers scoop up a wooden dipperful to wash their hands and mouths before clapping their hands three times to attract the deity's attention to their prayers.

In China the development of large families for the cultivation of rice fields was of great importance. The forms of worship used there were intended to promote fertility and these forms too found their way to Japan. The greatest offenses in the early days of agriculture were the breaking down of irrigation ditches and other acts which hindered the growth of rice. In the spring when the rice was planted and in the autumn when it was gathered, religious ceremonies were held and harvest prayers like this were offered :

Because the Great Deity has bestowed upon him (the ruler) lands of the four quarters, over which her glance extends . . . as far as the blue clouds are diffused and the white clouds settle down opposite ; by the blue sea plain as far as the prows of ships can go without letting dry their poles and oars ; by land as far as the hoofs of horses can go with tightened baggage cords treading their way among rock roots and tree roots where

the long road extends . . . therefore will the first fruits for the
Great Deity be piled up in her mighty presence like a range of
hills, leaving the remainder for him (the ruler) tranquilly to
partake of.[8]

Even now, on a regular day in autumn rather like Thanksgiving in our churches, the best of the rice crop is offered
at the shrines with prayers and ceremonies.

When these emigrants from various homelands began to
settle in communities along the seashore and rivers of
Japan, they seem to have become keenly interested in claim-
ing new land as their own and in guarding it against invaders. They invented religious devices to help them in
this ; the idea of kami, superiors or gods of the land, each
with his own special region, thus had its beginning. The
many different beliefs and practices which the settlers had
carried over from their own countries were made to conform
with this new idea. Foxes and wolves became messengers
of the gods. Bows and arrows helped to extend their domains, while magic was used to confirm their plans. Sun
and water made them prosper and fertility practices, too,
enriched the gods and their worshippers. If a clan wished
to get a new piece of land, their deity proclaimed a desire
to dwell there. What else could they do but claim it for
him ? These deities had to be served on other occasions,
too, by the chiefs of the clans. In spring when the land
was divided up among the clan and the seed rice planted,
again at times of harvest, marriage or change of leader, the
deities had to be worshipped. The places where the people
met, bringing their offerings of rice and hemp cloth, birds
and animals from the hunt, fish and seaweed from the

water, became the real centers of community life. There, in addition to religious services, government and trade were carried on and weapons were stored.

The country was thus divided into many districts, each with its own god or gods. Frequently, rivalry and conflict arose in their names. When the dolmen era was at its height in the fourth and fifth centuries there were a few deities who, by the conquest or peaceful accession of their clans, had come to rule large portions of the land, with lesser deities taking orders from them. One such deity was the sun-goddess, Amaterasu, Shining in Heaven.

Ancient stories have it that in the beginning two deities stood on the Bridge of Heaven and wondered what was beneath. One dipped a sword into the water. The drops which fell from the sword when it was pulled out formed islands, and the pair descended and dwelt on the islands and had a daughter whom they called Amaterasu, Shining in Heaven and a son, Susanowo, Impetuous Male. These ancient stories go on to say that Amaterasu ruled one section of the islands while her brother ruled another. She was beautiful and gentle, giving light and life to all, while he disregarded all his duties and perversely raged between heaven and earth, ruining crops and tormenting people generally. Finally in protest to the most offensive of Susanowo's antics, Amaterasu locked herself up in a cave, leaving the world in darkness.

To devise a scheme for bringing her out again, the other deities assembled in the tranquil river bed in front of her hiding place. They took iron from the rocks in the river and made a mirror which they hung on a birch branch

decorated with a string of curved jewels like this 𝔶 .[9]
Then one of the deities danced with resounding rhythm on
an overturned tub in front of the cave, her breast exposed
and her skirt out of place.

At this the deities laughed so loudly that Amaterasu
opened her door and spoke thus from the inside : "Me-
thought that owing to my retirement the world would be
dark — how is it that the deities all laugh ?" [10]

"We rejoice because there is one more illustrious than
thou art," they replied, pushing forward the mirror. Amaterasu, more and more astonished at seeing in the mirror
what she thought was another deity of her own brightness,
gradually came forth and gazed upon it. She was seized
and prevented from returning ; and the world again became
light.

Susanowo for his misbehavior was banished to the under-
world, but on his way he stopped at Izumo on the northern
coast of Japan facing the Korean peninsula.[11] In Izumo,
Susanowo married and had sons and grandsons who ruled
that land until a delegation came from Amaterasu and
forced them to give it over to her grandson Ninigi.

Amaterasu had bestowed upon Ninigi as emblems of
imperial right, a marvelous sword which Susanowo had captured from a dragon's tail, the string of curved jewels and
the mirror which had lured her from the cave, charging him
to take in hand her affairs on the islands. "Regard this
mirror exactly as if it were our august spirit, and reverence it
as if reverencing us," the ancient legends quote her as saying. "This land is the region of which my descendants
shall be lords ; do thou proceed thither and govern it. Go !

And may prosperity attend thy dynasty; and may it, like heaven and earth, endure forever." [12]

Having descended upon the large southern island, Kyushu, Ninigi found such disorder and confusion among the many clans and chieftains that he was unable to make much headway. It was not until the time of his grandson, Jimmu, that Amaterasu's line proceeded to extend their control to the main island of Japan. Leaving Kyushu by boat, Jimmu ventured up the Inland Sea, stopping at a beach here and an islet there, until after several years he reached a place in central Japan which seemed to have many advantages. It was called Yamato, Mountain-Guarded. According to tradition, Jimmu proclaimed his rule over the land of Yamato and ascended the throne on February 11, 660 B.C. Later, when the title "Tenno" came to be the official designation of the Japanese emperors, Jimmu was included as the first of them, Jimmu-Tenno — Jimmu, Son of Heaven. [13]

Jimmu-Tenno, official history says, made friends with some people of Izumo. With their help he drove many earlier settlers off their lands and forced them to move farther to the northeast. Thus Amaterasu's descendants, with their center at Yamato, came to have under their control many other important tribes and lands.

According to another Japanese legend, a princess of the divine tribe of Yamato took from their sacred place in the palace the bronze mirror and the sword bestowed by Amaterasu, and established a shrine for them at Isé, on the frontier which bordered the Ainu's lands. As the Yamato group continued in power a weaving center also developed at this outpost of their influence. [14] The more primitive settlers must have been impressed with the treasures and the talents of their conquerors.

Isé has since become the most sacred shrine of all Japan. Its little wooden structures are rebuilt of fresh unpainted wood every twenty years according to their ancient architectural design. Every loyal Japanese at least once in his lifetime makes a journey to Isé, and there along a crystal-clear river, among moss-grown rocks and towering cryptomerias pays his respects to Amaterasu, the divine ancestress of the ruling family.[15]

CHAPTER II

THE DAWN OF HISTORY
(c. 400–700 a.d.)

ABOUT the beginning of the Christian era, when the early settlers of Japan and their Korean neighbors were beginning to know something of the use of metals, the great Han Empire was flourishing in China. The Han Empire had begun in the third century b.c., with the Great Wall, fifteen hundred miles long, already built to protect it against barbarous invaders from the north. It had expanded rapidly by opening trade routes to India, Persia and even to the Roman world. After the Great Wall was completed, large numbers of workmen, who had been employed on this enormous project, and wandering tribes, who found it blocking their forward movement, migrated along it into the northern half of the Korean peninsula. A Han colony of half a million people was established there with Chinese governors and the complete Chinese system of administration. The chief center of this colony was called Lolang.

Many Chinese officials of high rank and families of great wealth transferred their homes to Lolang. They brought with them skillfully made swords and spears ; and the saddles, girths and stirrups of their horses were sometimes ornamented with gold. Undisturbed in their splendid tombs

have been found lacquer trays and dishes, vessels of pottery and bronze together with coins, mirrors and jewelry of
exquisite gold filigree. There is good reason to suppose
that such things were used by the living as well as buried
with the dead.[1]

Although not one of the noble mansions of Lolang remains standing, and but few traces of them have been
brought to light, the foundations of the great government
house, when discovered, gave evidence of its former gran-
deur. This building seems to have been made of bricks
and tiles in a great variety of colors and designs, and to have
been surrounded by an earthen embankment six hundred
feet wide and eight hundred feet long. Here in a continual
stream came traders, officials and ambitious travelers from
far distant places. Even the primitive settlers "on the
island in the midst of the ocean" knew about the marvels
of Lolang, and many of them went back to the mainland
whence their ancestors had come to experience firsthand
its civilized life, or sent envoys to seek a share of its splendors. Lolang, in its prime, was a most attractive center,
radiating its culture for hundreds of miles around.

After four hundred years of power, however, the great
Han Empire broke down into three rival kingdoms, and
the Lolang colony waned. Then the nearby Korean countries, which before had been weak and backward in comparison with their great neighbor, struggled for possession
of the Lolang treasures. Even Yamato leaders and troops
went overseas and managed to found a small colony of their
own on the Korean peninsula. They won such a reputation
as daring, strong and skillful fighters that not seldom en-

voys from the Korean countries were sent over to the islands with valuable presents for the Yamato rulers, and also with urgent requests for Yamato troops to come help them battle against their rivals. When the Yamato rulers did not respond at once, more envoys came, bringing in addition to the highly prized jade beads, iron swords and bronze mirrors, more precious and novel gifts. At one time they brought an image of Buddha in gold and copper, several flags and umbrellas and a number of volumes of sutras — all accessories of a wonderful religion with which the Yamato rulers as yet were unacquainted. Another time, at the request of the Yamato ruler, they brought "a man learned in divination, a man learned in calendar making, a physician, two herbalists and four musicians." [2]

Conditions on the continent, however, became more and more unsettled, so that whole villages of people from the Han and Korean countries began moving to the islands where they could foresee more security and greater opportunities for themselves. With this wholesale migration the real history of Japan begins.

Men of Yamato returning to their homes brought with them all they could of Chinese coins and medicines, personal finery and household furnishings such as silks, mirrors, lacquered boxes and stands, pottery, silver and glassware and writing materials ; and many of the foreigners who came knew how to make such things themselves. They were familiar with ways of fertilizing the soil so as to raise better crops, with methods of caring for silkworms so as to get fine strong silk to color and weave into beautifully patterned cloth. But more important even than this they knew how to read and write and could keep accounts of taxes and trading arrangements.

Since the Japanese themselves had never learned these arts, men who were accomplished in writing and reading seemed very wonderful to them and were treated generously. They were employed as scribes by the most important clan leaders who, though quite ignorant, realized that they would seem greater themselves if they had remarkable men around them. In return for their services, the Korean and Chinese refugees were given lands where they could build homes for their families, and abundant provisions for living. Often they were excused from the taxes of rice and cloth or the forced labor that ordinary Japanese rendered to the clan heads for the use of the land, and often because of their ability they were granted the best government positions and honored with official rank. Under such favorable conditions they increased in number ; they prospered and began to play a very important part in building up the Japanese nation ; "men of T'sin and Han" they were called. In the year 540, it is recorded there were seven thousand households of men of T'sin — or about one hundred thousand individuals — and in a Japanese Peerage compiled at the end of the seventh century over a fourth of the noble families listed claimed either Chinese or Korean descent.[3]

At first the Yamato leaders simply hired the scribes as they might have hired sculptors to make a statue of a great man, thinking the art of writing to be a special gift, not something which they themselves could learn. But soon they were eager to learn more of the new religion that newcomers had brought over along with their material treasures and for which they made glowing claims. "This teaching is among all teachings the most excellent, but it is hard to explain and hard to understand. It can lead to a full appreciation of the highest wisdom. Imagine a man in possession of treasures to his heart's content so that he might satisfy all of his wishes. Thus it is with the treasure of this wonderful teaching. Every prayer is fulfilled. Nothing is wanting. It has come from India to us and there are none who do not receive it with reverence as it is presented to them." [4]

Naturally enough the Yamato men wanted to be able to read for themselves the books of such teachings as these, so they began to study Chinese writings.

The new religion was Buddhism. It had begun with the simple, truth-revealing teaching of a young man in the villages of India, but had seemed so good to those who heard it that they began to spread it and add to it, just as the early Christians five hundred years later did with Jesus' teachings. Just as Christianity gradually spread all over Europe and was adapted to the habits of different peoples, so Buddhism had spread all over Asia and taken as its own the best of many other teachings. Buddhist priests had been the bearers of civilization to uncultured masses. They had developed a powerful organization in Asia as Christianity afterward did in Europe, and built beautiful temples filled with sacred paintings and statues of Buddha, their great "Enlightened One," surrounded by many of his saints.

It was about one thousand years after the founder of Buddhism lived that his teachings were brought to Japan. At first the Yamato rulers were afraid that by worshipping

Buddha they might offend their own land deities, the kami, and very few would take this risk.

Although their native religious beliefs and practices were not organized into any sort of system, and in fact did not even have a name, there were two families prominent in Yamato affairs who for generations had been responsible for the proper performance of ceremonies and rites. In return for the services which they performed these families enjoyed many special privileges. They were, therefore, not at all enthusiastic about the introduction of a new religion. To distinguish their own cult from the new one they dignified it with a name, Shinto, "The Way of the Gods," and did everything they could to encourage Shinto practices and to discourage Buddhist ones. When a plague broke out in the country they announced that this was a sign of the kami's jealous wrath. They threw the statue of Buddha into a canal and burned the building where it had been enshrined.

On further acquaintance, however, Buddhism grew to be acceptable. It could hardly be otherwise since the constantly increasing immigrant population which enjoyed such favor was entirely Buddhist. Buddhism stood for progress and the Yamato rulers were not without ambition. Prince Shotoku, a regent who governed for his empress aunt around the year 600, was the first to set an example for the people. He was so deeply interested in the teachings of Buddha, it is recorded, that he became the pupil of a Korean Buddhist scholar so that he might learn to read the scriptures for himself. Many others, like him, learned to read and write because of this new religion.

Prince Shotoku became one of the most loved rulers the Japanese ever had. They still call him "The Father of Japanese Culture." With his Korean tutors he is thought to have studied not only Buddhist writings but also the writings of Confucius and other Chinese classics which inspired him to make of Japan an ideal nation. He aimed to do away with rivalry between the big landowners, not by force of arms but by moral teachings and persuasion, and to have one ruler over all the clans who would deal justly with the people and keep harmony throughout his realm. To help carry out his aims he is said to have written what is known in Japanese history as "The Seventeen-Article Constitution." In form this was very different from the Constitution of the United States, but like that venerable document it was designed to inspire the confidence and cooperation of the people in a new government experiment. Prince Shotoku's Seventeen-Article Constitution is given here in brief : [5]

Harmony is to be valued, for when there is harmony between the ruler and the ruled and between neighbor and neighbor what can not be accomplished.

Sincerely reverence the three treasures : Buddha, his teachings and the priests.

When you receive imperial commands, fail not to obey them carefully.

Let your behavior be orderly and proper.

Chastise that which is evil ; encourage that which is good. Conceal not the good qualities of others, nor fail to correct wrong when you see it.

Flatterers and deceivers lead to the overthrow of the state and the destruction of the people.

Let the court officials attend early and retire late for the whole day is hardly enough for accomplishing the business of the state.

In everything let there be good faith, for without it everything ends in failure.

Let us not be resentful nor look angry when others differ from us, for each heart has its own leanings. We are not unquestionably sages nor are they unquestionably fools.

Let not the provincial authorities levy taxes on the people; the sovereign is the master of the people of the whole country. They have not two masters.

Let no official sacrifice the public interest to his private feelings.

Let the people be made to do forced labor only when they are not engaged in agriculture or the care of silk worms.

Let all important matters be discussed by many persons.

Needless to say, not all of these ideals of Prince Shotoku were realized, but he sowed seeds which later bore much fruit. It was he, they say, who first encouraged the building of temples; Horyu-ji, one which he had built as a teaching center, though repaired many times in its thirteen hundred years of existence, still bears close resemblance to the original. There on lotus blossom pedestals two statues still remain in marvelous preservation from Prince Shotoku's day — one of bronze inscribed with a date corresponding to the year 607 — and one of wood covered with gold leaf.[6]

In early times the Japanese had counted the years by the reigns of their rulers. Instead of saying that Prince Shotoku was appointed regent in the year 593 A.D., or according to some such continuous system, they said he was appointed in the first year of Empress Suiko. As a result of this system, or lack of system, there was much uncertainty and confusion about early dates in Japanese history.

During Prince Shotoku's regency, however, a scholar came to his court with books on astrology, calendar making and geography. The Chinese had developed these sciences with great skill. They had two cycles for counting years : a ten-year cycle called after the elements, wood, fire, earth, metal and water ; and a twelve-year cycle in which each year was named after an animal, the year of the rat, the ox, the tiger, etc. These names were suggested by the forms of constellations and were similar to our twelve signs of the zodiac.[7] The first year of the ten-year cycle coincided with the cycle of twelve only once every sixty years. Sixty years was therefore used as a unit corresponding to our century. The twelve months were named like the twelve-cycle years, and each month was divided into three parts. The days in each part were named like the ten-cycle years. There were no seven-day weeks but for convenience the months and days were simply numbered as they sometimes are with us. The days were divided into twelve parts instead of twenty-four so their hours were twice as long as ours.

In the seventh century the Japanese adopted this Chinese system of keeping track of time. Then, figuring back, systematically they gave dates to all their emperors. Like the Chinese, they seem to have exaggerated the lengths of many reigns in order to give themselves a more impressive past. Though modern scholars think it was more likely at about the beginning of the Christian Era when the Yamato clan came to power, officially Jimmu-Tenno, the great-great-grandson of Amaterasu, the sun goddess, is said to have ascended the throne on February 11, 660 B.C., and

this day is still celebrated in Japan with parades and patriotic speeches.[8]

After this new system of dating was introduced Prince
Shotoku, together with the leader of a clan named Soga,
is said to have compiled the first history of the Japanese
emperors, but this work was later destroyed when the Soga's
home was burned. Shotoku seems to have been interested
in music and dancing too because, according to Chinese
books, music softened men's hearts and made them easier
to govern. When an immigrant came who knew the Chinese style of music and dancing, the prince regent lodged
him in the palace, and had young people come there to
learn these arts.

While this progressive regent was governing Japan, the
Chinese kingdoms that had been divided since the fall of
the Han Empire were united and strengthened again by
the Sui Dynasty. Prince Shotoku decided to send an envoy to their new capital, for China, he realized, was the
source of all the knowledge and culture of his Korean tutors. The envoy took with him a letter which began, "The
emperor of the country where the sun rises sends greetings
to the emperor of the country where the sun sets." [9] History says the Sui emperor resented this note of equality
from the ruler of a mere island in the ocean, but nevertheless, the following year he sent back with the envoy two
representatives from his court and a number of books. The
Yamato envoy soon returned to China, this time with a
band of eight students, the sons of Korean families who
had been welcomed and well established in Japan. They
went to study Buddhism and Chinese government ; two of

them stayed in China studying for thirty years. Before they returned to the country of their adoption, Prince Shotoku passed away.

There was great disorder in Yamato then, for the Soga clan usurped the imperial rights. They had held important positions from very ancient times and had been closely associated with the finances of the ruling clan. When immigrants had begun coming from the continent, the Sogas had employed large numbers of them, thus increasing their own prestige and extending their own power. They were the first clan to worship Buddha and they had supported Prince Shotoku during his regency, but as soon as he was gone they took the reins of government into their own hands, not even hesitating to do away with his sons and grandsons. They brought in half-wild Ainu soldiers from the northeast and ferocious fighters from Kyushu to keep other powerful clans in submission to them. Added to the Sogas' ruthless arrogance, many chieftains had other worries; the immigrant groups by this time, grown large and ambitious, were constantly making greater demands on native clans. The Japanese colony on the Korean peninsula was in a precarious position, for a new dynasty in China was making startling conquests. And Shinto leaders were very much disturbed at the success the Buddhists were having in obtaining gifts of land and other favors from prominent people.

In the midst of all these troubles grew up a young man named Kamatari. One of his ancestors was supposed to have accompanied the first members of the Yamato race who came to Japan, and the family from ancient times had been one of those engaged in performing religious rites in honor of the deities of the imperial clan. Because of political and religious differences they had often come into conflict with the Sogas.

At this time there was really no well-organized central government; the country was dominated by a number of clans, each administering certain lands which they had occupied for many generations. Everything these lands produced belonged to the clan and constituted its living and its wealth. The head of the clan directed all its affairs and had full command over all the clan members. Between clans were continual rivalries which drained their strength and enabled the imperial clan to become larger and more powerful. Though the imperial clan had no acknowledged right over any other clan, many of the other clans became willing to take orders from it. As a system of government for the whole country, however, this could work only when the imperial clan was headed by a ruler who commanded the respect of the other clan leaders, and who could persuade or intimidate them into cooperation. Kamatari saw clearly that such a system was no longer adequate. Times were changing, and the growing numbers of immigrants in the country not only created problems, but also offered opportunities such as the Japanese had never had before.

Kamatari consulted with the students recently returned from China. Just before Prince Shotoku died the Sui Dynasty in China had been replaced by the T'ang, and the excellently governed T'ang Empire was now the brilliant marvel of all Asia. It was the largest and strongest country in the world, extending from Manchuria to Siam, and from the Caspian to the Pacific.

At its head was an absolute monarch, called "Son of Heaven." According to the teachings of Chinese sages the man of greatest virtue in their country was commissioned by the ruler of heaven to be their sovereign — while men of only slightly less virtue and wisdom were to serve him loyally as ministers and advisers. The empire was divided into many provinces, with a governor appointed to each. Then to all grown persons in the country were allotted equal portions of land. The entire government of T'ang was based on agrarian economy. Irrigation canals were dug for the benefit of the farmers, and storehouses were built where the surplus products of good years could be saved for years when the crops were poor. For students were provided schools and a university ; a sort of civil service examination was given for the selection of public officials. Merchants from all over the world flocked to their capital, which is said to have been gorgeous beyond description.

Kamatari, having learned much about the great T'ang Empire from the young men who had lived and studied in China for many years, resolved to make of Japan a small but worthy copy of her continental neighbor. A son of the nominal empress, Prince Naka, was found not only to share Kamatari's hopes, but to have the energy, courage and patience which would be needed to fulfill them. One day as Kamatari was playing football with some young noblemen — not football as we know it but a popular game of that time played by kicking a big soft ball — Prince Naka was playing too, and when he kicked the ball his shoe flew off after it.   Kamatari picked up the shoe and returning it to the young prince knelt down and put it on for him. After that they were frequently seen walking and talking together, but since they carried in their hands the yellow scrolls of the Chinese sages and went often to the homes of the students returned from abroad, it was not suspected that they were plotting the downfall of the Soga clan and the building of a new Japan.

The Sogas were so well guarded when they traveled out of doors that it was hard to get at them.   It was, therefore, decided to attack the young Soga at court during a celebration of welcome for a Korean envoy.   A swordsman was appointed to do the killing, but at the crucial moment he reneged and Prince Naka himself had to carry out the plan. All the other clans who had had grievances against the Soga but had been afraid to do anything now turned to Kamatari and Prince Naka, and within a few days the Soga leaders were all done away with and their palace burned.   This was the fire in which Prince Shotoku's history of Japan was destroyed.

Then the First Great Change was begun.   It was the keen ambition of Yamato progressives in the middle seventh century to have their country regarded by the T'ang Court not as an inferior state, but as a neighbor worthy of respect.   Yamato leaders had been treated with deference by the Korean kingdoms and they must continue to maintain their position and influence there.   But they must also establish a court of their own as nearly like the T'ang as possible — to which T'ang envoys could be welcomed with proper ceremony, and from which officials of real dignity could be dispatched to China. It was clear that to accomplish this many clans would have to unite their energies and resources, and there would have to be one man among them with absolute and direct control over all the people.

Though Kamatari and Prince Naka were the guiding spirits of the Great Change, they did not attempt to bring it about in their own names. Realizing that there were other great clan leaders to be considered and conciliated, all their acts were done, all their plans accomplished, on behalf of the imperial clan. They recognized the quality of genius in the family which based its claim to power on the revelations of a divine ancestress. A ruler who bases his right to rule on conquest has constantly to be looking to his fighting forces, for the first man stronger than he is eligible to replace him. But when a family has been commissioned by a heavenly deity to govern a land forever, it has a title as unchallengeable as any can be. Such was the traditional title of the imperial clan ; and as official envoys from the continent continued to bring treasures and scholars to this family, its wealth and prestige were further enhanced.

When the Great Change was slowly but surely under way, not Prince Naka himself but his uncle was made emperor. Kamatari and the prince kept themselves in the background and proceeded carefully. First they adopted the Chinese system of using period names. (When some happy omen or outstanding event occurred the Chinese would start a new era and call it by an appropriate name.) Kamatari and Prince Naka called the era they were begin-

ning, Taikwa, Great Change, to prepare the peoples' minds
for something new and interesting. Then they appointed
governors for the northeastern border provinces to replace
the local chieftains who had only recently won their lands
from the Ainu. These governors were to take a census of
all the people living in their districts, to collect all the spears
and bows and arrows the people had, and to store them in
government armories to lessen the danger of revolt. Their
next step was to grant to all the people the right of appeal
to the emperor. This was to make the people feel that
they were being given a special privilege, and also to lessen
the power of the clan heads. Before this, if a man had a
grievance against his chief he could do nothing about it,
the chief's word was final ; but now, theoretically at least,
a man could ask the emperor to get justice for him. Thus
clan rule began to give way to centralized government.

Since no great trouble arose as a result of these changes,
as soon as the New Year's celebrations were over in 646,
Kamatari and Prince Naka had the emperor issue their
Edict of Reform. This contained four new provisions : [10]

I Private administration of land was to be abolished. All
the property of the country was to be returned to the emperor.

II A central government was to be organized with a capital
modeled after a Chinese city, and a system of roads, ferries,
barriers and post horses to be provided through the provinces.
Provincial governors were to be appointed and assisted by
clerks familiar with writing and arithmetic.

III A census was to be taken of all the people, and the land
returned to the emperor was to be given back in equal parts to
all the people for them to use.

IV The old taxes and forced labor required by the clan

chiefs were to be replaced by new taxes to be paid to the central government whereby communities which produced special products like silk, flax, cotton, salt, horses, weapons, flags or drums, for example, could substitute these for the regular taxes of rice and labor.

To set an example for the people Prince Naka, himself, though a member of the imperial clan, and in line for the throne, gave up all claim to the lands and people he had formerly controlled and turned them over to his uncle. Many of the chief landholders followed his lead. Afterwards they were appointed as governors or salaried secretaries to oversee the lands and people they had been managing right along. They were paid salaries by the emperor for their service, not in money, for there was still practically no money in Japan, but in the natural products of their district, in fish and timber, salt, silk and such things. These clan chiefs had been so proud of the titles of respect by which they were called, titles like "Lord of the Family," or "Superior of the Clan," that Kamatari and Prince Naka were afraid they might be dissatisfied at now being called only governor. A Chinese system of ranks was, therefore, revived which, it is said, Prince Shotoku had introduced forty years before.

At elaborate ceremonies the important people of the country were honored with names like "Greater Benevolence," "Lesser Benevolence," "Greater Righteousness," "Lesser Righteousness." Each name stood for a rank or grade of social superiority and political importance. The people of the various grades were distinguished at special court functions by the colors of the robes and caps they wore. Those belonging to the grade of "Greater Righteousness" wore red, while those belonging to "Lesser Benevolence" wore blue. The most loyal supporters of the emperor, of course, were given the highest ranks, and only a man of a certain grade could hold a certain official position. The emperor gave special gifts of land corresponding to official rank. Amounts were frequently changed, but at one time they ranged from one hundred and sixty acres for each one of first rank down to sixteen acres each for members of the lower fifth rank, and gifts of produce from the imperial treasury were given to persons of rank below this. So people were eager to please the emperor in the hope of being advanced in rank and of receiving correspondingly increased rewards. No person of rank was required to pay taxes to the imperial treasury.

The Great Change which Kamatari and Prince Naka hoped to see in Japan, however, did not take place at once. Even a hundred years later in many parts of the country it still was not effective. Their efforts to retain some shade of Yamato authority on the Korean peninsula ended in a crushing defeat and expulsion by T'ang reinforcements in 662. And though during their regime four official embassies were sent to the T'ang capital, neither of these great men lived to see in their own country a permanent capital built like a Chinese city. Ten years before he died, Prince Naka, succeeding to the throne as Emperor Tenji, moved his court away from the stronghold of the old clan leaders and landowners in Yamato, into a region on the shores of Lake Biwa where there was a large settlement of Korean immigrants who favored his new policies. And it was Tenji-

Tenno's envoys who requested the T'ang court in future to call their country Nippon, or Sunrise Land, instead of Yamato. (Yamato proper was only the small central district where the imperial clan had very early established its control.)

Kamatari was well rewarded for his faithful efforts on behalf of the imperial clan : he was granted large estates in a region called Fujiwara, close by Yamato. From this advantageous position he and his descendants continued to watch over the interests of succeeding emperors. They came to be called Fujiwara after the region which was granted to them, and Fujiwara came to be the greatest family name in Japanese history.

After Kamatari's death in 669 no official embassies were sent from Nippon to T'ang for over thirty years. The enemies of the Great Change had a moment of victory and Tenji's son was done away with, but Tenji's younger brother, Temmu, had strengthened his own position by marriage with Tenji's daughter, and succeeded to the throne. Temmu-Tenno established himself at Asuka near a flourishing settlement of Chinese immigrants and with their encouragement, no doubt, his court continued to develop its knowledge and use of Chinese literature and social practices.

Though there were no official exchanges of envoys during this period, there was great law-making activity, regulating in the Chinese way everything from the functions of public officials to the style of ladies' coiffures. No end of time and energy was consumed by Chinese ceremonials of one kind or another, and temples were encouraged with generous gifts and elaborate festivals. Court people began to write Chinese poetry and, more important still, appointed a committee to write an official history of the country as they did in China. The efforts of this committee resulted in the Kojiki and the Nihongi.

In the first year of the eighth century another official embassy was sent to the T'ang court and, soon after, plans were well under way for building Nara, the first capital city of Nippon.

CHAPTER III

NARA, THE FIRST CAPITAL
(EIGHTH CENTURY)

IN APRIL of the year 710 the Yamato court moved into its first real capital. Before that the center of government had been wherever the head of the imperial clan had happened to live. In their own artless dwellings (Tenji-Tenno's is recorded as made of logs with the bark still on) the rulers had conferred with other clan leaders who in turn had given orders from their rustic homes. But the more they learned about the splendors of T'ang cities the more the Japanese nobles wanted to have a real capital of their own. And so Nara was built.

The site chosen was in a valley sheltered on three sides by gentle slopes, a place where as an ancient poem says, "When the bright spring showeth upon the hillsides, the cherry blossoms surpass all the world in beauty and the warblers are ever singing." [1] Several Buddhist temples, already established there on large estates, lent great dignity to the new center. Materials and builders poured in from near and far. Hewn timber, copper, tin and silver, clay products, dye stuffs, silk cloth and hempen cloth, together with skilled laborers, were brought from the various provinces of Japan, while architects, sculptors and painters were

37

brought from the continent, together with works of art and treasures of various kinds. Priests also came who knew the science of building roads, bridges and wells. It was a great age in which to be alive. The Yamato people had never seen such marvels before.

The city, covering thirty-five square miles, was laid out with broad streets crossing each other at right angles. Instead of the thatched-roof houses of simple construction to which they had been accustomed, now the imperial family and some of the high court officials built palaces of more massive architecture with roofs of colorful tiles.

Since all of these were destroyed a thousand years or more ago, it is not possible to give a clear picture of Nara in its prime, but many of the most treasured palace furnishings and personal belongings which were used by the imperial family in the eighth century are still preserved in a storehouse called Shoso-in.[2] Among them are thirty-one rugs of felt with intricate conventionalized floral designs in rich colors, and arm rests of wood in graceful shapes decorated with inlays of ivory, wood, mother-of-pearl and gold. These on special occasions were placed on the floor beside the silken cushions which served as chairs. For serving food there were low lacquered tables and dishes of glazed pottery from China. Many of the treasures appear to have been brought from distant places. A graceful glass ewer has curves strongly reminiscent of Persian design, while the inlaid camels on a mandolin-shaped instrument, and an exquisitely made game-board are suggestive of Central Asia. There are cups of rhinoceros horn believed to destroy or disclose poison. There are flutes, foot rules and dice of

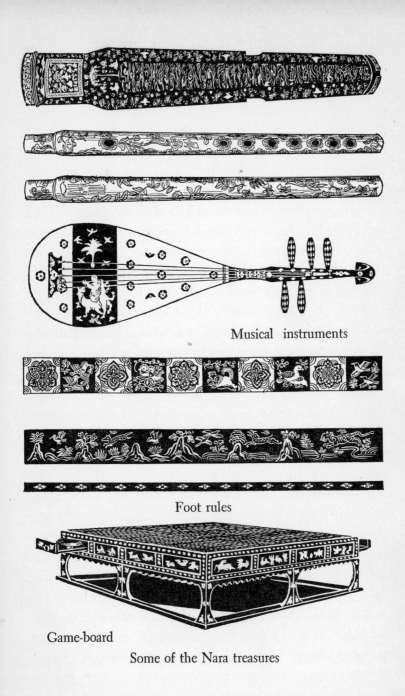

Musical instruments

Foot rules

Game-board

Some of the Nara treasures

carved ivory, which probably came from India ; ornaments
of jade and amber, furniture of red sandalwood, and a log
of incense wood, none of which were native to Japan. There
are two kinds of harps from Korea — one with twelve strings
and one with twenty-three. There are standing screens,
decorated with Chinese writing — some of it done by
famous Chinese scholars, and some of it colorfully appliquéd in duck feathers. There are scissors and pad-
locks of gilded copper, and spoons of gilded silver.

Also in this collection of Nara treasures are large needles
about a foot long, made of silver, copper and iron, which,
it is thought, were offered at the Weaving Maiden's Festival by young girls who desired special skill in needlework.[3]
In another festival of Chinese origin held on the first day
of the rat in the first month of the year, brushwood brooms
and lacquer plows were used. There is a broom in the
Shoso-in with colored glass beads strung on the brushwood, the handle bound with purple leather and gold
thread, with which, it is thought, the empress swept the
silk workroom as an act of worship to the deity of sericulture. And there is a lacquer plow decorated with gold and
silver with which, it is thought, the emperor plowed on the
same day to encourage agriculture. Fragments of two New
Year's cards, sent about twelve hundred years ago, are still
kept among the Nara treasures. They had cut-out designs
of gold leaf pasted over thin colored silk, with a message
that reads, "Auspicious occasion. Renewal of happiness.
Peace ten thousand years. May life last a thousand springs."

Everyday life in the Nara palace was copied as closely
as possible after that of the T'ang court. The affairs of the

imperial household were directed by a government official in accordance with prescribed forms of Chinese ceremony. People had to speak in honorific terms. They had to bow just so, and have a certain number of attendants. Differences of rank were strictly observed. Only persons of the fifth rank or above were allowed to enter the imperial presence.

Court costumes were constantly changing in response to the latest styles from China, but in general ladies wore loosely draped gowns with high necks, and flowing sleeves covering their hands. They had fancy girdles decorated with appliquéd designs, silk cords and glass beads. Courtiers wore voluminous long trousers gathered in at the ankles. They, too, wore ornate belts ; an especially fine one was of moleskin with rhinoceros horn ornaments and a silver buckle. On very festive occasions plum blossoms were worn in the hair. The emperor and empress had head-dresses made of lacy gold, set with pearls, rock crystal, coral and colored glass beads. The emperor had a pair of scarlet leather shoes with turned-up toes ; the backs above the heels were decorated with gold ribbon and silver flowers set with pearls and colored beads. The soles were scarlet leather like the rest, but the inside was lined with white leather and a pad of white silk. On all formal occasions courtiers wore very long and elaborate swords. These were not intended for use, but the length and splendor of the sheath bespoke the rank of the wearer.

The favorite sports of the Nara nobles were archery, rowing, horseback-riding and hunting with falcons. The ladies rode as well as the men either astride or sidesaddle.

For less active pastimes they had various gambling games and a sort of checkers. Often they were entertained by musicians, acrobats, jugglers and dancers. On one day a year, old, young, high-born and low gathered together on the streets or in open fields to sing and dance, to dance and sing, to flirt and fall in love.

Musicians (Nara period)

But Nara court life had a somber and serious side as well. Responsible officials were earnest in their desire to make their country orderly and prosperous ; and since the T'ang government was the very best they knew, they studied T'ang practices carefully with the idea of adopting and adapting them for their own needs. The Fujiwaras were leaders in this. Kamatari's son, Fubito, headed a committee of ten for devising a code of laws to apply to all the people. Many attempts had been made to do this since Prince Shotoku's time ; but the Taiho, Great Treasure, Code was the culmination of them all. This code was based on the idea that all persons, whatever their rank or from whatever family they came, were indebted to the state and were to be rewarded only as they showed their ability in service. When the Taiho Code was first completed, experts in legal matters were sent with it to provincial governors to explain it and to see that it was put in practice.

The range of things it sought to regulate was very wide :
official titles, the duties of officials in various royal households, services to the gods, Buddhist priests, the family,
land, taxation, the descent of the crown and dignity of imperial persons, salaries, army and frontier defenses, ceremonies, official costumes, public works, the mode of ad-
dressing persons of rank, storage of rice and other grain,
stables and fodder, duties of medical officers attached to
the court, official vacations, funerals and mourning, markets, arrest of criminals, finding of lost goods, and various
other matters.

The most important part of the Taiho Code was probably that which dealt with the administration of the provinces. It was very important that the government be extended to the provinces outside the capital, for it was from
the provinces that the court derived its income. According
to the new code, provincial governors were supposed to be
appointed by the emperor to hold office for from four to six
years. Their official duties included supervision of the
shrines of local kami, registration of land, the taking of a
census, and the selection of able-bodied men to be soldiers
or workmen for roads, palaces and timber lands. They were
also supposed to settle disputes and mete out justice.

It was the privilege of the provincial governors to recommend officials for the districts into which the provinces
were divided. Men whose families had lived on the land
for generations and who knew the farmers well were usually appointed. They really did most of the actual work,
while the provincial governors remained in Nara to enjoy
the exotic novelties of capital life. The chief duty of both

provincial and district officials was the collection of taxes. Most of the taxes they were supposed to send to the capital, but they were allowed to keep a certain share of all they collected as salary.

The bulk of the taxes which farmers had to pay was in rice which the nobles of the court not only used for food but exchanged instead of money for other things that they wanted. There was little money in Japan in those days. Some coins had been brought from the continent and some were minted in Japan after mines were discovered there, but neither kind was circulated widely. The court controlled the issuing of coinage as a special and profitable privilege. Whenever extra funds were needed it issued a new coinage of poorer quality but greater designated value than the previous one, and continued its efforts to put money into general use. The people, however, finding money increasingly to their disadvantage, preferred to use rice as their standard of value in buying and selling. And the court had to be content to collect as taxes, not metal coins, but cloth of silk and fiber, purple, red and yellow dye-stuffs, hemp, many kinds of fish, garlic, salt, oil (both fish and vegetable), iron spades, paper, willow branches for weaving into baskets, bamboo screens, mattresses, deer's horns for medicine, and barrels of saké, the rice wine of which Japanese have always been fond.

The Taiho Code did not become effective for a long, long time ; some of its regulations were never practiced. People were not accustomed to anything like it, and where it affected their privileges they often failed to see any advantage in it. Those who had always inherited their father's lands, slaves and titles continued to do so ; the system of inheritance was deep-rooted in Japan. Though a university was provided for the training of court officials, only noblemen's sons were allowed to enter, and the T'ang civil service system was never introduced. Influence still continued to play its part also (and where does it not ?) in the punishment of crimes.

The condition of slaves, however, was somewhat improved by the Taiho Code. From earliest times there had been large numbers of these ; some were prisoners of war, some criminals, some debtors, some sold into slavery to save the rest of their family. Able-bodied slaves could be bought for about a hundred bundles of rice ; then they and their children continued as the personal property of the purchaser. Like rice, they were also used as a medium of exchange and were one of the units in which wealth was measured. When the clan system began to break down, slaves were especially important for carrying on the cultivation of the land. The period is sometimes called the "period of slave economy." [4]

In addition to provincial government, literature was a serious concern of the Nara court people. Instead of depending entirely on scribes they were now beginning to be able to read and write themselves. It may be that some of the earlier settlers once had known some form of writing, but scholars have not yet been able to find any proof of this. The early rulers of Yamato had had a "Be," that is, a company or guild of reciters called the Katari-be, who kept in their minds the stories and traditions and important happenings of the leading families, reciting them on special

occasions. In the fifth and sixth centuries when large numbers of immigrants had begun coming into Japan from
Korea and China, those among them skilled in writing and
keeping records had been employed as scribes by the
Yamato chiefs. But when continental priests came, with
rolls of scripture, teaching the way of Buddha, the Yamato
people began to study how to read and write themselves.

After one really knows how, it does not seem at all hard
to read and write. If one remembers, however, the time
and effort spent on learning to write well in a single language which everyone around was using, and then thinks
of the Yamato people, grown men and women who had no
schools and had never done such things before, having to
learn from a few foreign teachers the several thousand
"characters," more complicated than letters, in which the
foreign books were written, the difficulty of their task will
be appreciated. Then, having learned to read and write
Chinese, they had the added problem of trying to use the
foreign characters to write their own language.[5] The process took a very long time.

Two languages more different than Japanese and Chinese
were in the eighth century are hardly possible. English
and German, or English and Greek, though they have different scripts, in grammar and vocabulary have many things
in common. But not so spoken Japanese and Chinese.
When Japanese first tried to write their language with
Chinese script, everyone had a different idea as to how it
should be done. Three distinct ways developed which may
be illustrated very simply like this. Suppose a Japanese
wished to express "man." In his own language the word

was "hito." The Chinese sign for man looked like this 人 . This sign the Chinese pronounced "jen." One thing the Japanese could do was use this just as the Chinese did and remember that 人 called "jen" means "hito." Or they could use the sign 人 and call it "hito" instead of "jen." And there was still another way. They could find a Chinese sign which was called "hi" and another "to" and put them together to express "hito," regardless of what the signs meant in Chinese. They did all three of these things in their writings in the Nara period. Four literary works from this period have been preserved by editors and copyists down to the present day. These are the two histories called Kojiki and Nihongi, and two collections of poetry called Kaifuso and Manyoshu.

The Kojiki appeared first. It was written in the second of the three ways given above, with Chinese signs in their proper meaning but arranged and pronounced in the Japanese way. The Nihongi and the Kaifuso were done in regular Chinese style, while the Manyoshu was written for the most part with Chinese signs which had the desired sound, regardless of their meaning. The use of these three different methods was very confusing, and it took a vast amount of study afterward to decipher them.

For five or six centuries Chinese court officials had been keeping records of events in the heavens, like comets and eclipses, together with those of important government affairs. Usually when a change of dynasty occurred these were compiled into an official history — such as the ones from which accounts of Japan were quoted in the first chapter. It was only natural that when the Japanese learned to read and write they should attempt to provide themselves with similar chronicles. Prince Shotoku and Soga, you will remember, are credited with the first venture of this kind. The Kojiki and Nihongi were produced by a historical committee originally appointed by Emperor Temmu. The preface to the Kojiki states that it was based on the facts stored up in the memory of a remarkable member of the reciters' guild, the Katari-be, and that it was written to sift the true from the false before it was too late. At this time, class rivalries had become intense, and preposterous claims were made by ambitious families in the name of their ancestry and relations. To rectify this situation, the court proceeded to guard itself with an authoritative record of genealogies. The Kojiki, completed in 712, was the result.

The Kojiki begins with the creation of Japan by heavenly deities, and the sending of the sun goddess' grandson to rule over the land, he and his descendants forever. And it goes on with stories of the imperial family, their conquests and relationships with other leading families, glorifying their loyal supporters with superior ancestors like their own. There are no dates in the Kojiki and the emperors are called by the names of the places where they had their home and court.

Eight years after this was completed, the Nihongi appeared. Neither of these writings were books as we think of them now. They were written with brush and ink on long strips of paper and rolled up on cylinders of ivory or some other semi-precious material instead of being folded flat and cut into pages. They were not printed in thousands. Copies had to be made by hand.

The Nihongi showed much greater literary accomplishment than the Kojiki ; it was much better calculated to impress the T'ang court. The compilers had introduced it with a Chinese theory of creation and embellished it throughout with Chinese literary forms. Emperors in the Nihongi often were given Chinese names, and dates were figured out according to the Chinese system, which put the founding of the Japanese nation by Jimmu-Tenno way back in antiquity.

Though the contents of the Kojiki and Nihongi are similar, the former concludes soon after the death of Prince Shotoku while the Nihongi carries the story on till the end of the seventh century. What evidence there is seems to indicate that some of the same people worked on both and that they added descriptions and anecdotes to their later work which they thought would interest Chinese readers. And, indeed, in the later histories of the T'ang Empire in China the Nihongi was often quoted when Japan was mentioned.

The Kojiki remained obscure for several centuries. But when the Nihongi was completed, it is said, a great court banquet was held in celebration and many poems were written in honor of the occasion. For years and years thereafter courtiers and officials were required to attend special lectures by outstanding scholars on various sections of the Nihongi. This document has served as an official textbook for over a thousand years and is still read as part of the New Year's celebrations of the court.

The writing of histories was limited to a very small group of men. In poetry, on the other hand, by the end of the

Nara period everyone of any education aimed to partici-
pate, from the emperor in the capital to the soldier on the
frontier, and from the royal princess to the Buddhist nun.
The writing of poetry in Japan has never been a profession
as it has with us.   It became in the days of Nara, as it is
now, an accomplishment to be expected of every person of
refinement.

The first poem said to have been composed in Japan is
credited to Amaterasu's brother, Susanowo, in honor of his
Izumo bride, and the only ones recorded in the Kojiki and
Nihongi were supposed to have been composed by members of the imperial family.   But in the Kaifuso, a collection of one hundred and twenty poems written in Chinese
for grand occasions such as enthronements and court ceremonies, sixty-four different courtiers are represented.   Over
six hundred writers, seventy of them women, are known to
have contributed poems in Japanese to the Manyoshu,
Collection of a Myriad Leaves.[6]

According to the Kojiki and Nihongi the Japanese were
fond of dancing even in the age of the gods.   There is the
very amusing story of the deity dancing on an overturned
tub to lure Amaterasu out of the cave where she had hidden, leaving the world in darkness.   The earliest songs of
the Yamato race were no doubt made to go with their dancing.   They made them as long as they wished and put from
four to eight syllables in a line.   The ideas they expressed
were plain and simple.   Most of them were love poems.
Others are about experiences we would scarcely think poetic.   There is one written by the Emperor Tenji which in
Japanese goes like this :

Aki no ta no,
Kari ho no iho no,
Toma wo arami
Waga koromo de wa,
Tsuyu ni nure tsutsu.

A literal translation is :

Autumn rice fields,
Sort of temporary house,
Rush matting may be,
My clothes on that account
With dew are getting wet.

One man says this means that the emperor was sitting in his palace weeping at the thought of the miserable shelters of the farmers on the land. Another says, "Oh, no, Emperor Tenji himself was working in the field setting an example for the people." [7]

That is the way many Japanese poems were twelve hundred years ago and still are — spontaneous expressions of emotion. If one is familiar with the man and the situation which gives rise to his poem, then it is perfectly understandable. But if one does not know these things, then there seems to be great leeway for personal interpretation. For this reason poems were often accompanied by brief prose prefaces describing the circumstances in which they were composed.

In the early days Yamato people had been accustomed to singing whatever came into their heads without much regard for the propriety of either form or content. Even Kamatari is represented in the Manyoshu with an outburst to this effect : "Wow ! I've won her. All men said she was hard to win, but I've won her !" [8]   Sentiments direct from the heart are characteristic of the Manyoshu poetry. At this stage the Japanese had learned enough of Chinese script to express in writing what they really wanted to say — but they had not yet developed the smooth facility with which, a century later, court ladies and nobles devoted themselves to poetry for poetry's sake.

Chinese influence, however, was tending to formalize everything in Nippon, and poetry was not an exception. Toward the end of the Nara period the majority of Japanese poems had assumed the standard form called tanka. This form had only five lines. The poetry of the T'ang court in China usually had either five or seven syllables in each line, and the Japanese adopted these line patterns, first a line of five syllables, then one of seven, another of five and then two of seven, making the five lines have thirty-one syllables in all. As you have noticed in Tenji's poem, the tanka has no rhyming pattern. Since Japanese has only five vowel sounds and every syllable ends in a vowel or "n," rhymes would be very stupid. It has no meter either of the compelling sort we are accustomed to in western verse. The rhythm is given instead by the natural arrangement of the two and three syllable elements in the five and seven syllable lines.

Nine out of ten poems in the Manyoshu and practically all the poems written in Japanese for over eight hundred years were in the tanka form. They had little of the variety we have in sonnets and quatrains, iambics and dactyls, and in the brief space afforded by the tanka it is obvious one could say but little. One could give only a hint, leaving the rest to the understanding and imagination of the reader. Sometimes a little trick of economy was performed and a lot more meaning was packed into the verses by the quoting of a few suggestive words from some supposedly familiar Chinese poem. It was considered very clever and elegant to do this, but it made severe demands on the reader's knowledge of literature.

The writing of poetry at the Nara court was certainly less of a social pastime than it came to be at the Heian. A number of the poems of this period were written on the occasion of deaths and accessions and were of a ritualistic and ceremonial nature. At farewell banquets, however, poems were sometimes written for the departing guest ; lovers often delighted each other with verses of recollection, longing and anticipation. Journeying courtiers also carried writing materials along with them and described in five and seven syllable lines, sent to their friends at home, sights and thoughts which occurred to them on their way. A long one in the Manyoshu gives this description, for those left at home, of the events of a voyage :

Like the shining mirror my dear holds in her hand each morn-
    ing
Is the shore from which we launched our tall ship manned by
    many oars.
We drifted on the tide to open ocean where white waves
    surged across the water.
When we sighted Lone Isle, darkness fell on the cloudy mar-
    gin of the sea,
As night still deepened we could not see our further course.
And, therefore, tarried in a bay in wave-rocked slumber.

I watched the fisher-girls casting lines from crowded boats in
    a row,
And, as the day grew brighter, screaming wild fowl hastening
    to the reed marsh.
The sailors shouted making ready, and the fishers launched
    their boats across the breakers.
Rowing our tall ship further we affronted huge ocean billows
    that rose and curled and toppled.
In the cloudy distance we passed Home Island which my eyes
    had longed to view,
And onward fared to the hollow Bay of Jewels.
While we tarried there my thoughts returned to homeland
    and tears fell from me.
I thought I would gather pearl shells such as deck the sea
    gods' arms,
And send them as gifts by runner to my home,
But, finding no runner, left them lying there.[9]

It is an interesting fact that practically all we know of
life away from the capital during the Nara period is contained in the Manyoshu in the poems of traveling priests
and court officials.

It was troublesome to travel in those days, for the roads
were poor and occasionally blocked by robbers. The frequent streams had but few ferries or bridges across them
and persons of rank either rode their horses through the
shallows or were carried over on the backs of common people. Since there were no inns, all provisions for the journey had to be carried along.

Ordinary farmers in the country lived in the crudest sort
of shelters with bare earth floors strewn with wisps of straw
on which the family huddled together at night to sleep.

If they labored from sunrise to sunset and had good fortune they could raise enough rice to live on and make enough cloth to cover themselves, but a poem [10] in the Manyoshu says, "Then would come the village head-man with his rod in hand calling for taxes or service in loud and angry tones." If their crops were poor on account of heavy rains or droughts or insects, then "No smoke rose from their hearths but spiders wove their webs about the iron cooking pots, forgetting rice was ever cooked in them." If some member of the household was called away to do forced labor building a governor's mansion or fighting on the frontier, the rest of the family had not only to do his share of the work at home, but in addition to their regular taxes provide his livelihood and equipment wherever he might be for as long as he was away. A courtier sent out from Nara as counsellor to the governor of a distant province was passing along a mountain trail when he saw a shrunken corpse lying by the wayside and wrote in a poem his thoughts : [11]

> White clothes made by a dear one
> From dried hemp grown in the garden.
> A girdle bound three times
> Around the wasted frame —
> Returning home from having done forced labor
> Hurrying on in pain,
> Eager to see wife and parents
> Here the gentle soul departed.
> The hair is disheveled, the body looks chilly —
> His family ? His native place ?
> No answer.

From poems in the Manyoshu we also learn how Nara
people felt about overseas voyages. They were indeed experiences to strike terror in the heart. When parties were
about to embark on the "Dread Way Perilous of the Great
God of the Sea" they gathered with their families and
friends at the Sumiyoshi Shrine (near the modern city of
Osaka on the Inland Sea, which even in those days was a
great port). Praying here for the voyagers' safe return,
they made offerings of jars filled full with rice wine and of
cloth of mulberry bark.

It is no wonder that any Japanese who went to China to
study was thought of very highly and honored by his countrymen. There was one man named Kibi no Mabi who
left Japan in the early days of Nara when he was twenty-
two years old, and remained in China studying for seventeen years. Later he went again as an official envoy to the
T'ang court. Japanese official history says that the Chinese were favorably impressed by his dignity and sincerity
and were inclined to think well of the country he represented.[12]

When Kibi no Mabi returned to Japan the first time, he
brought with him a great store of knowledge and books on
many subjects. He gave many lectures to the Nara court
on the forms of etiquette and ceremony considered proper
in China, and on the classics of Chinese literature. He
was made head of the university established at Nara for
training officials and before he died had become an important minister of state. Kibi no Mabi is also said to have
been the inventor of a simplified set of phonetic symbols
called katakana, which the Japanese use for writing as we

use our alphabet. Though the katakana more likely were
developed later, the fact that Kibi is credited with their in-
vention shows how great and clever a man people thought
he was, and how much they respected him.[13]

Even toward the end of the Nara period, after considerable experience with navigation, a voyage was a terrifying
undertaking. One mission returning from China set out
from the Yangtze River with four ships, each carrying over
a hundred people. These included the chief envoys, their
subordinate officials, secretaries, interpreters, doctors and
diviners, carpenters, seamen and crew. Soon after setting
out they ran into a storm. One envoy and forty of his followers were washed overboard and drowned. After a day
or so at sea a mast snapped and a ship broke into pieces.
Those who could clung to the pieces which floated and
were finally washed ashore. One ship reached Japan safely
after only nine days of battering at sea, while another took
forty days to make the trip. The last ship of the four was
wrecked on an island and the passengers were made cap-
tives. This was perhaps a more unlucky mission than most,
but such disasters were not uncommon. Even with fair
skies and smooth sailing the discomforts of a hundred or
more people crowded together for many days on one of
those small ships may well be left to the imagination.

But discomforts and dangers notwithstanding, official
embassies continued to go from the Nara court to the T'ang
at approximately fifteen year intervals. What they especially desired to bring home with them were books — books
on government, on writing and phonetics, on calendar
making and astrology, and the official historical works of

the Chinese court. Not only did court officials by their courageous voyaging prove the intensity and sincerity of their interest in T'ang culture, but Buddhist priests also, continually coming and going between the continent and the islands, gave convincing proof of their faith in the possibilities of Nippon. Famous priests from China and even from India came out to the islands to teach and ordain new followers ; while less famous, perhaps, but no less zealous priests from Nippon made the perilous trips to China to study and bring back treasures for their temples. Indeed it seems more than likely that the Buddhist priests played a very important part in inspiring, directing and sustaining the interest of the Japanese people in things Chinese.

CHAPTER IV

BUDDHIST PRIESTS AND THEIR
NARA TEMPLES
(EIGHTH CENTURY)

FROM the good start Prince Shotoku gave them the
Buddhists had continued to go forward improving
their economic condition, extending their public works and
making their influence felt in ever widening areas. Before
the Nara capital was built an imperial edict was issued ordering every family to have a Buddhist altar and read the
scriptures daily in the home. Since very few people knew
how to read, this edict probably was not generally effective, but it is recorded that there were already thirty-four
temples and fifteen nunneries built throughout the country, and that several Ainu even had been prepared for the
priesthood and sent out as missionaries to the northeastern
frontier.

Buddhist temples were large institutions. They spread
over several acres of ground in the midst of beautiful scenery, and were enclosed by walls too tall for a passerby to
look over. In the south side of the wall was an ornamental
gateway covered with a gently sloping roof. The whole
enclosure represented a realm of enlightenment. In the
center was the Golden Hall where the statue of Buddha

was enshrined. Surrounding this were the pagoda, in which his earthly life was represented, the bell tower, the drum tower and various other buildings connected by covered

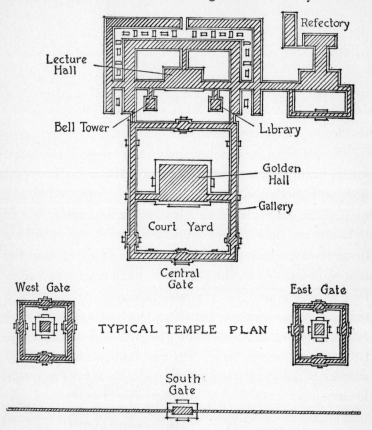

TYPICAL TEMPLE PLAN

passageways and porches. There were buildings where the priests slept, ate and studied, and others where they cared for orphans and aged people, where they taught lay students the holy scriptures, where they dispensed medicinal herbs to people who were sick, or prayed and performed rites for invalids.[1]

The Golden Hall was not a very large building but it was as beautiful as its priests knew how to make it — and this is saying a great deal, for Buddhist priests had had long and rich experience in all forms of art. A gilded statue of Buddha occupied the central place, surrounded by wall paintings, ceremonial banners of richly colored silk brocades, and other accessories of worship made of precious materials by devoted hands. Here on regular occasions the scriptures were solemnly intoned and priests in slow and rhythmic procession performed the sacred rites accompanied by the beat of hand drums and the music of wooden flutes. Attendants, either standing or sitting in worshipful pose on the floor, could not help but be impressed by the mysterious and exotic beauty of the sacred ceremonies.

It was not only a great honor but also a very profitable thing to be a priest in those days. The temples had the best of everything in the country. They received in addition to gifts of land the very best the people had to offer in rice, wine and sea food, in silk and hempen cloth. They owned most of the books and the works of art imported from the continent. The temples were the homes of all the best scholars and artists. As such they provided more luxury, more culture and more security than any nobleman's palace. Their number, however, was limited and it was a much sought after privilege to be a priest.

Prominent priests and abbots of the temples were all able men of wide experience. Most of them had either been brought up and trained on the continent, having taken refuge in Japan from wars and political disturbances in their native lands, or had gone to China to study with Chinese

masters and teachers ; one had even come from India. All of
them had traveled. They knew the ways of the world.
There was a loved and learned priest who tried five different times to come to Japan from China but each time was
shipwrecked and nearly died. On the sixth attempt, a very
old man and completely blind, he arrived safely on the
same boat with the famous political scholar Kibi no Mabi,
mentioned in the previous chapter. Another priest named
Gyogi was a great personality. Gyogi traveled all over
Japan and wherever he went drew such crowds to listen to
him that he was jailed for a while as a disturber of the
peace. He taught the people how to build roads and
bridges, how to dig wells, and how to make harbors safe
for ships. He planted small trees and gardens of herbs
which were good for medicine, and brought the people relief from famine, pests and plagues. He also solicited offerings for the building of an enormous statue of Buddha
at Nara which he did not live quite long enough to see
completed.

There are two kinds of Buddhism, one the teachings of
the historic Buddha himself, and the other, teachings which
later grew up about Buddha. It was the second kind,
"about Buddha," which was brought to Japan. The entire
collection of these teachings is called the Tripitaka. The
Tripitaka is to the Buddhist what the Bible is to the Christian, and as the Bible is made up of many separate books
written at different times and places by different people, so
the Tripitaka (of the "about Buddha" kind of Buddhism)
is made up of over four hundred and fifty different "sutras." Just a few of these became great favorites and sects

were founded which emphasized the teachings of one sutra alone. The Lotus Sutra and the Sutra of the Benevolent King were the most popular ones at Nara. These sutras had been written originally in Sanskrit, then translated into Chinese as the religion was carried eastward. They were still copied in Chinese when they reached Japan.

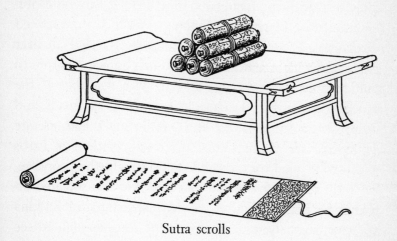

Sutra scrolls

One of the first requirements for a priest, therefore, was that he be able to read Chinese script. For this reason most of those who aspired to the priesthood in early days were members of Chinese or Korean families who had migrated to Japan and had brought some knowledge of reading and writing with them. But there were many native Japanese, too, who by diligent effort were able to qualify for the advanced studies of a temple. The advantages of the priesthood were a great stimulus to learning.

The copying of sutras was not confined to temples — a special government bureau was organized for this purpose.

Only men who had learned to write very beautifully were allowed to copy the texts and only the most excellent of all was allowed to write the titles.   There were proofreaders who re-read each copy twice and imposed penalties on the copyist if they found more than five errors on a sheet. Then there were "dressers" who joined the separate sheets of paper into a long strip, dyed it with a brownish stuff distasteful to insects, mounted it on a roll and fastened it with a silk cord.   There were specialists to make writing brushes from rabbit, deer and badger fur, and paper polishers who rubbed the paper with a boar tusk to smooth it.   Paper was made at two different places in Nara from mulberry bark, hemp, straw and rags.   Painters were employed also to decorate the ends of the rolls and a space at the beginning of the scroll.   The full staff included more than two hundred people and could complete about six thousand copies a month.[2]   This Sutra Copying Bureau was one of the most important factors in the development of Japanese art ; from it later came the families of official artists for the service of the court.

Besides reading, writing and religion, medicine and civil engineering, the Japanese learned from the Buddhist priests the science of blending metals and the art of casting and engraving them.   In the course of years they became especially skilled in this.[3]

Buddhist priests also encouraged the raising of silkworms, silk weaving and dyeing.   In the early days of Nara, textile experts were sent to twenty-one provinces to teach the advanced art of weaving brocades and twills. These experts had recipes for the exact amounts of various

kinds of plants which would give exactly the desired shade
to a fixed length of silk when it was boiled with exactly so
much vinegar and wood ash over exactly so much fuel.
There are fragments of silk still remaining from the Nara
age, some of which though dyed with madder root twelve
hundred years ago are even now a fresh rich red. Blue and
green were derived from a kind of marsh grass and a shrub
called the wild orange. Fragrant jasmine blossoms supplied the yellow. The designs used often included birds,
flowers, trees and insects.[4] While much of the silk used
by princes and priests was imported from the continent,
the best of the native textiles also were sent to the court
and temples as tribute.

The Buddhist priests were certainly an inspiration for
Yamato. "Look forward," they taught, "not backward ;
build temples, not tombs ; cremate your dead and make
your monumental offerings works of art which may bring
enlightenment to children yet unborn." Though they
kept the favor of the powerful and wealthy, they did not
scorn the poor. The most beautiful pagoda, they demonstrated, may be built from the roughest timber.

The Yamato people admired these priests greatly and
trusted them ; trusted them for advice in dealing with their
continental neighbors ; trusted them for the healing of
their ills and the satisfying of their desires. And for these
things the Yamato people paid well.

The Buddhist priests had advanced so far and so fast
that they did not think it enough to be merely the rulers
of temples. They began to see Japan as a Buddhist kingdom entirely under their control. To that end they ap-

pointed officials of the Buddhist order similar to the officials of the state. Some of the shrewdest members of the
court, seeing danger ahead, tried to put brakes on the Buddhist progress and develop within their own ranks leaders
of equal merit. The strongest of these were the Fujiwaras,
the descendants of Kamatari. It was they who promoted
the codes of law for governing the country. One of Kamatari's sons named Fubito became prime minister soon after
Nara was founded, and his four capable sons all held important offices. One of his daughters was the mother of
the heir to the throne, and another daughter by another
wife was a likely person for the heir to marry. With the
Fujiwaras in such a good position to defend the imperial
interests the day when a Buddhist priest would take the
place of the emperor seemed very far away. The Fujiwaras
themselves, to be sure, were not beyond Buddhist influence, but they had their own talents and their own ambitions.

Fubito's younger daughter did marry the emperor, and,
though not immediately, was proclaimed Empress of Japan
a few years later. This was the first time in the history of
the country that such an honor had been bestowed upon a
girl not born of the imperial family. Fubito, however, had
not lived to enjoy it. Not long afterward some poor fishermen from Korea landed in Japan with smallpox which
spread through the population like wildfire. Among those
who lost their lives were Fubito's four promising sons.

As the plague raged on, priests advised the court to turn
to Buddha. In Buddha, they said, lay the only hope for
the nation. Emperor Shomu allowed two and three thou-

sand persons at a time to become priests and nuns and attach themselves to the more than two thousand temples then existing in the country. Lavish offerings were made for prayers at the Nara temples. And still the plague raged on. Then it was decided to build a bronze statue of Buddha over fifty feet high and a special sanctuary to contain it. To help this project along Emperor Shomu ordered that in every province a temple be built with a seven-story pagoda and a nunnery. "Let the sound of the tools that are raising the image of Buddha reverberate in heaven!" urged Fubito's daughter, Shomu's Empress Komyo. "Let it rend the earth asunder! for the sake of the fathers, for the sake of the mothers, for the sake of all mankind!" [5] Thus she encouraged the people in their giving and toil.

Metals, timber and fuel were brought from all over the country. A million pounds of bronze were to be melted and molded. Such an enormous metal statue had never been cast before nor has one of such size been cast since. Six attempts at casting ended in failure, and then the son of a Korean immigrant who had come to Japan in Tenji-Tenno's time finally succeeded. He turned out a perfect figure of Buddha sitting on a pedestal shaped like a lotus blossom, backed by an enormous halo studded with minor statues of Buddhist saints all united in adoration, and for his remarkable achievement was honored with the fourth rank of the court.

At this point, the priests did some clever propagandizing. They had it announced far and wide that gold was discovered for the first time in Japan and this was a sign that the deities were well pleased. They had some of the precious metal transported to Nara with great ceremony and gilded the great bronze Buddha. Emperor Shomu abdicated his throne and gave it over to his daughter so that he might be relieved of government duties and devote himself wholly to worship — or so it was reported. Such a thing had never before been heard of in Japan. Though his daughter was no longer young, she was still unmarried and had no heir to succeed her. The chances for the Buddhist kingdom looked very bright indeed.

On the two-hundredth anniversary of the date when Buddhism is officially supposed to have been brought to Yamato, the dedication ceremony for the great bronze Buddha was held. A grand procession moved solemnly along the broad avenue from the palace toward the Todai temple, led by the new Empress Koken followed by her father and mother, the retired Emperor Shomu and his wife the Empress Komyo. Hundreds of lesser court people followed, robed in voluminous gowns of colored silk. At the entrance to the new sanctuary the procession was greeted with music and feasting.

"Ten thousand" priests and musicians in brocade robes were there performing with rhythmic motion. On two stages outside the temple groups of figures wearing large, grotesque masks performed rhythmic dances. Inside the temple was candlelight, incense and perfume. A crimson cloth covered the floor. Before the great Buddha offerings were laid ; gilded copper flowers on six silver stands, crystal balls, white tortoise-shell cups.[6]

At the climax of the ceremony Ex-Emperor Shomu and

his empress proclaimed themselves "servants of Buddha and the three treasures." [7]   Then wearing a crown he mounted a platform forty feet above the crowd while the priests and musicians chanted.   A very large brush was there with endless yards of light-blue silk cord suspended from it.   Shomu clasped the brush in his hands.   The spectators below clasped the cord that they too might have a part in the rite of painting black pupils on the great gold eyes and making the Nara Daibutsu an image filled with the spirit of light.   This image was not thought of as the real deity any more than the statues or crosses in Christian churches are thought to be really Christ.   It was a symbol which made the deity seem near, real and understandable.

These were great days for the Buddhists in Japan.   It was their golden age.   Their ambitions seemed scarcely to exceed their grasp ; their highest hopes seemed all but fulfilled.   A priest named Dokyo was their head.   By gift, purchase and reclamation they had come into possession of as much land as was controlled by the imperial household itself.   And temple land was free from taxes.   Dokyo was given rank higher even than the prime minister, and his annual income was very large.   Empress Koken jilted the Fujiwara whom previously she had extravagantly favored with affection, lands and titles, and took Dokyo for her lover.   Only one more step to the throne !

But this step never was taken.   The landlords rebelled against Buddhist domination and the best soldiers in the country refused to fight for it.   "Since the establishment of the state," it was proclaimed, "the distinction between

sovereign and subject has been observed. The successor
to the throne must be of the imperial family. The usurper
is to be rejected." [8]

The country was in a turmoil. Before long the Empress
Koken passed away and Dokyo was made an ordinary priest
again. Conditions in Nara made it expedient for the court
to establish itself elsewhere, and so the first capital was
abandoned and a new one started thirty miles across the
valley.

The temples, however, remained at Nara, and on the
grounds of one, Todai-ji, was the Shoso-in, the temple
storehouse mentioned in the last chapter, which was built
of rough-hewn logs and which, alone of all the buildings
that stood in the heyday of Nara, was to survive the ravages of storm, fire, war and time. In the Shoso-in were
stored all the treasured possessions of Emperor Shomu
which his widowed empress, Komyo, had dedicated to the
Todai temple after his death in 756. The document of
dedication reads:

His Majesty the late Emperor was illustrious and his virtue
filled the universe. . . He suppressed wickedness and exalted
the doctrine of Buddha. . . Priests of the purest virtue and
deepest learning came to his empire from afar. . .
. . . Alas, of his term on earth there could be no prolonga-
tion and his spirit has departed. . . Nine and forty days have
now elapsed, but each day my grief grows deeper and sadness
weighs ever heavier on my heart. . . I have therefore resolved
by the performance of good deeds to give succour to his august
spirit. To this end, and in obedience to the will of his late
Majesty, these his relics, that in truth are national treasures,
I donate to the Todai-ji by way of offering to Buddha for the

repose of the Emperor's soul. May these gifts I humbly pray, help its progress to the Temple in the Lotus World. May he there always enjoy heavenly music, and may he finally be admitted to the Sacred Hall of the Buddha of Light ! [9]

A list with detailed descriptions of over six hundred and fifty items followed this devout dedication, and a number of these are still carefully preserved. More offerings were made a little later and many of the temple treasures used in the great Eye Opening and other ceremonies were also stored in the Shoso-in, together with one hundred suits of armor, eighty swords, one hundred and three bows, ninety-six quivers full of arrows and twenty-one chests of medicines.

In the course of centuries, some of these objects were withdrawn by members of the imperial family and twice thieves broke in through the floor, but nearly five hundred dated objects from the eighth century are still preserved in the collection. The expansion and contraction of the logs with the weather, it is explained, has guarded the precious contents well against both dampness and dryness. They are further protected now by an imperial seal which keeps the building locked except during a few weeks of good weather in the autumn.

For the annual opening a messenger arrives from his Imperial Majesty in Tokyo, and with officials of the Imperial Household Museum proceeds up the freshly raked sand path to the threshold. Here all slip out of their footgear and with fresh water from a wooden dipper cleanse their hands ceremonially, drying them on soft white paper. Great formality attends the unsealing and unlocking of the massive

wooden doors before they swing open on their wooden piv-
ots. Then the treasures are officially inspected and cared
for, and by very special permission visitors with electric
flashlights may view the remains of the glory that was
Nara : palace furnishings and personal adornments, mirrors and musical instruments, swords, saddles, bows and
arrows, scepters, masks, and rosaries, brocade banners,
bronze censers and flower baskets.

An interesting though unspectacular part of the collection
are the medicines in their little earthenware jars. These,
too, were given to Todai-ji in adoration of Buddha, and
theoretically any person suffering from illness and in need
of them could apply to the head priests of the temple. The
clergy had a practical monopoly of medicines and their ap-
plication. One priest was sent to China especially to study
medicine. Its chief use in those days was to promote
long life and to keep men virile ; the curing of disease was
secondary.

The parts and organs of the body, in accordance with
Chinese philosophy, were designated Yin or Yang, i.e.,
passive or active in essence, and also by the five elements
— wood (liver), fire (heart), earth (spleen), metal (lung) and
water (kidney) ; and medicines were similarly designated
according to their origin and properties. Sickness, like all
other evils, they thought was caused by a lack of harmony
between the active and passive elements, and medicines
were chosen to restore a harmonious relationship between
them in the body.

A kind of pepper was used to warm the stomach, cure
rumblings in the intestines, pain in the shoulder, headache,

toothache or nasal catarrh. Croton seeds from India were used to open the passages of the body, kill worms and cure snake bites. Magnolia wood from Cochin-China was pulverized and made into pills or given with ginger juice for typhus, diarrhea or nervousness. Petrified dragon bones "with a simple sweet taste" were supposed to protect one from devils and to quiet the mind; powdered and heated they were a dose for malaria. Rhubarb was used as a tonic and laxative; mica powder, for carbuncles; nutgall, to prevent perspiration and for dyeing the hair; a form of arsenopyrites for rat poison; hedgehog skin from northwest Asia and Africa for hemorrhoids; and sheep fat from Korea to cure colds and gout and to expel wind. These remedies and many others are still to be found in the Shoso-in.[10]

All in all this collection of treasures in the Nara temple storehouse is unique. Nowhere else in the world is an age represented by such a variety of objects so carefully preserved throughout more than a thousand years.

CHAPTER V

THE IMPERIAL COURT
(NINTH AND TENTH CENTURIES)

AFTER the affair of Empress Koken and Priest Dokyo the whole country was in confusion, and naturally enough. Only two hundred years before, the Yamato people had had very little of what we call civilization. They had been entirely illiterate, and practically ignorant of both organized religion and organized government. In the two centuries from 600 to 800, they had tried three great experiments. They had learned to read Chinese script and tried to adapt it for writing their own language. They had tried to attain the fulfillment of their desires by following the teachings of Buddha and his priests. And they had made an effort to establish a centralized government such as there was in China.

It is small wonder that disorder followed change. It is small wonder that each of the several Japanese books written in Chinese script used the foreign symbols in a different way, or that the Buddhist priests to whom the Yamato leaders had looked for guidance had attempted to seize the supreme power themselves. Nor is it very surprising that government by public officials could not be made effective throughout the country at once, for both the geography of the land and the psychology of the people were very different from those of China.

Instead of the broad, fertile plains and the few wide torpid rivers separating vast areas, here were rocky slopes, stony valleys and innumerable little torrents cutting the country to bits. Instead of worldly wise philosophers were men and women of ambition and action.

Japan was still a young country with frontiers beyond the reach of court officials where small farmers could escape from burdensome tax collectors and where energetic leaders could develop their own domains. On the large island to the south and west were independent clans of bold seafarers ; in the north and east beyond Mount Fuji were the Ainu and a vigorous breed of settlers.[1] The Nara priests had enshrined the sea god in one of their temples, hoping thus to win the cooperation of seafaring clans in importing treasures from China, but these worshippers of Hachiman had refused to fight for Dokyo. The settlers on the northeastern frontier rose up in revolt when the government tried to expand and take toll of their forests, fields and mines. Even among the clans close to the capital there was keen rivalry. But now a new generation of Fujiwaras had grown up since the great epidemic, as determined as their ancestor Kamatari had been to establish the supremacy of the imperial family.

Fujiwara Momokawa was determined that the emperor should be an able man. He stayed forty days in the palace refusing to move, until at sword's point it was agreed that the prince of his choice was to succeed to the throne.

Though this prince was a great-grandson of Emperor

Tenji, his mother was a girl of Korean descent, not of the Yamato nobility, and his position, therefore, had not been very high. He had belonged to the Junior Grade of the Fifth Rank and had earned his living as head of the imperial university at Nara. Fujiwara Momokawa saw in this, however, an excellent recommendation for his protégé, for in the university little respect was paid to Buddhism. There they were concerned with the study of Chinese history, Chinese institutions and the teachings of the Chinese sages, which had to do with the responsibilities of rulers, with loyal and proper conduct toward people of higher and lower rank, and were closely associated with good government. Furthermore, through his mother's relations this prince had the support of a large colony of continental immigrants who had settled in the province of Omi near Lake Biwa and who had grown very rich and important because of their great skill in weaving silk and their monopoly of saké brewing. Both of these industries had flourished when the Nara temples flourished, but when the clergy fell from favor, they had to look for other patrons. Thus, in addition to being a Chinese scholar, and more independent of the Buddhist priests than were many courtiers of his day, this prince united the interests of the wealthy and progressive immigrant group with the interests of the Yamato leaders, chief among whom were the Fujiwaras.

When he became emperor, Kwammu began planning at once for the removal of the capital from Nara. The priests of the Nara temples were very loath to have the court carried away from their control since it meant the loss of the many gifts and favors which they had enjoyed under Shomu and the empresses. There were also old clan leaders whose interests were closely affiliated with Nara who opposed the move in every possible way and for ten years struggled to prevent it. The Fujiwara minister in charge of the plans for the new capital was assassinated. Even after the new capital was built, a rebellion was instigated within the imperial family and an attempt made to move back to Nara. But plans for the new capital were carefully laid.

A new site was chosen some thirty miles west of the old which had three chief advantages. It was away from the center of the scheming Buddhist priests ; it was convenient to the settlement of Chinese and Korean immigrants, willing to support the new regime ; and it was on the direct route from the Inland Sea via Lake Biwa to the northern frontier where uprisings were growing more serious. Emperor Kwammu's capital was called Heian-kyo, Capital of Peace, and the new era which it instituted was called the Heian Era. People often referred to Heian-kyo simply as Miyako, The Capital ; later it came to be better known as Kyoto, and since that is the name most familiar today, Kyoto it will be called in this book.

The great cities of the world all seem to be on rivers. The T'ang Chinese had a superstitious saying which they applied when they chose the site for their capital : "For a capital, three hills and two rivers." [2] And it is said the Japanese court thought of this also when they chose the location for their new center of government and planned to model it after the magnificent T'ang capital. Kyoto was supposed to be a very fortunate choice, for it lay in a valley protected on three sides by mountains which opened toward the south, and through this valley ran two beautifully clear streams.

To separate the city from the surrounding fields a wall was built enclosing a section of land about three miles square. A moat was dug just beyond the wall and through it flowed fresh water. In the northern part of this enclo-

Typical Palace and Garden

sure was the imperial palace. Its grounds stretching for about a mile in each direction were also surrounded by walls with three gateways on each side. The Kyoto of Kwammu's day was not such a splendid city as is often imagined. The imperial palace and the government buildings around it were built in part with materials transported across the valley from the demolished Nara palace.

The most spectacular edifice was the Great Hall of State.

It stood on a spacious stone platform, surrounded by red lacquered balustrades ; its roof of blue-green tiles was up-held by fifty-two pillars painted a rich red. The imperial throne stood on a dais in this hall with a canopy and golden phœnix over it, bespeaking the schoolmaster emperor's fondness for things Chinese.[3] Near by was the hall where nobles and court ladies gathered to attend official entertainments, and the Hall of Martial Virtues with its field for archery, riding and equestrian games. Further se-cluded were the hall in which state ministers and nobles of high rank conferred with the emperor, and the living apartments of the emperor and his consorts, called the Cool Refreshing Hall. Just outside the wall on the southern side was a large estate, comprised of several buildings, which Kwammu gave for the university. Here also, many of the nobles had residences.[4]

Broad avenues traversed that part of the city not occu-pied by the official enclosure, dividing it into equal districts called First Ward, Second Ward and so on to the Ninth. The avenues, wide enough for ten bullock carts abreast, were traversed by narrower thoroughfares lined with one-story unpainted houses roofed with shingles or thatch, where the common people lived. Shrines and temples too were located here and there — shrines to the old deities of the land — and temples to Buddha and the Chinese sage Confucius. The booming of the temple bells let people know how time was passing.

Merchants were not scattered everywhere in the city as they are today. They were established in a large market where, on scheduled days, people would display the products and wares which they wished to sell. These were brought from many provinces. Business was still carried on chiefly in terms of rice : thirty bundles of rice, let us say, for a roll of silk ; three bundles of rice for a hoe, and so forth.

Market scene

Modes of transportation in Kyoto varied with the rank of the traveler. High officials sometimes sat in curtained palanquins which were carried around on poles in the hands of a group of servants. Sometimes they rode in two-wheeled carts drawn by oxen and attended by many servants walking. Those of lesser rank and importance rode on horseback. But the common people, by far the greatest in number, went everywhere on foot.

The Japanese capital was small compared with the Chinese one it copied, but was none the less lovable for that. People flocked to it as if charmed, and as time went on built nearly forty thousand homes there.

Emperor Kwammu did everything he could to make Kyoto the real center of the country with government authority extending from it as far as possible in all directions. He built new roads, repaired bridges and improved old ferries to facilitate travel between the provinces and the capital.

Government through the ages, as everyone well knows, has been a great system for collecting taxes, and this was the chief concern of the Heian regime. The Nara government had failed because it had paid little attention to the collection of taxes. Large areas of the land, whose yield was its greatest source of revenue, had got away from it and into the hands of priests and officials who were immune from taxes. That is why Emperor Kwammu, when he came to the throne, issued an edict forbidding the gift or sale of land to religious organizations, and limiting the building of temples and the number of men and women who might become priests and nuns. Many officials, too, had added to their own lands at the expense of the government which they were supposed to serve. They not only accepted lands from farmers who could not pay their taxes but also reclaimed land from mountain slopes and river beds by using forced labor, and held it as their own instead of turning it over to the emperor. By these methods district governors who handed their office down from father to son were able to build up very large estates for their families. Then there was also the possibility that a dishonest tax collector might simply keep the taxes for himself and report that he had been unable to deliver them to the capital because a bridge was down, the roads were bad, or the storehouse where the tax rice was kept had been struck by lightning.

All these malpractices Kwammu-Tenno sought to remedy. He tried to put into effect the Chinese system of office based on merit instead of inheritance, and made a great effort to do away with officials who sought special privileges for themselves. When lightning struck too often in the same district the governor was investigated. Inspectors were appointed to audit the tax records in all the provinces, and the emperor himself often performed official tasks until he found a man whom he thought honest and efficient to relieve him. The farmers who had left their lands and migrated toward the frontier, he ordered to return to their native places, and for their protection he had granaries built and stored up rice for times of need. He also tried to get people in the provinces to pay their taxes in money if they had any, for money was more convenient than rice to use in the capital market, and was of less use than rice in the country. There had never been very much money, however, and now more and more of it, instead of fulfilling its intended function, was being melted and made into huge bells and Buddhist statues.[5]

The Ainu up in the northeast, supplemented by rebellious farmers, were another one of Kwammu's great problems. While his father was ruling, they had won a victory over the provincial defenders, and again not long afterward had defeated them on sea as well as on land, causing the death of over a thousand of the emperor's soldiers. Whenever a court official was sent there to try to collect taxes they were stirred to fresh revolt and finally began pressing down toward Isé. "They gathered together like ants and dispersed like birds."

Then Kwammu, whose name means Prosperous in War, organized imperial troops from among the sons and younger brothers of provincial officials. Two thousand suits of leather armor he provided for them, and three thousand suits of iron armor. He appointed a man named Tamura Maro, of extraordinary height and hawk-like eyes, as permanent Sei-i Tai Shogun, Great Barbarian-subduing General. Tamura Maro drove the rebels farther and farther back and killed some of their chiefs. At last many of the ringleaders who survived fled to the northernmost island, Hokkaido. Those who remained agreed to obey the shoguns who were sent to rule them. An occasional burst of resentment occurred later and there were a few rebellious sons of courtiers on the frontier, but aside from these minor disturbances the country enjoyed peace for three hundred years. Tamura Maro was the first warrior to be given the title of shogun, and the last shogun of any importance during the Heian era. At the end of the twelfth century, however, the whole of Japan came to be ruled by a shogun and continued to be until 1868.

But to return to the early ninth century and Emperor Kwammu. He had broken with the Nara Buddhists, it is true, but he did not fail to appreciate all the good their priests had done in developing civilization in Yamato. Though his own interests centered more largely in the wisdom of Chinese sages, his courtiers and court ladies were enthusiastic attendants at the beautiful temple ceremonies and willing believers in the power of Buddhist prayers to save them from disaster, disease and death. Kwammu did not attempt to suppress Buddhism entirely; he merely tried to free the government from Buddhist domination.

As it happened there were two brilliant young priests who saw things much as he did and were willing to work with him. One was Saicho; the other, Kukai.[6]

Saicho belonged to a family of Chinese immigrants who had settled near Lake Biwa. He was ordained at Nara when he was eighteen years old, but growing dissatisfied with the conduct of the Nara priests, went off into the mountains near his native place to think and pray alone. When Kwammu founded Kyoto, a little monastery built by Saicho already stood on Mount Hiei, north of the site, to defend it from the evil spirits which Japanese seem to think always lurk in that direction. Before long there were many places of worship and learning on the slopes of Mount Hiei, but the priests devoted themselves to religious services and did not meddle in politics during Kwammu-Tenno's lifetime.

Kukai was a descendant of a warrior clan which had for generations served as imperial guards at Isé, but which had been implicated in a plot to prevent the removal of the capital from Nara and were, therefore, in disfavor with Emperor Kwammu. Young Kukai, however, managed to go to China with Saicho, as some modern scholars think, to restore the fortunes of his family.[7] There he remained three years, studying with both Indian and Chinese masters, traveling and collecting many books and works of art. Upon his return he had no more than begun to make a good impression on the Heian court when another relative was indicted for plotting against it. Though this made Kukai's position difficult, it could not prevent his rise. He personally contrived to be on good terms with everyone of influence, made friends of Shinto priests and courtiers as well as rival Buddhists. His name is written with the Chinese symbols for "sky" and "water" which signify "broadminded" and this he surely was.

Before Kukai died he succeeded in establishing a teaching center similar to Saicho's though not so near the capital, on Mount Koya, winning the support of Kwammu's emperor sons and the loyalty of many of Saicho's disciples. His monastery later became "the largest and perhaps the most flourishing in Japan. His memory lives all over the country, his name is a household word in the remotest places, not only as a saint, but as a preacher, a scholar, a poet, a sculptor, a painter, an inventor, an explorer, and — sure passport to fame — a great calligrapher. Many miraculous legends cluster about his name. A great light shone when he was born, a bright star entered his mouth, by his prayers he could cause wells of pure water to spring up from foul places, could make rain fall in times of drought and conjure away the pains of an ailing emperor." [8] His tomb is still visited every year by hundreds of pilgrims. Approached through a mile-long cemetery with mossy monuments to thousands of faithful followers, it rests in the dim shade of tall cryptomerias and fragrant incense smoke. In the quiet beauty of its surroundings worshippers find exaltation and peace.

For a time Mount Hiei and Mount Koya were at odds, but gradually Saicho's group was won over to Kukai's teaching. "Everything in the world," he declared in his most important writing, Ten Steps in the Development of Religious Consciousness,[9] "has something of the God spirit in it, and there is no real difference between man and nature or body and soul, but all are essentially one." According to the doctrines of Kukai's sect, every human desire could be fulfilled by the performance of prescribed rituals, the details of which were kept secret among the priests. Certain rites assured health and long life — others wealth, fine weather or promotion in official rank. No teaching was so full of hope and promise as this. It made the people feel as though anything were possible. This was most encouraging for a young nation which was trying to appear as dignified as ancient China.

Court people flocked to the temples and made generous offerings to the priests for performing mysterious services. Their gifts were sometimes so extravagant that the court found it necessary to issue an edict limiting the amount that might be given by persons of different ranks. Princes of the imperial family might give five thousand yards of cloth — members of the sixth rank not more than three hundred. This new Buddhist movement, however, as already noted, had its centers on mountain tops rather than in the capital and offered no political threat to the government.

In an energetic attempt to make practical use of his Chinese studies by building up a body of able government officials competent in bringing about order and peace in his domain, Kwammu-Tenno gave the Yamato people a sense of self-confidence greater than any they had known since they lost their standing on the Korean peninsula and their country was flooded with immigrants far more gifted than themselves. The feeling of inferiority and helplessness which made the Nara court depend entirely on the foreign priests was disappearing, and native leaders of Yamato were ready to direct affairs themselves in their impressive new capital. Fortunately for them, the T'ang Empire which had seemed all-powerful was now beginning to be weakened by Tatar invasions.

The first code of laws in Japan had been issued by Kwammu's great-grandfather, Tenji, from his palace in Omi in 662. Japanese officials after that time seem to have been very much interested in legislation. Tenji's code underwent a revision from 672 to 686, and in its revised form was distributed throughout the government offices in 689 or a few years later. Then in 701 the Taiho Code was compiled and it also was revised seventeen years later. These revisions represent the process of adaptation of the Chinese models on which the Japanese codes were based.

Many differing opinions developed concerning these laws, and as a result Kwammu appointed one of his ministers to prepare a version of them with a commentary which should be considered authoritative and official. The resulting document, called Ryo no Gige, Commentary on the Code, is still in existence. It deals with the functions of the departments of state and the duties of officials. While the Nara court had provided statutes on paper, the Heian court put into practice a classical system of government. At the head were the Emperor and the Department of Religion and under them eight ministries of state, with officials and employees totaling well over six thousand people. These were associated with the Central Government alone, and did not include provincial officials. There were one hundred and seventy ministers or directors of departments ; seventy secretaries ; one hundred and fifteen clerks or recorders ; one hundred and seventy-eight scribes ; nine hundred and fifty-eight attendants ; ninety-four inspectors ; one thousand three hundred and fifty-four servants and one hundred and eighteen watchmen and messengers. A list of the various bureaus, with a brief description of their functions as given in the Ryo no Gige, affords a good idea of what an elaborate, complex and costly business the Heian court was as early as the ninth century.[10]

THE EIGHT MINISTRIES OF STATE

I Ministry of Central Affairs

The chief officer of this ministry is in constant attendance upon the sovereign and advises him on matters of ceremonial and precedent. He scrutinizes the drafts of imperial edicts and transmits memorials to the throne after examining them. He supervises the compilation of official chronicles, the keeping of lists of court ladies and palace women and the records of their services, promotions, and ranks — the registers of population, land tax and labor tax of all provinces ; the registers of monks and nuns. This was the most important of the eight ministries and its chief was usually a prince of the imperial family. A secretary of this department was supposed to enquire into the conduct of court officials so as to decide promotions, etc., and eight chamberlains belonging to it were supposed to be in constant attendance to maintain discipline at court. Ninety palace attendants who were to wear swords and keep guard within the palace and to act as escort before and behind the imperial carriage were also members. Then there were inspectors to oversee the receipts and orders of the palace storehouses, to receive and return the keys which were kept by a palace woman official. Masters of the Bells were for despatching communications from the central government to the provinces. Bells were given as tokens of the right of an official to use post horses, and seals were used to make the despatches authentic.

Under the Ministry of Central Affairs were bureaus and offices as follows :

(1) The Office of the Empress' Household which managed the affairs of the highest ranking ladies of the imperial court.

(2) Attendants' Bureau
Eight hundred young men of good family and appearance were employed by this bureau to carry messages, act as escorts and wait upon the great people at court.

(3) Bureau of Books and Drawings
In charge of the custody of books, documents, maps, drawings ; the collection and arrangement of national chronicles ; the copying, revision, mounting, binding and repairs of sacred writings used for court ceremonies. Four paper makers, eighteen brush makers and four ink makers were among the employees of this bureau.

(4) Bureau of Palace Storehouse
To keep custody of gold, silver, jewels, precious utensils, brocades, rugs, hangings, clothing and other personal properties and furnishings of the emperor and his household. Two bootmakers and saddlers and eighteen needleworkers were employed in this bureau.

(5) Bureau of the Wardrobe
In charge of lists of princesses, ladies-in-waiting and women servants, reports on their conduct, and the cutting and sewing of robes and accessories.

(6) Bureau of Divination

Experts in Onyo, the science of Yin and Yang, the passive and active principles of nature which by their interaction produce and control events. This bureau was held to be of great importance. Its director was in charge of astrology, calendar-making and the appearances of clouds and winds. Belonging to this department were :

Six masters of divination and six doctors of divination, one doctor of calendar-making and one doctor of astrology, each doctor in charge of ten students ; one doctor of chronology in charge of twenty time-keepers who watched the water clocks and struck the hours on gongs or drums.

(7) The Office of Painting

In charge of the execution of drawings and paintings. Four master painters and sixty members of the official Painters' Guild were employed by this office.

(8) Office of Medicine

Included four physicians-in-waiting and ten apothecaries to supply drugs and perfumes for the palace and to compound medicines.

(9) Office of Palace Discipline

To be responsible for the behavior of persons within the palace and to admonish offenders for breaches of etiquette.

II *Ministry of Ceremonial*

To keep registers of officials, central and provincial, to recommend promotions, transfers and dismissals, and to supervise the behavior of officials at court.

(1) The Universities Bureau

Responsible for the examination of students and the celebration of the festivals in honor of Confucius and his disciples. Doctors in this department lectured upon the Chinese classics, taught the students to read and write and pronounce Chinese, and to do arithmetic. Provision was made in the state university for about four hundred and thirty students.

(2) The Bureau of Court Ranks

To keep a register of court ranks and arrange for the reception at court of the provincial delegates.

III The Ministry of Civil Administration

To scrutinize genealogies and to regulate succession, marriages, funeral rites, national mourning and the reception of foreign envoys.

(1) The Bureau of Music

In charge of civil and military music and dancing for solemn occasions, and the selection and training of male and female singers. Among those employed by this bureau were : professors of singing, dancing, Chinese and Korean music, flute playing and drum playing ; eight flute makers ; and about three hundred and fifty singers and students.

(2) Bureau of Buddhism and Aliens

In charge of the register of Buddhist temples, the arrangement of Buddhist services, the reception and entertainment of foreign guests.

(3) The Office of Imperial Mausolea

Responsible for worship at the tombs of members of the imperial family, burials, funeral services and guilds of grave wardens.

(4) Office of Funeral Rites

In charge of funeral ceremonies and the supply of necessary equipment.

IV The Ministry of Popular Affairs

Responsible for the registers of population, the labor taxes, family obligations, rewards for meritorious conduct, servants and slaves, bridges and roads, harbors, fences, bays, lakes, mountains, rivers, woods and swamps and rice lands in all provinces.

(1) Bureau of Statistics

To keep account of taxes, and to estimate and balance revenue and expenditure.

(2) The Tax Bureau

Responsible for the receipt, custody and issue of the actual grain delivered as tax ; also for its hulling and milling.

V   The Ministry of War

In charge of registers of military officers, records of their services, transfers, promotions, rewards, the allocation of troops, arms and equipment for war service and ceremonial fortifications and beacons.

(1) The Remount Office

In charge of feeding and training horses for military use, post stations, public and private horses and oxen.

(2) The Arsenal Office

In charge of the manufacture of arms and equipment and the register of artisans' guilds.

(3) The Military Music Office

In charge of the supply of instruments and instruction in playing drum and flute.

(4) The Ship Control Office

In charge of public and private vessels and their equipment.

(5) The Falconry Office

In charge of the supply and training of hawks and dogs.

VI   The Ministry of Justice

Responsible for the investigation and judgment of offenses, imprisonment, claims for debt.

(1) The Office of Fines

In charge of matters concerning the investigation and disposal of property, fines and ransoms, abandoned property.

(2) The Office of Prisons
In charge of the imprisonment of criminals, their labor, rewards and punishments.

VII *The Ministry of the Treasury*

In charge of the receipt and issue of tax goods from the provinces, coins, gold, silver, jewels, copper, iron, bones, horns and leather, fur and feathers, lacquered hangings and curtains, weights and measures, the system of prices for sale and purchase, miscellaneous tribute goods.

(1) The Mint Office
In charge of the casting of gold, silver, copper, iron.

(2) The Housekeeping Office
In charge of the supply and maintenance of palace furnishings such as mats and blinds, etc., and the cleaning and arrangement of the apartments.

(3) The Lacquer Office
(4) The Needlework Office
(5) The Weaving Office

VIII *Ministry of the Imperial Household*

The administration of crown lands producing taxes and food stuffs for the palace.

(1) The Palace Table Office
Chiefly concerned with the provision of meals for the palace officials and of state banquets.

(2) The Woodworkers' Bureau
(3) The Palace Kitchen Bureau
(4) The Intendance Bureau
Responsible for the supply of carriages and palanquins, sun shades, fans, blinds, curtains, etc., the cleaning and lighting of palace apartments and gardens, the furnishing of firewood, charcoal, etc.

(5) The Bureau of Medicine

Connected with this bureau were professors and students of medicine, acupuncture, massage, and exorcism, herb gardeners and a guild for providing cows' milk.

(6) The Imperial Family Office
(7) The Imperial Table Office

Responsible for the supervision of his Majesty's table, the proper heating, cooking, testing and service of his food.

(8) The Imperial Wine Office
(9) The Smith's Office

In charge of the making of copper and iron articles.

(10) The Public Slaves Office
(11) The Ponds and Gardens Office
(12) The Clay-workers' Office

In charge of making bricks and tiles.

(13) The Palace Women's Office

In charge of girls of good family and appearance who were chosen for service in the palace.

(14) The Water Office

In charge of water supply and ice chambers.

(15) The Oil Office

In charge of oils and fats for lighting and cooking.

(16) The Inner Housekeeping Office

Responsible for the upkeep of the apartments used by the sovereign.

(17) The Office of Receptacles of Wood and Pottery for Food and Drink
(18) The Palace Dyeing Office

To supply this great body of court officials and court servants called for by the Ryo no Gige there were, according to a genealogical record of the time,[11] eleven hundred and eighty-two families of rank. These were divided into three important classes and a few miscellaneous ones. Those of imperial lineage, descended from Amaterasu herself, numbered three hundred and thirty-five; four hundred and four families were descended from the companions of Amaterasu's grandson, Ninigi, and his son, the first emperor, Jimmu; and three hundred and twenty-six families of nobles were of Chinese or Korean origin. These must have been a very impressive group. From their numbers also were appointed provincial officials and the Kebiishi, Transgression Inspection Agency. The function of the Kebiishi was to apprehend law breakers. Operating at first only in the capital, it later extended its activities into the provinces and helped to increase the government's prestige.

Young sons of these noble families were educated for office at the imperial university or in the private schools of their own clan, where studies were based entirely on Chinese writings. The Heian court held in highest esteem not only the wisdom of the ancient Chinese classics, but also the minutest details of the manners and customs of the contemporary T'ang court and endeavored with earnest enthusiasm to deport themselves according to T'ang standards.

Throughout the greater part of the ninth century, groups of students and scholars traveled to and from the T'ang court at frequent intervals in their effort to establish a perfect reproduction of it in Japan. Toward the close of the ninth century, however, Japanese returning from the mainland began to report that the T'ang Empire was no longer what it had been; orderly government no longer existed; trade and the arts no longer flourished. A favorite adviser [12] of the emperor's then offered his opinion that Japan no longer had anything to gain by sending official envoys overseas; he recommended that the Heian court, instead of persisting in imitation, make an effort to digest what had already been learned and develop new ways for putting the knowledge to use.

This advice was followed and brought about noteworthy changes not only in government, but in literature and art as well. The resulting forms of the latter, which today are held to be classical and representative of the Golden Age of Japanese court life, will be described more fully in the next chapter.

In the realm of government, the new tendency led to the passing of more and more of the actual administration into the hands of an able few. The Fujiwara family came to be "The Court." They exercised the real power and controlled the country, while many official titles were borne by men who performed no serviceable duties. The imperial family, to whose prestige the official recognition of Chinese rulers had contributed largely, now came to be of less and less importance in affairs of state. The emperor's function became increasingly that of a high priest. The performance of religious ceremonies made such demands on his time and energy that he had little left for politics and statesmanship.

Even during the century of Buddhist domination the old cult called Shinto, "The Way of the Gods," had persisted.

Though Japanese worshippers had given a large share of their attention and offerings to the Buddha of Light, still they had not forgotten Amaterasu, their own Shining-in-Heaven goddess. The majority of the people, not only farmers on the soil but great property owners and provincial leaders, had never turned wholly away from their native deities of heaven and the land. The government took most respectful cognizance of this and encouraged the populace in the worship of their local divinities, as well as in the worship of the divine ancestors of the rulers.

In the Ryo no Gige the Department of Religion, with the emperor as its high priest and object of worship, was given precedence and held greater authority than the Departments of State. This department was made responsible for oracles and divination by which government officials were supposed to be guided, as well as for the traditional ceremonies connected with the accession and enthronement of the sovereign. It also had to perform a number of prescribed observances throughout the year : rites held in early spring for freedom from calamity and bountiful harvests, prayers for freedom from sickness offered at the end of the third month ; and in the fourth, festivals in honor of food and wind deities together with offerings of summer garments at the Isé shrine. On the last day of the sixth month rites had to be celebrated at the crossroads outside the capital to induce the gods of the crossroads to prevent evil spirits and pestilences from entering Kyoto. The prayer recited on this occasion had no doubt been in use for generations. It beseeches the deity of the crossroads :

Whenever from the Root-country, the Bottom-country, there may come savage and unfriendly beings, consort not and parley not with them, but if they go below, keep watch below ; if they go above, keep watch above, protecting us against pollution with a night guarding and a day guarding.

And it goes on :

The offerings furnished in your honor are bright cloth, shining cloth, soft cloth and rough cloth. The tops of the saké jars are raised up, and they are filled, and the bellies of the jars are ranged in order. Of things that dwell in the mountains and on the moors, the soft of hair and the coarse of hair are offered. Of things that dwell in the blue sea plain, the broad of fin and the narrow of fin, even to the weeds of the offing, and the weeds of the shore. Peacefully partaking of these plenteous offerings laid before you in full measure like a range of hills, hold guard on the highways, preserving from pollution the sovereign grandchild firmly and enduringly, and make his reign prosperous.

Also be pleased peacefully to preserve from pollution the imperial princes, the ministers of state and all the functionaries, including moreover the people of the Under-Heaven.

An official of the department of religion humbly fulfills your praises by this celestial, this great pronouncement.[13]

Following the celebration at the crossroads, was one required for preventing the destruction of the imperial palace by fire. This included a somewhat similar prayer in worship of a fire kindled by the official in charge rubbing together two pieces of wood.

In the eleventh month there was a very important thanksgiving ceremony in which the emperor, together with the gods, partook of wine and food made from rice of the new crop. There were many other rites and services also, less important perhaps than these, which had to be performed.

Before each festival those participating were required to observe a period of abstinence and purification. This varied from one day to one month, depending on the importance of the occasion. During periods of abstinence, officials were not permitted to pay visits of condolence upon a death, call upon the sick, or eat meat. During such times death sentences could not be pronounced nor criminal cases judged. No music could be played and no unclean or inauspicious tasks performed. Complete abstinence meant that all work was suspended and the only duties performed were those having to do with the ceremonial observances. The court observed partial abstinence for one month, and complete abstinence for three days, at the time of the accession of a new emperor. Complete abstinence for three days was also observed at the end of the sixth and of the twelfth month, when purification ceremonies regularly were held. Special great purifications were held on such occasions as the appearance of a comet, the outbreak of epidemics, the finding of a dead body in the palace, or the officiation in a festival of a Shinto priest who had recently performed Buddhist rites. The great purification included a very careful preliminary washing of the bodies of those taking part, the presentation of offerings, and the recital of a formula in which the emperor, by virtue of the authority transmitted to him from Amaterasu, declared to his ministers and people that he was "graciously pleased to purify them and cleanse away all their offenses."

Once a year there was prescribed a ceremony of "Luck

Wishing for the Great Palace," when a procession of officials from the Department of Religion and virgin priestesses entered the palace carrying two eight-legged tables on
which were boxes of precious stones, cut paper, mulberry
bark, rice and bottles of saké. The officials read the ritual
while the priestesses went throughout the palace, even to
the emperor's bathroom, sprinkling rice and mulberry bark
and saké, and hanging strings of precious stones at the four
corners of each room.

A not insignificant part in Heian religious observances
was played by the sacred mirror, one of the Three Imperial
Regalia.[14] Every new moon, offerings of rice cakes, paper,
cloth, eggplant, fish and shellfish were presented by ladies
of the palace at the "Place of Reverence" where the mirror
was kept, and many other special rites were performed at
Isé.

At many Shinto festivals gaiety prevailed; saké cups
were passed around, and the voices of official singers joined
with the flutes and harps. Ceremonial dances were performed by priests and priestesses, sometimes by even the
Vice-Minister of Religion himself. Not seldom those taking
part later proceeded to the race course, and the festival,
which began with ritual very early in the morning, was concluded in the evening with galloping matches.

In and around the capital there were over seven hundred
shrines, and in the provinces over two thousand others,
kept up at the expense of the imperial treasury. The offerings presented by the emperor on ceremonial occasions
were divided by the Department of Religion and given to

representatives from these various shrines who were supposed to offer them to the gods in their own localities. This network of shrines and elaborate program of rites and festivals served to perpetuate the power of the imperial court in a peculiarly Japanese manner.

CHAPTER VI

THE POWER AND GLORY OF THE FUJIWARAS

(TENTH AND ELEVENTH CENTURIES)

FROM 669, when Kamatari won for the family its name, until 1016, when Michinaga became regent and brought the Fujiwaras to the zenith of their power and glory, was over three centuries. After this Fujiwaras were still to rule Japan for another hundred and fifty years. No other family in history has continued to dominate a nation for an equal length of time.[1] The secret of their success lay in adherence to three principles, two of which may be stated briefly in familiar Western phrases : The first, knowledge is power ; the second, in unity is strength. The third is more distinctively Japanese — it is the principle of ancestor worship and blood relationship as the foundation of the state.

Kamatari's greatness had lain not so much in breaking the power of the Soga clan as in setting for his own family an example of intelligent eagerness to learn. He had devoted himself for years to studying the teachings of scholars returned from China, and though the voyage was filled with perils had sent his eldest son to the continent in search of firsthand knowledge.

In the latter part of the seventh and in the eighth century when they became keenly aware of their own limited knowledge, young Fujiwaras, with determination, turned their minds to learning everything they could from the cultured priests and other talented immigrants in their midst. Quick to absorb experience from others, they became the leaders in all the legislative activities in the court, and headed the committees for compiling the official histories throughout two centuries. In spite of the loss of four promising sons in the smallpox epidemic and the efforts of the clever Nara clergy to thwart their best-laid plans, the Fujiwaras, by diligent self-improvement, were able to create new opportunities for extending their influence. It was due to their leadership that the government overcame its trusting acceptance of Buddhist authority and moved away to establish an independent center of its own.

Had only a few members of the family been fired with ambition they could not have gone so far, but the Fujiwaras worked together with remarkably little friction. Daughters as well as sons cooperated in furthering the fortunes of the family as a whole. Marrying their daughters into the imperial household was one of their best devices for consolidating political power. Fujiwaras very early realized the advantages of uniting their interests with those of the imperial family, administering for the emperor and in his name, rather than taking possession of the throne themselves. In this way they not only strengthened themselves politically against possible rivals, but also greatly improved their economic position. The emperor from the taxes he received had to pay the expenses of government, a large part of which were the salaries of Fujiwara officials. In addition, he had continually to be rewarding special services, usually with the gift of a manor, so that his acreage of taxable land was continually decreasing. The Fujiwaras, on the other hand, were the most frequent recipients of these grants of land, on which they were not required to pay taxes, but from which they were free to collect as much as they could. Their income was thus constantly increasing.

By installing their daughters in the imperial household the Fujiwaras were able to keep well-informed of what went on there and to make their influence felt at all times. Further than this, they emphasized the importance of the divine ancestry of the imperial family, as shown by the high priest function of emperors in the previous chapter, and encouraged filial piety in general ; disrespectful acts or attitudes toward parents were considered the height of immorality. Little princes, well-trained in these precepts, were willing to trust their grandfathers in everything. With the sanctions of this Chinese principle of ancestor worship, Fujiwaras were often able to keep boy rulers on the throne and act as regents for them. Before one grew old enough to take matters in his own hands he was retired and replaced by one still younger. Emperors of superior piety showed their grandfathers greatest honor by retaining them as regents even after coming of age. Such emperors were usually kept so involved in choosing the colors of the robes to be worn by officials of various ranks, deciding the proper length of jeweled swords, learning Chinese etiquette, and performing Shinto rites that they had little mind for more pressing problems of government.

Occasionally able scholars of attractive personality appeared who won favor with an emperor though they were not of the Fujiwara clan. But when any of these threatened to oppose the Fujiwara will, they found themselves in trouble. On one such occasion the Fujiwaras let loose a herd of wild horses in Kyoto and the whole city was thrown into a panic, just by way of suggestion that the country would end in anarchy if they did not keep a firm control on affairs of state. Scholars of political bias different from theirs were always dismissed from the court and usually sent to some place of obscurity.

Soon after the cessation of official relations with the declining T'ang Court in 895, there was a period during which the line of great Fujiwara statesmen seemed to have run out. One emperor was able to take the actual power into his own hands and rule the country without dictation from his Fujiwara ministers for almost a quarter of a century. For two or three generations, though they continued to fill official positions, no great men were produced in the distinguished family, and it was further weakened by jealous rivalries between its various members over which should provide the mother of the next emperor. But the Fujiwaras by this time had vast resources at their disposal, and the strength of their reputation carried them on. Then came Michinaga!

Michinaga had the good judgment and good fortune to enlist in his service a rising military clan named Minamoto. The Minamotos were strong-armed men, experienced in rural administration, the collection of taxes and the enforcing of law and order. They gave Michinaga the power he needed to reunite the Fujiwara family, and forwarded to him regularly in the capital revenues from estates much more extensive in area and much more rich in yield than those belonging to the emperor himself.

Five of Michinaga's daughters were married to successive sovereigns and he became the grandfather of five crown princes. He was the supreme power in government for many years. "This life of mine," Michinaga wrote in a poem, "is akin to the full moon, nothing seems to me wanting." And over his cups he muttered, "It is no disgrace to make one's daughter a princess. The empress is not so badly off in having a father like me. Her mother must be very glad to have such a husband." [2]

For his family Michinaga had a marvelous palace built. Provincial officials vied with each other in bringing treasures for it, aiming to surpass their rivals for the great man's favor. According to the description of a court lady of the time this palace was as beautiful as a polished jewel and surrounded by exquisite landscaped gardens with pools that shone like spotless mirrors. On the clear surface of the waters, whence pure white and pale pink lotus blossoms raised their lovely heads, were reflections of the palace, its towers and storehouses, which looked like a painting of Buddha's paradise.

Close by was the Fujiwara family temple. When it was being built treasures were taken even from the imperial palace, and a provincial governor was ordered, "Though you neglect your official duties, do not neglect to furnish materials and labor for Hojo Temple." Here, amid its other glories, in a venerable row stood a Buddhist figure thirty-

EXCERPT FROM CARICATURE SCROLL

SCREEN SHOWING COURT LADIES DRESSING PRINCESS

Two excerpts from the Heike scroll

Byodo-In

two feet high and a hundred other gilded Buddhist statues.

In the early eleventh century when Michinaga was in his prime, life in both temple and palace was very gay. Priests talked of a paradise where court life continued on a more colorful and more luxurious scale, and where all the sins of the flesh were forgiven by the mere mention of a sacred name. They fostered a belief in their special powers to keep away ill fortune, disease and death, and encouraged the building of temples and monasteries in connection with palaces, where spectacular ceremonies could be performed for the enjoyment of courtiers and court ladies.

There was such a demand for Buddhist statues at this time that distinguished artist families and schools of sculptors began to appear. Priest sculptors had always been able to supply the demand hitherto, but when Michinaga began to build Hojo-ji he hired a sculptor named Jocho and his school of assistants. Jocho and his school did not simply copy Chinese statues (ardor for things Chinese had somewhat subsided), rather, they gave their deities the distinctly Japanese forms of beautiful human models such as they saw in the palaces and temples of Kyoto with lovely bodies, round faces and slender eyes and brows.

These statues were all carved from wood, but not necessarily from a single tree trunk as statues had been in earlier times. Now methods of joinery were developed and the head, arms and hands were carved separately and fastened to the torso. Figures of Amida Buddha had their faces and bodies covered with gold foil, but lesser deities and saints were given a heavy coat of ivory-white flesh paint. Their robes, lying in smooth, graceful folds, were painted to represent the richest of silk brocades with a variety of gorgeous colors and intricate patterns of gold foil. Often they wore crowns, necklaces and arm bands of most elegantly carved gold. Figures attending the deity often resembled court ladies in beautiful flowing draperies, riding or dancing on clouds or playing musical instruments. For background they had gilded wooden canopies of most marvelously lace-like perforated carvings in designs of flames, flowers, vines, clouds and saints. The interior of the temple, the pillars, walls and ceilings, were elaborately decorated with paint-ings, mother-of-pearl inlays and open carving.

But the sculptors of the days of Fujiwara splendor did not surpass the painters. One large scene of paradise, al-most seven feet high and fourteen feet across, still preserved from that era, shows Amida Buddha on a cloud in the midst of a happy host of celestial beings who look very much like priests and court ladies. They are playing on various kinds of drums, flutes and stringed-instruments, and one is singing with a broad smile on her face. All are adorned with elaborate jewelry. The figures are drawn in fine lines of lively red and filled in with vividly contrasting olive-green, rich blues and yellow-reds, lavishly overspread with gold.[3]

Other paintings of which Fujiwara court folk were very fond showed the beautiful and merciful Amida Buddha coming over the green hills of their own beloved Kyoto landscape to welcome the faithful believers. This deity is represented in such lovely form that Westerners sometimes refer to it as "Amida, the Goddess of Mercy." But among

Buddhist deities sex is transcended. There are neither male nor female, but only perfect, all-sufficient beings.

When noble ladies fell ill, priests rather than doctors attended them. Handsome young priests, according to one court lady's diary, in elegant brown robes and mantles of thin, lustrous silk murmured incantations and fanned themselves the while with clove-dyed fans.[4] Everything was done esthetically.

For this the court had the smooth-running Fujiwara government to thank. It is easy to skip over the orderly processes of administration, the steady working of a well-regulated organization, and pass quickly on to more spectacular activities, but the important functions which the Fujiwaras performed in maintaining law and order ought not to be overlooked. Their strong, able government, which gave the country peace for over three hundred years, played a larger part than their brilliant court life in making their regime the Golden Age of Japanese history.

The characteristic orderliness of the Fujiwaras penetrated even the social sphere. Most of the activities of the court were prescribed ones, regulated in accordance with the annual calendar of court functions. Two-thirds of this calendar was devoted to religious ceremonies, both Shinto and Buddhist: the New Year's service to the sun goddess, followed by services throughout the year to important deities of nature and state, and homage to the imperial forefathers ; many and various Buddhist rites, visits to temples of different denominations, and an elaborate practice of prayers. Time was also prescribed for a drinking bout on January

2d., poem contests on several occasions, contests of archery and polo, picnics in spring to view cherry blossoms, outings in autumn to see the red maples and golden grasses and to listen to the chirping of insects. Dates were set for horse races and parades of decorated ox carts, fetes for wistaria and chrysanthemum, for new-moon and full-moon festivals, wrestling matches, exhibitions of shells and pictures, and initiations of dancing girls.[5] The court at certain periods had as many as two hundred and fifty men musicians and fifty dancing girls to enliven its ceremonies.

When little princes became twelve years old they were feted with initiation rituals. Their long childish locks were cut off and, dressed for the first time in man's attire, they danced "The Dance of Homage" before the assembled court. The hero on such occasions was given presents, such as fine horses from the royal stables and trained hawks from the royal falconry. His friends and followers in uniform robes of violet, pink, white or yellow, according to their rank, were showered with baskets of fruit and delicacies, and boxes of cakes. Sometimes on this day the young prince was betrothed. Then the "Moon Lords" and "Cloud Gallants" as the courtiers were called, all assembled to drink a love cup and the initiate took his place among them. Other court entertainments are vividly described in "The Tale of Genji," a lengthy narrative of the adventures, mostly amorous, of the shining Prince Genji and the Fujiwara court circle.[6]

Here like figures in a picture of fairyland they spent the day gliding away across the lake to the pleasant strains of the tune called the Royal Deer. Suddenly the boats halted, and the ladies were invited to go ashore at the fishing pavilion which was finished in a manner combining elegance with extreme simplicity.

As the parties spread along the empty galleries and across the wide deserted floors, there was such an interweaving of gay colors as would have been hard to outdo. The musicians were again called upon and soon were joined by a troupe of dancers. It seemed a pity that darkness should be allowed to interfere with these pleasures.

When night came on, a move was made to the courtyard in front of the palace. Here flares were lit, and on the mossy lawn at the foot of the great steps not only professional musicians, but also various visiters from court, and friends of the family, performed on wind and string, while picked teachers of the flute gave a display in the mode beginning on alto A which symbolizes spring. Then all the zithers and lutes belonging to different members of the household were brought out onto the steps and carefully tuned to the same pitch. A grand concert followed, the piece "Was Ever Such a Day?" being performed with admirable effect.

Even the grooms and laborers who were loitering amid the serried ranks of coaches drawn up outside the great gates, little as they usually cared for such things, on this occasion pricked up their ears, and were soon listening with lips parted in wonder and delight. The concert continued till dawn — already the morning birds were clamoring in a lusty chorus.

Part of the race course was not far away from this side of the palace and a good view could be obtained from the porticos and outer galleries which soon were thronged. Persons of quality were hidden behind green shutters or curtains, dyed in the new-fashioned way, with color running down into the fringe. Among the dresses of the visitors were many elaborate Chinese costumes specially designed for the day's festivity, the color of the young dianthus leaf tending to prevail. Some were in their summer gowns, green without and peach-blossom color within. There was a great deal of rivalry and harmless self display, which was rewarded from time to time by a glance from one of the young courtiers who were assembled on the course.

Genji arrived on the scene at the hour of the sheep (1 p. m.). It was interesting to see the competitors, so differently arrayed, each with his following of smartly dressed squires and assistants. The sports continued till evening. The ladies, though understanding very imperfectly what was going on, were at least capable of deriving a great deal of pleasure from the sight of so many young men in elegant riding jackets hurling themselves with desperate recklessness into the fray.

The races were followed by a game of polo played to the tune of "Hitting the Ball." Then came a competition of rival pairs in a Korean dance. All this was accompanied by a great din of bells and drums, sounded to announce the gaining of points on one side and another. When it began to grow dark there was indoor entertainment with a distribution of prizes among the successful riders and a great banquet. It was very late indeed when the guests began to withdraw.

With a continuous round of prescribed ceremonies and entertainments such as these to keep them busily amused, and most of the luxuries of the nation concentrated in Kyoto, it is small wonder that the Fujiwara court people had little interest in life beyond their own circle. They went on short trips to mountain temples and to country places near the capital, but they never traveled into other provinces if they could possibly avoid it. Even courtiers who were appointed to provincial posts sold their offices to others and remained in the capital whenever they could so manage. It is interesting to read of their reactions to things outside their customary environment.

Lady Sei, for example, jotted down the following notes about a spontaneous little excursion to hear the cuckoos singing at a place just outside the city : [7]

Presently we came to the house of Akinobu and someone suggested we should have a look at it. The house itself was a poor affair and very cramped, but quite pretty in its way. Everything was very simple and countrified — pictures of horses on the panels, screens of wattled bamboo, curtains of plaited grass — all in a style that seemed to be intentionally behind the times. Sending for some stuff which I suppose was husked rice our host made some girls — very clean and respectable — along with others who seemed to come from neighboring farms, show us how the rice was threshed. Then the grain was put into a sort of machine that went round, two girls turning it and, at the same time, singing so strange a song that we could not help laughing. Then refreshments were brought on a queer old tray-stand such as one sees in Chinese pictures. As no one seemed much interested in its contents, our host said :

"This is rough, country fare. If you don't like it, bother your host or his servants till you get something you can eat. We don't expect you people from the capital to be shy."

"You don't want us to arrange ourselves around the tray-stand like a lot of maid servants sitting down to their supper," I protested.

He ordered the things to be passed around, but while this was going on rain threatened and we hurried back to our carriage.

And again she writes :

When one thinks of it, to be in a boat at all is a terrible thing ! It is bad enough, even in reasonably shallow water, to trust oneself to such a conveyance ; but where the water may be any depth — perhaps a thousand fathoms — to embark upon a thing loaded up with goods and baggage of all kinds, with only an inch or two of wood between oneself and the water ! However, the low-class people who manage the boat do not seem to be in the least frightened, but run up and down un-

concernedly in places where a single false step would lose
them their lives.

Even the loading of a ship, when they bang down into the
hold huge pine trees two or three feet in circumference, sometimes half a dozen at a time, is an amazing thing. Rich people, of course, go in ships with cabins, and those who are
lucky enough to be in the middle of the ship do not get on so
badly. But those who are near the sides get very dizzy.[8]

The writing of notes such as these and of diaries was a
favorite pastime of Fujiwara court ladies. A charming
literary style was thus developed which became one of the
chief glories of the Fujiwara age.

As the Japanese had grown familiar with Chinese script,
different groups had begun to invent abbreviated forms for
the symbols, a sort of shorthand which they could use
among themselves. There were several styles of Chinese
writings for them to copy ; one was an angular, discon-
nected style, which had been used before the days of brush
and ink, when the Chinese wrote with chisels on stone, or
with lacquer on strips of bamboo ; another was an informal
running style much more convenient to use when one
wanted to write quickly. The first style was called in Chinese "writing in the house," and the informal style "writing
in the field."   In the Nara period about four thousand different Chinese symbols came into use in Japan.

Scholars liked to use as many different symbols as they
could, just to show how learned they were. If they wished
to write a Japanese sentence, for instance, in which the
sound "wa" occurred six times, they might use six different
symbols all of which the Chinese pronounced "wa," even

though they had no connection whatever with the meaning of the sentence. The result was something like a rebus puzzle, only much more difficult to read.

As Japanese came, however, to read not only Chinese, but also Sanskrit, the language in which Buddhist scriptures originally were written, they discovered that the sounds of their own language could be classified ; there were just forty-seven pure ones. Then different groups chose forty-seven

ン	ワ	ラ	ヤ	マ	ハ	ナ	タ	サ	カ	ア
	ヰ	リ	イ	ミ	ヒ	ニ	チ	シ	キ	イ
	ウ	ル	ユ	ム	フ	ヌ	ツ	ス	ク	ウ
	エ	レ	エ	メ	ヘ	ネ	テ	セ	ケ	エ
	ヲ	ロ	ヨ	モ	ホ	ノ	ト	ソ	コ	オ

Katakana

Chinese symbols, one for each sound, abbreviated them a little, and used them phonetically as we do our alphabet. One temple would have a set of symbols abbreviated in a certain way, another temple would have an entirely different set, abbreviated in an entirely different way. Officials had sets peculiar to themselves, and sometimes lovers made up sets for their own private use. Two such sets came to be used much more than others. One based on the "writing in the house" was called katakana, part sign, and one based on the "writing in the field" was called hiragana, handy sign.

It is sometimes claimed that Kibi no Mabi, the great scholar-minister of the Nara period, who went to China twice and made such a good governor of the Dazaifu, invented the katakana, but so few of these abbreviated symbols have been found in the writings of his time and even

いろはにほへと
ちりぬるをわか
よたれそつねな
らむうゐのおく
やまけふこえて
あさきゆめみし
ゑひもせすん

Hiragana

later, that this is hardly likely. It seems more probable that the katakana now in use developed in the ninth century from studies of the sutras, mainly under the guidance of two abbots from Mount Hiei, and that this particular set came to be better known than many others because of the great influence of this center of religion and learning. The hiragana, though said to have been invented by Abbot Kukai, the founder of Mount Koya, were also the result of a lengthy process of selection and change and a sort of survival of the fittest. There was not an official standard set of either kind of "kana" until after the Restoration in 1868.[9]

After the annals, Kojiki and Nihongi, and the anthology, Manyoshu, had appeared, several other official chronicles and collections of poetry had been compiled; there were legal and religious writings too, but the earliest Japanese fiction we know of was written in the Fujiwara age. It was a humorous sort of fairy tale and legend called "The Old Bamboo Hewer's Story," [10] which pretended to explain why smoke always rose from the summit of Mount Fuji. This story was soon followed by several others which made very popular entertainment for courtiers and court ladies.

Courtiers and officials seemed to think it much more dignified to write in the Chinese language (just as lawyers and college officials in America even today seem to think it more dignified to use phrases of Latin or Greek); they spent no end of time and effort trying to write things which could be mistaken for the work of Chinese scholars and poets.

But the ladies wrote in Japanese, in their own natural way of talking. The novels, notes and diaries which flowed profusely from their brushes now are known as the classical literature of Japan. The prose works of several of these Fujiwara court ladies have been translated into English as have the verses of a great number more.[11]

Along with this natural style of writing a new style of painting also developed, called Yamato-e. Yamato-e were pictures of Japanese people in Japanese settings, drawn and colored in a typically Japanese manner. Two outstanding characteristics are the amusing way in which artists drew an eye or a nose with a single stroke of the brush, and left off the ceiling instead of a side wall to show the inside of a room.

Many Yamato-e were graceful illustrations for the "Tale of Genji," others with none of the elegance of these were caricaturish drawings of street crowds or of miraculous happenings at some shrine or temple. They usually told a story, either in a series of different views or in a continuous scroll picture.[12] Like Japanese books, which are made to begin where Western ones end, these Yamato-e narratives start at the right and proceed toward the left of the scroll.

The age of Fujiwara supremacy was a golden age for women in Japan. A beautiful and clever girl had unlimited possibilities for social advancement ; her chances were much better than a man's. The empresses were all Fujiwara girls in their early teens who needed counsel and coaching in etiquette, the arts, and the ways of life. Their parents were ready to go to any length to secure the most talented companions for them. Many of these more experienced ladies also found favor with the emperors themselves. Fujiwara princes were able to bestow on amiable and entertaining beauties gifts of rank and riches to satisfy the most ambitious. With every detail of everyday life as carefully prescribed as it was in the late days of Heian, no courtier presumed to be spontaneous or original ; court ladies offered his only chance of adventure. Since they also played principal roles in political intrigues, they were very important indeed and acted accordingly with very great freedom.

For example, Lady Murasaki, authoress of the "Tale of Genji," in her early twenties had been left a widow with a baby daughter, but being keenly admired by the great Michinaga she was appointed as companion to one of his empress daughters, and had every opportunity of knowing intimately the ways of the court life she described so well.

Fujiwara power and glory was brought to its climax by Michinaga, and Japanese classical culture reached its greatest height during his regime. His life was a perfect pattern of the classical tradition even to the end. When his faculties began to weaken, according to time-honored custom, Michinaga took the tonsure and became an ordained layman. This provided a pleasant relief from the performance of court formalities and was supposed to insure salvation in the future. His ordination ceremony was held at Nara and, if one may believe the poetic description of it given by a court lady in her historical novel [13] of the Fujiwara supremacy, equalled in splendor the spectacle of the "Great Eye Opening" of the Nara Daibutsu. In the year 1028, at the age of sixty-two, Michinaga passed away.

CHAPTER VII

COURTIER GIVES PLACE TO PROVINCIAL SOLDIER

(TWELFTH CENTURY)

THE JAPANESE have a very old hymn that says :

> The sound of the temple bell
> Echoes the impermanence of all things.
> The flowers of the teak tree declare
> That they who flourish must be brought low.
> The proud ones are but for a moment,
> Like an evening dream in springtime.
> The mighty are destroyed at the last ;
> They are but as dust before wind.[1]

Even the Fujiwaras' "moment" at last drew to a close. Unproductive themselves, they had depended on the tillers of the soil and the tax collectors to provide them with luxuries, but the limited agricultural resources of the country were no longer sufficient to satisfy the desires of the ever-increasing court circle. More and more absorbed in the fastidious life of Kyoto, courtiers had gradually passed on their provincial duties to the less favored ones of their number. But these, as the wheel of fortune turned, became the real power of the nation.

The working people of the country were called by court

officials "The Great Treasure" and a very great treasure they were indeed. Patiently the farmers levelled and cultivated their little pieces of ground, piled firm banks of earth around them and covered them with water. They sowed the seed-rice and transplanted the tiny, grasslike shoots when they began to grow. The whole summer long they guarded the delicate plants ceaselessly against insects, storms and droughts until the time for harvest. When they handed over to the tax collectors a large part of the fruits of their labors, there was scarcely enough left to feed the family through the winter.

Japan was little suited for rice cultivation. In tropical countries where the warm season was long, as many as three crops a year could be gathered ; their broad, flat river valleys seemed specially made for the growing of rice. Under such conditions, rice was capable of sustaining an enormous population. But in Japan it was different. The warm season was shorter, interrupted with heavy storms and typhoons, and the land consisted chiefly of volcanic mountain slopes. The Yamato court ate rice because the Chinese court did ; Yamato farmers raised it because they were required to. For their own food they planted hardier grains like millet, oats and barley.

The peasants' wives and daughters made cloth of bark, hemp and cotton. Some of them raised silkworms and wove silk. This, too, required an enormous amount of labor. Trays had to be carefully prepared for the cocoons to be spread out on ; then bushels and bushels of fresh green mulberry leaves had to be picked for the ravenously hungry little worms when they hatched. When cocoons of the next generation were finished they had to be dipped in boiling water and the fine silk filaments of which they were made had to be unwound with very steady hands and even tempers before they were ready for spinning into threads for weaving into cloth. It was a long, painstaking process, and when it was over a generous share of the precious fabric was sent as taxes to the capital.

Taxes were based on units of land. It was found by experience that a square patch of ground two paces, or six feet, long on each side would yield about as much rice as an average man would eat in a day. Their years being made up of twelve months of thirty days each, for a year's supply of rice to feed one man, three hundred and sixty of these units, or a plot about one hundred and fourteen feet square, would be required. Ten such plots were called one cho. One cho, or about half an acre of rice fields, may be thought of as the holding of an average peasant's family; in addition, they sometimes had some ground planted in other cereals, and in mulberry and lacquer trees.

By the twelfth century, the rice tax had mounted to thirty-two and one half per cent of the total yield; thirty per cent was for the court in Kyoto and two and one half per cent for the support of the provincial governor. For each cho of land it held, a family was also supposed to pay in taxes : one piece of silk fabric ten feet long and two and one half feet wide, three pieces of pongee and four pieces of cotton goods of the same size, and a proportion of the other things produced in the district. It was said that in the latter days of the Fujiwaras the court took seven-tenths of the produce of the land and left to the people only three-tenths. In addition to taxes, every man from twenty-one to sixty-six years of age was likely to have to give one month of labor a year, cutting and hauling timber, mining iron ore and sulphur, making repairs on roads, official residences and public buildings.

Japanese farmers have always been marvelously hard-working and loyal to their masters, but under such conditions they could not pay their taxes and live. Very often they turned their land over to some provincial landlord who was less exacting than the people in the capital.

The court at the time of the First Great Change had claimed that all the land of the country belonged to the emperor and that theoretically he had the right to collect taxes from it all. But he also had to reward officials for their services and pay for other expenses of the court. The best way to do this, it seemed, was for the emperor not to try to have all the taxes collected and brought to the capital and then divided and turned over to the various members of the court, but to allot a certain section of land to each official and let him be responsible for collecting his own share. Since the Fujiwaras held most of the highest-ranking positions in the court, they also were allotted most of the land. Other officials, however, had received grants from time to time, and provincial manors were also given by emperors with large families to their younger or less favored sons whom they could not afford to support in the expensive style of Kyoto.

These sons were expected to go out and secure their own living, and many of them did so very successfully. They were looked up to by the country people because of their ancestry and admired for their skill in horsemanship, hunting with hawks, and writing. Because they did not have to keep up with the extravagances of life in the capital these ex-courtiers could get along very nicely by taxing the farmers much less than the Fujiwaras or the emperor did. Farmers, therefore, much preferred to work their lands for them rather than for the central government; and these men were glad to increase the number of fields and farmers from which they might draw income for themselves. When agents from Kyoto came around, such provincial landlords sometimes used force to defend their gains; they began to enlist in their service men experienced in handling spears and bows.

Two of these families of provincial landlords prospered and flourished remarkably. One was named Taira, or Heike; the other Minamoto, or Genji. Taira and Minamoto are the Japanese pronunciations of the Chinese symbols Hei and Gen; ke and ji mean "family" or "clan."

Clever Fujiwara regents saw that the way to treat these growing warrior clans was not to oppose them but to get their cooperation. They used them for collecting taxes from Fujiwara estates and for settling disputes with rivals. This system worked very well indeed at first; warrior clans, gratified to receive the recognition of this great court family, vied with each other for favor by adding lands to the Fujiwara domain. They reclaimed large tracts of land from mountain sides, river beds and marshes, and sent very generous gifts up to the court. It was the cooperation of the Minamoto warriors that made it possible for Michinaga, the most spectacular of the Fujiwaras, to achieve the supreme power and glory of his family. But any government that delegates to others its right to collect taxes is in imminent danger.

The Heike and Genji were more vigorous and energetic than the Fujiwaras. They had lived on the land and they loved it ; they sympathized with the hard-working farmers. Gradually they began to lose their respect for the Fujiwaras and to gain some notion of their own importance and possibilities. They realized that they were the real power of the country on whom the government depended and from this consciousness grew a military caste.

While the Taira and Minamoto were the most powerful families of this military caste, they were by no means the whole of it. There were several other families only slightly less strong, with bands of loyal followers recruited from among the farmers. These families, seeing that the government was no longer able to enforce its laws, made rules and regulations of their own. They paid little attention to orders from the court, but they saw to it that their own family regulations were strictly enforced. This created a situation very much like the one which existed in the very early days of Japan — before Prince Shotoku tried to organize a central government, when there were many clans.

Japanese soldiers had always worshipped a special deity, and now this deity came to play an especially important role. In the chapter on the early settlers you may remember there was a story from the two oldest annals of Japan about an empress who commanded an army and went overseas to fight. For divine aid, guidance and protection in this undertaking, she had appealed to a sea god called

Yawata, Bubbling-Tremendous-Waves, who was enshrined on the coast of the island Kyushu. When she returned victorious and gave birth to a son, he was held in high esteem as a symbol of victory. In the course of centuries the memory of this son seems to have become merged with that of the deity, and the old sea god still called Yawata continued to be worshipped in Kyushu as the god of wars and victories.[2]

During the Nara period, when the Buddhist priests were trying to build the Daibutsu, they found it to be very desirable to enlist the support and friendship of the whole country and so they summoned these rugged Yawata worshippers to bring their deity to the capital and enshrine him among the temples. There the highest ranks were conferred upon him and he was given a new name in Chinese script, pronounced Hachiman, Eight Banners. The priests said that these stood for the eight right ways of Buddha. They thought Hachiman would thus be induced to cooperate with them in importing religious articles from China and Korea. Not long afterward a messenger was sent to his shrine at Usa to ask his approval for letting the priest, Dokyo, become emperor. The answer brought back to Nara was, "Since the establishment of the state the distinction between sovereign and subject has been observed. There is no instance of a subject becoming sovereign. The successor must be of the imperial family, the usurper must be rejected." [3]

This patriotic stand had made Hachiman very popular with the Fujiwaras while they were still trying to consolidate their position with respect to the throne, but once they were in power they neglected Hachiman. In the days of peace and splendor people worshipped chiefly the Fujiwara ancestral deity, Kasuga, and the merciful Buddha Amida. No matter what they did, they were forgiven by simply believing in Amida. This must have been a great comfort to dissipated courtiers.

With the rise of the military caste, however, Hachiman again came into his own. New shrines were built in his honor and old ones repaired. His spirit inspired, unified and strengthened the warrior class.[4]

After the middle of the eleventh century there were emperors who took advantage of the Fujiwara laxness toward official duties and began to rule the country themselves. But they could not succeed in reverting their lands to a paying basis. Their revenues were almost nil. Taxes were collected and kept by the military clans.

It had been the policy of the government originally to keep these provincial soldiers engaged in defending court interests in distant places. But as court incomes were reduced, the gifts and favors of the court were necessarily curtailed. This meant that many temples accustomed to enjoying the generosity of princes and nobles also began to feel the pinch of circumstance. Instead of resigning themselves to the new situation they blamed it on the extravagance of the Fujiwaras and gave open expression to their resentment. Armed monks from the temples of Nara and Mount Hiei several times came to blows and pitched battles in the streets of Kyoto, three thousand of them threatening the negligent Michinaga's son. Then it became necessary to call provincial soldiers into the very capital. Once there, these soldiers became more and more in demand as support for ambitious officials. In the middle of the twelfth century the Tairas and Minamotos took opposite sides in a dispute about who should become emperor and a war developed between them. The Minamotos were defeated and the Tairas had the court in their hands.

Previous to this Taira victory all offices of the Fifth Rank and higher had to be filled by the nobility. No military man could hold them. Tamura Maro, the first shogun, who had finally subdued the Ainu was the only exception in history. He had been raised to the Third Rank and made a councilor. Now upon Taira Kiyomori likewise was this honor conferred.

Kiyomori's father had been a member of the imperial guards, a member braver than most, who was appointed governor of a province on the Inland Sea to rid its shores and waters of pirates. The boy grew up familiar with the ways of the sea and ships. He came to feel very strongly that the future of the nation lay, not in agriculture, but in export and import trade.

While still a provincial governor, Kiyomori had had convenient channels in the Inland Sea deepened and widened for the passage of merchant vessels, and had reinforced the shore of an inlet to make a safe anchorage. On this work, it is recorded, fifty thousand laborers were employed for twelve years, all men from his own estates. The harbor which they made was the beginning of the port of Kobe which today is one of the busiest in the world.

Kiyomori also had a lighthouse erected so that ships might sail in safety at night; and when he became head of his clan he adopted as a sort of guardian deity for his family Beautiful-Island-Princess, one of the three guardian deities of the sea, enshrined at Itsukushima. In honor of this deity he built a very beautiful shrine on an island in the Inland Sea, the red lacquer gateway of which is often seen in tourist pictures today.[5]

Victorious over the Minamotos at the age of forty-two, the far-seeing head of the Heike was a great influence in Kyoto. His clan came to have thirty of the sixty-six provinces of Japan under its control; and soon Kiyomori succeeded in replacing many Fujiwara officials by members of his own family. His daughter was married to an emperor. He whose father had been laughed at for his awkward dancing and rustic squint when first he came to court was now the arbiter of fashion, and "Not to be a Taira was not to be a man!"

Kiyomori's palace, according to later courtly raconteurs, consisted of one hundred and seventy buildings in a park which covered more than ten square miles. Other buildings occupied by his family and retainers numbered over twenty-five hundred.

In their many gorgeous costumes, his sons and daughters were resplendent as the flowers of the field. Nobles and illustrious people crowded before their gates like throngs in a market place. Gold, jewels, damask, brocade, no rarity or treasure did they lack. And for poetry and music, fishing and riding, even the emperor's palaces were not more renowned.[6]

Kiyomori was granted special permission by the retired emperor to enter and leave the court riding in state in an ox-wagon or palanquin, acting as one who holds, alone, the whole power of the government. But Kiyomori had not forgotten his maritime ambitions.

In the first chapter, on the early settlers of Japan, three influences were traced in artifacts, language and religion. As the country developed into a nation these three influences continued to play their part, represented by the rugged, hard-working farmers in the northeast, the adventurous seafarers of the southwest and the cultured court group in the center. Impressive at first on account of its treasured swords and mirrors, and then on account of its entourage of artists and scholars, the court group with the official recognition of China had always maintained a certain prestige. But they had never been independent ; threatened by the Nara clergy they had called upon the followers of Hachiman in Kyushu ; threatened by revolting Ainu they had called upon troops from the northern districts ; and always they had relied for their safety upon a certain balance between the northeastern and southwestern elements.

Two hundred and fifty years before Kiyomori's day official relations with China had ceased and during all that time Japan had had practically nothing to do with her neighbors on the mainland. Only seldom during that interval had trading boats come to Japan, and more infrequently still had student priests gone to China. What little intercourse there had been was carried on through the southwestern part of the country.

Now Kiyomori allied himself with that southwestern interest. He could see only plodding poverty in the limited land resources on which northeastern farmers based their ideas of economy, and this did not suit his temper. Kiyomori was an original thinker, unbound by the conventions of his day — a man of will, and a man of action. He succeeded in getting Chinese and Korean traders to bring their ships and cargo to his port, and advocated expanding this trade as a means to national prosperity. And yet, withal, Kiyomori was very naïve. He took great pride in the success and high position he had achieved through his own efforts and outdid the Fujiwaras in showy, luxurious living. When at last he was able to make his grandson emperor, with little regard for the strong undercurrent of ill-feeling and resentment that was rising up against him, he pushed the interests of the southwestern element still further.

The better to establish Japan on a maritime basis he required the whole court to leave Kyoto and move to a new capital on the coast of the Inland Sea. Very much against their will did officials, nobles, court ladies, artisans and tradesmen leave their sheltered capital, founded by Emperor Kwammu and glorified by the Fujiwaras, and expose themselves to the fogs, salt winds and discomforts of a city in process of construction. They could not even imagine any good existing anywhere outside Kyoto. The older ones among them, large landowners especially, kept raising bitter opposition to the seacoast capital. The great temples, too, more than indignant at having their patrons transported from their midst, joined forces with the court and called in Minamoto soldiers from the northeast. Six months after it was moved the court returned to its sheltered valley and three months later Kiyomori died. Since his sons were not men of the caliber to carry on his plans, the first attempt at Japanese trade expansion came to an untimely end.

The court moved back to Kyoto in December, 1180, but it was never the same again. Despoiled by the removal, frequently beset by the fires of malcontents, shaken by typhoons, it was a wretched place. The whole country was in upheaval.

"Misfortunes succeeded each other," wrote an eye witness. A great fire reduced to ashes the southern gate of the palace, the Hall of Audience, the University buildings, the Home Office and the houses of sixteen nobles, and took the lives of an immense number of people and cattle. A great whirlwind blew all the houses of three or four city wards flat on the ground and crippled countless people. Then came the miserable moving, and after that: [7]

Either there was drought in spring or summer or there were storms and floods in autumn and winter, so that no grain came to maturity. In all the provinces people left their lands and sought other parts, or, forgetting their homes, went to live among the hills. All kinds of prayers were begun and religious practices revived, but to no purpose whatever. The capital, dependent as it is on the country for everything, could not remain unconcerned when nothing was produced. The inhabitants in their distress offered to sacrifice their valuables of all kinds, but nobody cared to look at them. Buyers made little account of gold, and much of grain. Beggars swarmed by the roadsides, and even respectable-looking people, wearing hats and with their feet covered, might be seen going from door to door. Sometimes they fell down before your eyes. Countless persons died on the roadsides and their bodies were not removed. It was worse on the river banks where there was not even room for horses and vehicles to pass. Porters and woodcutters became so feeble that firewood got scarcer and scarcer and people pulled down their houses. It was strange to see pieces of firewood adorned with vermilion and gold and silver leaf.

Such conditions did not arise in a moment. They had existed in varying degree ever since the splendor of the Fujiwaras had begun to bankrupt the country in the tenth century and social upheaval had begun to take place.

In the course of this confusion, the Tairas went down and the Minamotos rose once more. Those who had once been serfs and peasant farmers became equals of the best. Court people were allowed to continue as well as they could in the capital, but all the business of government (as described in the next chapter) was carried on in camp headquarters at Kamakura, a sort of fishing village three hundred miles northeast of Kyoto near the modern port of Yokohama. Young Yoritomo, of the Minamoto clan, was the new leader of the nation.

Courtiers who once had spent all their days in idle song and dance and poetry now had to earn their own livings. Many of them turned their talents to account by composing flattering narratives about the new military heroes which they recited or sang to the accompaniment of a zither. The new rulers, and the country people, who had had but slight acquaintance with the talents of the court before, were very enthusiastic about this form of entertainment. Some of the stories which were sung in this way were later written down and also frequently represented in painting.[8]

In the era which these chanted tales describe, the court was giving way to military dictatorship ; the center of the stage was shifting from the capital to rural districts and social leaders spent their time, not in ceremonies and festivals, but in battles and preparations for battles.   In this era personal valor came to count for more than rank or family ; affability and stylized conduct gave place to reckless egotism and defiance of established authority.   Lacquer armor replaced the colorful brocaded robes of court officials with silk trains several feet long.   Religion, which had been taken so lightly, now began to receive serious consideration.[9]

The "Tale of Heike," the most elaborate of the heroic narratives describing the conquest of the Tairas by the Minamotos, was composed by destitute courtiers and, perhaps, a bit over-embroidered by their elegant hands.   Several descriptions and episodes from it give such a vivid picture, however, of life in this age of transition that they seem well worth quoting.[10]

The commander-in-chief of the Taira forces was at this time twenty-three years old and his costume and bearing were beautiful beyond the power of brush to depict.   His general's armor, an ancestral treasure, laced with Chinese leather, was carried in an armor box before him, and on the road he wore a robe of red brocade under light-green body armor.   He rode a dappled gray horse and his saddle was mounted in gold.   The second in command wore a robe of blue brocade under armor with black lacings and rode a large and powerful black horse. His saddle was ornamented with powdered gold lacquer. With their horse trappings, armor and helmets and even their swords and bows flashing and glittering as they rode they were a splendid spectacle.

When the commander-in-chief summoned his guide to the eastern provinces and asked "Are there many samurai in the eight eastern provinces who are as mighty archers and as bold as you are?" the guide replied with a scornful smile, "Do you consider me a mighty archer? Why I only draw an arrow of thirteen handbreadths and in the eastern provinces there are any number of soldiers who can do that. A really famous archer never draws a shaft of less than fifteen and his bow is so strong that it needs four or five ordinary men to bend it. They are bold riders too, and their horses never stumble even on the roughest ground. When they fight they do not heed even if their own parents or children are killed, but ride on over their bodies and continue the battle. Men of the western provinces are different. If their parents are killed they retire and perform Buddhist rites for the repose of their souls — if their children are slain they are overcome with grief and can fight no more. They dislike the summer because it is hot and grumble at the cold of winter."

The hour of the hare (6 a. m.) was the time fixed for the beginning of the battle between the Heike and the Genji, and so on the preceding evening the outposts of the Heike went forth to observe the disposition of the enemy. The farmers and inhabitants of the neighborhood, in terror at the movements of the armies, had fled away, some to the moors, some to the hills and some in boats on the sea and river and had kindled their cooking fires everywhere. The Heike, seeing them on all sides, exclaimed, "Ah, see! The camp fires of the Genji are without number. The mountains, sea, river and plains all are full of warriors. What is to be done?"

About the middle of the same night the water-fowl of the marshes of Mount Fuji were startled by something or other and rose suddenly with a whirring of wings like the sound of a mighty wind. The Heike soldiers hearing it, shouted, "It is the Genji army coming to attack us from the rear — we must fall back to the river or we shall be cut off."

Panic stricken, they abandoned their positions and fled without even taking their belongings with them. Some snatched up their bows without arrows or arrows without a bow, springing onto each others' horses and even mounting tethered animals and whipping them so that they galloped round and round the tie post. Some had procured singing girls and dancers and were making merry with them when the alarm took place. These women were hustled, thrown down and trampled in the confusion and their cries added to the uproar.

Then at the hour of the hare the Genji advanced to the river and shouted their war cry three times. The heavens echoed and the earth shook, but from the Heike side there was only silence. When the vanguard approached their camp there was not a man to be seen, not so much as a fly stirring, so they gathered up the armor left behind and bore away in triumph the curtains of the headquarters that had been left standing.

Then Yoritomo alighted from his horse and taking off his helmet washed his hands and rinsed his mouth. Turning toward the imperial palace he reverently made obeisance and said, "This victory is owing to the favor of Hachiman."

Now since the priests of Nara had made clear their feelings for Kiyomori and had shown many signs of rebelling against him, Kiyomori sent troops to attack them. Though it is said nothing drastic was intended, one of the soldiers set fire to a few houses; the wind veered around in all directions so that flames spread hither and thither and most of the temple buildings were soon in a blaze. Even the great Buddha of gold and copper whose eyes the Emperor Shomu had painted was fused with the heat so that its full moon features fell to the pavement below. Never before had there been such a destruction of sacred treasures.

The Genji forces continued to gain in power and before long one of their number named Yoshinaka had made common cause with the monks of Mount Hiei and was pressing on the capital. The Heike abandoned all hope of saving the city and planned to take the emperor with the sacred jewel, sword and mirror away to places of safety. As they fled from Kyoto to the Inland Sea they set fire to all their mansions and the houses of their followers. Though in former days the Heike had flourished like the flowers of spring, now they were falling like the autumn leaves. Looking for some safe refuge they were driven from one place to another by threats of the Genji or Genji allies.

A faithful friend gave them one hundred large boats to replace the little ones in which they had been keeping themselves. Then they sailed to a large island and on its shore built a palace of rough timbers, but it was so common they shrank from permitting his eight year old majesty (Kiyomori's grandson) to live there, and the real palace was a ship. Courtiers spent their days in the thatched huts of fishermen and their nights on shipboard.

Plunged in sorrow deep as the tide, their lives were frail as frosted grasses. At dawn the clamor of the sea birds increased their anguish and at night the grating of the ships on the beach tormented them. When they saw the flocks of herons in the distant pines their hearts sank wondering if they were the white flags of the Genji, and when the cries of the wild geese were wafted from the offing they trembled lest it might be the oar beats of the foe by night. The keen breeze lashed their blackened eyebrows and painted faces, and the salt spray penetrated their delicate eyes which homesick longing often filled with tears. For their green-curtained chambers of scarlet they had exchanged the earthen walls of the reed-hung cottage, and instead of the scented smoke of their braziers rose the briny fumes of the fisherman's driftwood. The features of the court ladies bereft of cosmetics and swollen with continual weeping were changed almost beyond recognition.

While the Taira still held possession of a few provinces in the west, Yoritomo ruled supreme in the north and east; and Yoshinaka lorded it over the capital. His soldiers wearing on their backs quivers of twenty-four arrows tipped with falcon feathers swarmed everywhere in Kyoto. They entered any place at their will to plunder, broke into people's storehouses and even waylaid citizens on the street and robbed them. Yoshinaka was ordered to stop this violence, but he just laughed and said his men had to be taken care of. His swaggering was more unendurable than that of the Heike. Even

Yoritomo thought he was going too far and sent his younger brother, Yoshitsune, to put Yoshinaka in his place.

After one desperate battle Yoshinaka fled from the city with a small band of followers. He was arrayed in a robe of red brocade under a suit of armor laced with Chinese silk. By his side hung a magnificent sword mounted in silver and gold and his helmet was surmounted by long golden horns. Of his twenty-four eagle-feathered arrows most had been shot away in the previous fighting; only a few were left drawn out high from the quiver and he grasped his rattan-bound bow by the middle as he sat on his famous gray charger, fierce as a devil, on a saddle mounted in gold. Rising high in his stirrups as he met a band of his enemies, he cried with a loud voice, "Yoshinaka you have often heard of — now you see him before your eyes! Come, take my head and show it to Yoritomo!"

Then he and his three hundred fell upon their six thousand opponents — cutting, slashing and swinging their blades in every direction until at last, only five of them still surviving, they broke through the enemy ranks. Among these five was a girl named Tomoe who had taken the field many times with Yoshinaka and handled her sword and bow so well that she had won matchless renown in encounters with the bravest captains. Now in this last desperate struggle Yoshinaka called Tomoe to him and said, "As you are a woman it were better that you now make your escape. I have made up my mind to die either by the hand of the enemy or my own; and I would be shamed to die with a woman." But Tomoe was still in fine mettle and would not forsake her lover. "Ah, for some bold warrior to match with," she exclaimed, "that you might see how fine a death I can die." A band of thirty valiant men rode up at that moment. Plunging into them she seized their captain, dragged him from his horse and calmly cut off his head. Then stripping off her armor she fled away to the east.

Then Yoshitsune, determined to wipe out the Heike and restore to the capital the three imperial regalia (the jewel, the sword and the mirror) which the Heike had carried off with them, set out with a band of followers. The Heike at this

time had made their way back toward Kyoto and were en-
camped at a place on the seashore, protected on all sides by
steep cliffs. "Is it possible for a stag to pass there?" Yoshitsune enquired of an old hunter who knew the country well.
"Where a stag may pass, there can a horse go also." And
Yoshitsune rode over the cliff at the head of his thirty retainers. The whole force of three thousand followed after them.
For more than a hundred yards the slope was sandy with small
pebbles so that they slid down and landed on a level place.
Thence downward it was all great mossy boulders, steep as a
well and some fifty yards to the bottom. It seemed impossible to go any further and the soldiers were recoiling in horror
thinking they were in a trap, when one sprang forward shouting, "In my part of the country we ride down places like this
any day to catch a bird. We would make a race course of
this !" Down he went, followed by all the rest, and the Heike
in a panic fled out of their stronghold and onto the sea once
more.

One of the Heike leaders then seeing that all was over,
turned toward the west to repeat the death prayer. "O Amida
Nyorai who sheddest the light of Thy Presence through the
ten quarters of the world, gather into Thy Radiant Heaven all
who call upon Thy Name !" Just as his prayer was finished a
Genji soldier from behind swept off his head. Not doubting
that he had taken the head of a noble foe, but quite unaware
whose it might be, the Genji soldier, searching the armor,
came across a piece of paper fastened to the quiver on which
was written the verse :

> Tonight my lodging,
> The shelter of a pine tree
> And my host, a flower.

Another Genji captain seeing a single horseman attempting
to escape to one of the ships in the offing beckoned with his
war fan crying out, "Shameful to show an enemy your back !
Return ! Return !" Then the Heike warrior turned his horse

and rode back to the beach. Springing upon him and tearing
off his helmet, the Genji captain beheld the face of a youth of
sixteen or seventeen, delicately powdered, with blackened
teeth and features of great beauty. "How pitiful to put this
youth to death," the Genji captain thought, mindful of his
own son, and was about to set the Heike warrior free when a
troop of Genji horsemen rode up. "Though I would spare
your life," the captain explained, "the whole countryside
swarms with our men. You cannot escape them. If you
must die, let it be by my hand, and I will see that prayers are
said for your rebirth in bliss." His eyes swam with tears and
his hand trembled so that he could scarcely wield his blade.
"Alas," he cried, "what life is so hard as that of a soldier?
Only because I was born of a warrior family must I do such
cruel deeds." And he pressed his face to the sleeve of his
armor and wept bitterly. Stripping off the young man's armor
he discovered a flute in a brocade bag that he was carrying in
his girdle. "Ah," he exclaimed, "it was this youth and his
friends who were amusing themselves with music within the
walls this morning. Among all our men of the eastern provinces I doubt if any has brought a flute with him. What
esthetes are these courtiers of Heike!" The flute was named
Saeda, Little Branch, and had been given as a present by an
emperor.

One evening as the sun was sinking and both forces on the
shore were preparing to rest for the night a small Heike boat
appeared some seventy or eighty feet from the water's edge
and swung round broadside. A girl hung a red fan on a pole
fastened to the gunwale of the boat.

"Summon the best archer we have," ordered Yoshitsune,
"and show the enemy how we can shoot."

Yoichi was called, a lad barely twenty years old. He was
wearing a robe of greenish blue with the collar and edges of
the sleeves ornamented with brocade on a red ground. His
armor was laced with light green and the mounts of his sword
were silver. With bow under his arm and helmet slung to

his breastplates, he came into the presence of Yoshitsune and bowed respectfully.

"I cannot say that I can hit the fan for certain," Yoichi said, "and if I should miss, it would be a lasting reproach to the skill of our side. Would it not be better to entrust it to someone who could be quite sure?" This angered Yoshitsune. So Yoichi said, "If my lord commands, I will try." Then he mounted a fine black horse with saddle ornamented with gold and, taking a fresh hold on his bow, gripped the reins and rode into the sea till he came within bowshot of the boat. The wind was blowing strong; the waves were running high. The ships were rising and falling on the swell and the fan was fluttering in the breeze. The Heike had ranged their ships in a long row to see better, while on land the Genji lined the shore in expectation. Yoichi prayed to Hachiman and the deities of his homeland. "I pray you grant that I may strike the center of that fan, for if I fail I will break my bow and put an end to my life." Then he opened his eyes again, drew his bow with all his strength and let fly. The shore echoed to the whirr of the arrow as it flew straight to its mark. The Heike in the offing beat applaudingly on the gunwales of their ships while the Genji on the shore rattled their quivers till they rang.

The forces of the Genji increased while those of the Heike grew less with the continual desertion of their followers. On the twenty-fourth day of the third month of the second year of Genryaku, at the hour of the hare (6 a. m.), the final battle between the Taira and Minamoto began at Dan-no-ura.

The two hosts of the Genji and Heike faced each other scarcely thirty cho distant on the water, and as the tide was running strong the Heike ships were carried by the current against their will while the Genji were naturally able to advance on them with the tide.

One of the Heike leaders shouted, "These eastern fellows may have a great name for horsemanship but they know nothing about sea fights. Let their Commander Yoshitsune be the special object of your attack. He is a little fellow with a fair complexion and his front teeth stick out a bit so you will know him by that. He changes his clothes and armor often — so take care he doesn't escape you !"

The fleet of the Genji was more numerous, but as their men shot from various places here and there their force did not show to advantage. Yoshitsune himself who was fighting in the forefront of the battle was greatly embarrassed by the arrows of the foe that fell like rain on his shield and armor. Elated by their victory on the first attack, the Heike pressed on and the roar of their shouting mingled with the booming of their war drums.

Both sides set their faces against each other and fought grimly without a thought for their lives, neither giving way an inch. As the Heike had on their side an emperor endowed with the ten virtues and the three sacred treasures of the realm, things went hard with the Genji. Their hearts were beginning to fail them when suddenly something like a cloud or a white banner floating in the breeze came drifting over the two fleets from the upper air and finally settled on the stern of one of the Genji ships.

When he saw this Yoshitsune, regarding it as a sign from Hachiman, removed his helmet and, after washing his hands, did obeisance, his men all following his example.

Later on, the men of Shikoku and Kyushu all left the Heike in a body and went over to the Genji, so the struggle was decided in their favor.

Then the widow of Kiyomori in an outer dress of dark-gray mourning color, with her glossy silk skirts tucked up, put the sacred jewel under her arm and the sacred sword in her girdle and, taking the emperor (her grandson) in her arms, spoke thus. "Though I am but a woman, I will not fall into the hands of the foe, but will accompany our sovereign. Let those of you who will, follow me."

The emperor was eight years old that year and his appearance was very lovely with his long black hair hanging loosely down his back. With a look of surprise and anxiety on his face he enquired, "Where is it that you are going to take me ?"

Turning to her youthful sovereign with tears streaming down her cheeks she answered, "Face the east and bid farewell to the deity of the great shrine of Isé, and then the west and say the prayer that Amida may come to welcome you in paradise. There is a pure land of happiness beneath the waves, another capital where is no sorrow. Thither am I taking our sovereign." Thus she comforted him and bound up his long hair in his dove-colored robe. The child sovereign put his beautiful little hands together and did as she had told him. Then holding him tightly in her arms she said, "In the depths of the ocean we have a capital," and sank with him at last beneath the waves.

Now the whole sea was red with the Heike banners and the insignia which Genji had torn off and cut away; it looked like a river in autumn flecked with the maple leaves the wind brings down. The deserted, empty ships rocked mournfully on the waves.

CHAPTER VIII

THE FIRST MILITARY DICTATORSHIP
(THIRTEENTH CENTURY)

MINAMOTO YORITOMO, who emerged from the struggle described in the previous chapter to become Japan's first military dictator, had a romantic career. As a boy of eleven he lived at the palace of the emperor's second wife who was the fashion leader of the time. Since his father, like Taira Kiyomori's, was a chief of the imperial guard, it seemed likely he would grow up in the fastidious society of leisurely and self-indulgent courtiers. When Yoritomo was twelve, however, his father was defeated in a skirmish with the Taira and had to escape from the capital in the dark of night. The boy, not wishing to remain in the hands of enemies, ran after his father's party, but somehow or other missed them and had to hide with peasants. His father was caught and killed. By natural succession Yoritomo became head of the Minamoto clan, and as such was in imminent danger from the Taira. But his mother was a very charming lady, and when she appealed to Kiyomori to spare the life of her sons, the heart of the great man melted.

Instead of being beheaded, Yoritomo was sent to live in the custody of a Fujiwara family in the Mount Fuji region.

Not at all broken in spirit by this experience, the boy at once set about making friends in his new surroundings. Though the leading families of the region were of Taira descent, instead of turning with Kiyomori toward the sea and the court, they had, like the Minamotos, kept up their interest in the land. They were not very kindly disposed toward their relatives in Kyoto. Chief among these eastern landlords and highly respected by them was a man named Hojo Tokimasa ; he was the father of Masa, a most remarkable daughter. Hojo Tokimasa was favorably impressed with Yoritomo, and willing to cast his lot with this heir of the Minamotos rather than with some of his own blood relatives. His daughter, Masa, seemed to share his sentiments. On the night set for her marriage to a Taira governor deputized by the court she eloped with Yoritomo.

This rather raised than ruined Yoritomo in the estimation of the eastern landlords and, with the backing of his father-in-law, he became a sort of champion for them. Minamoto ancestors were fully as illustrious as the Taira's and the interests of Heike in the provinces were more closely allied with those of the Minamotos than with those of their Kyoto cousins. When Yoritomo led troops to the capital to free it of Kiyomori's domination, about as many Tairas as Minamotos followed him. When he returned victorious to the east the owners of large estates were willing to make him their chief.

Yoritomo established himself as Lord High Constable in the fishing village of Kamakura, and from there he directed the affairs of the surrounding country. After Kiyomori's death, the government in Kyoto was totally ineffectual. It could neither keep order nor collect taxes, and several of the able men in its employ were glad to enter the service of the new government at Kamakura, called the Bakufu, or Camp Administration. On the advice of these men of experience Yoritomo appointed three committees : one for carrying on general affairs, one for hearing and judging law suits and one in charge of soldiers. He also obtained permission from Kyoto to appoint military governors and land stewards to supplement and supplant the governors and officials appointed by the court. In this way he was able to reward those who had fought for him, and to extend his own influence. But, more important still, he was able to levy and collect taxes from all privately owned lands in return for the military protection which his government offered.

By leaving the court undisturbed, and restoring many of the old nobility to the offices and estates which they had held before the rise of Kiyomori, he won favor with them. By rebuilding many temples which the Tairas had destroyed, repairing the great Buddha at Nara and having another large one cast in Kamakura, he made friends instead of enemies of the Buddhist priests. Shinto priests and the followers of Hachiman were likewise gratified when they found the Lord High Constable lavishing gifts upon the shrine to the god of victories which had been erected near Kamakura by the Minamotos two centuries before.

In ten years Yoritomo, by negotiation and conquest, got under his control the entire eastern half of the country. Then he revisited Kyoto. Great preparations were made for his coming. Dwellings were furnished for him and his companions on the site where the Tairas' magnificent palace once had stood. The court was thrilled with curious anticipation for the coming of this wonder-working strong man from the east. Even the cloistered emperor went out secretly to watch Yoritomo and his followers pass.

Though he stayed five weeks in the capital, bestowing costly gifts on the court, the temples and shrines, Yoritomo's hope of being appointed shogun, with the right to move troops as he pleased, was not readily fulfilled. It was not until two years later that he won the coveted commission, Commander-in-Chief of the troops of the nation — a commission which he could hand down to his sons and grandsons.

And as fate would have it, neither Yoritomo himself nor his sons were long to enjoy this privilege. Returning from a bridge-opening ceremony in 1199 Japan's first military dictator was thrown from his horse and fatally injured at the age of fifty-three. His sons who fell heir to the family possessions and the title of shogun were soon put out of the way. His widow, Hojo Masa, however, rallied Yoritomo's followers and managed to maintain the stability of the Bakufu.

When some of the Kamakura generals, with their strong leader gone, were inclined to desert the camp government and try to make a name for themselves with the Kyoto court, she called them together and, with trembling voice, pleaded, from behind a bamboo screen as befitted a respectable lady :

Nobles and retainers of Kamakura, if ye recollect the past direct administration of the emperors, your fathers had to do military service at court for three years, besides bearing many burdens. It often happened that many, when discharged, had to return home barefooted because of poverty. But my late husband, touched by such conditions, reduced the term of court service to six months and abated many burdens. Now the court is trying to overthrow me. Is it possible that a government which has achieved so much should be punished? The loss of my beloved husband and two sons was already sufficient sorrow, yet I had to see my dear father pass away only recently. Now comes a moment of life or death for my government. Those of you who remember what my husband and father did for you, give me your hands in allegiance . . . But if some would prefer to render service to the court, speak out at this moment.[1]

Everyone present was touched by the earnestness of her appeal and the dignity of the soldiers' life as compared with the ways of the court. All swore to share the fate of the Kamakura government, and thereafter fought like one man for the victory of the Hojo regime.

The kind of life these military men had led on the frontier was the best possible training for ruling the nation at that time. Though originally they had been the less favored members of the nobility, or erring ones banished far from courtly ease and pleasures to atone for their misdemeanors, they were now the aristocracy of power. While courtiers had been dissipating their energies in idle amusements, these men had been working hard. In the great Musashi plain they had found more extensive fertile fields than anywhere else in Japan; the climate there was less fickle than farther south and west — but it was also sterner. Untiring industry and long perseverance had been required to develop the district ; and united action had been required to defend it. These men, therefore, loved the land to which they had given so much. And they knew full well the value of working together, sacrificing together, if need be, for the good of all.

For twenty-five years after Yoritomo passed away, Hojo Masa carried on the government he had planned. Ama Shogun, the widow or nun general, she was called. Though neither of her sons who succeeded their father had been allowed by rival generals to live long enough to amount to anything as rulers, Masa organized a Council of State which, under the leadership of her brother and his descendants, gave Japan a century of government as just, efficient, strong and economic as any the country has ever known.

The thirteen members of her Council of State swore a solemn oath that they would give no regard to ties of relationship, but would speak out unfearful of powerful houses. Every opinion the council expressed or order it issued was to be upheld by every member. There was to be no dissension or criticism of one member by another, for this would destroy their solidarity and give men a chance to laugh at them.

Law suits were settled promptly with good judgment. Even when an envoy from Korea came complaining of the ravages of Japanese pirates on the coast of his country, the matter was given prompt consideration, the pirate leaders were punished and their booty was restored to its owners. A real effort was also made to reduce the cost of government and lessen the taxes on the people as shown by the following anecdotes about various Hojo rulers.

Once, when the fence surrounding the Hojo regent's home was in need of repair, some government officials wished to replace it with an embankment, but the regent refused, saying the suggested change would take too much labor, and would not protect him nearly so well as the bravery of his comrades.

On another occasion when a young Hojo regent was coming to visit his mother she set about patching some torn places in the sliding paper walls. Her brother said, "Let me give it to So-and-So to do ; he understands such things." But she replied, "His work will not be any better than mine," and went on pasting square after square. "It would be easier to repaper the whole thing," her brother suggested, "and, besides, the patches look ugly." Then the regent's mother explained, "I am doing it like this on purpose, to teach young people to mend evils while they are small." [2]

There are also stories about Hojo regents who disguised themselves as pilgrims and traveled through the deep snow to find out how poor people were living. One of them wore only old clothing and ate only two simple meals a day as an example for his officials. Both he and they worked from dawn till dusk, devising and supervising effective measures of relief.

A Hojo regent's widow obtained permission from the government to establish a "temple of divorce" where helpless wives could stay for two or three years and be protected from cruel husbands.

The officers appointed to the provinces by the Hojo government were visited at regular and irregular intervals by inspectors from Kamakura, and people were encouraged to report any maladministration and dissatisfaction with officials. Every autumn inspectors were sent out through the country to estimate the crops and thus keep a check on tax returns of rice and produce. Storehouses were kept filled with rice, to be dispersed to the people in time of bad crops and famine. There were no longer any estates completely immune from taxes. All land holders were to receive justice and protection, and all were, therefore, required to pay taxes.

The emperor, resenting the thorough-going way in which the Hojo regents were taking over the functions of government, raised a revolt against them, but his efforts were worse than futile.[3] He himself was deposed, three ex-emperors were sent into exile, and the Hojos put on the throne a boy whom they knew they could manage. As a result of this unsuccessful coup the Hojo regents were enabled not only to clear many princes and courtiers out of the capital, but also to take possession of many lands valuable as rewards for faithful followers. Two officials were appointed to represent the Kamakura government in the capital and keep watch over the imperial family, to prevent further conspiracy. These officials used the buildings prepared on the Taira estates for Yoritomo's visit as their mansions and offices. The fire-swept imperial palaces and court office buildings were entirely neglected. The spacious grounds were frequented only by hunting parties. The university was no more. And emperors lived here and there in the homes of nobles.[4] But in spite of Hojo economy, the country was miserable. The national bankruptcy was aggravated by earthquakes, plagues and famines. While the country people, in general, were better treated under the new regime, court people were impoverished.

Buddhist priests who formerly had appealed chiefly to the upper classes, of necessity changed their programs. They now catered to persons of wealth and leisure by building temple hostels in beautiful scenic places, and encouraging the practice of making pilgrimages. They also encouraged courtiers and officials who found themselves in difficulties with their rivals, and their plans gone far awry, to withdraw from active life and retire to some temple.

Instead of the gay confidence and optimism that characterized the religion of Fujiwara days, now there was pessimism. Instead of saying, "Eat, drink and be merry and make generous gifts to us for obtaining your salvation," now they said, "The times are so bad that there is no use trying to do anything about life here. Shun it as much as possible and simply believe in Amida's all-embracing mercy and willingness to save you." Just repeating the deity's name, with faith, was sufficient for some denominations. They did away with learned discourses on the scriptures, with complicated theology and creeds, for the masses were ignorant and unable to read. They said, "You must look in your own heart for the truth, and work out your own salvation."

A fisherman's son named Nichiren turned preacher and went through the streets of Kamakura accompanied by followers, beating sticks and drums. "We have seen many signs in heaven and in earth! A famine, a plague, the whole country is filled with misery! Horses and cows are

FOUR WOODEN STATUES

dying on the roadsides and so are men ; and there is no one to bury them. One half the population is stricken, and there is no house that has entirely escaped, hence many minds are turning to religion," thus Nichiren addressed the people. "Others again in accordance with the secret doctrines of Shingon use copious sprinklings of holy water from the five vases. Some write the names of the seven gods of luck on pieces of paper and affix them by the hundreds to the door posts of their houses, while others do the same with the pictures of various gods of heaven and earth. But let men do what they will, the famine and the plague still rage, there are beggars on every hand, and the unburied corpses line the roads. The truth is missed and distorted by squinting eyes . . . Repent and be converted to the true faith before the hour of utmost disaster arrives." [5]

Nichiren felt sure that Japan was to be a fountain of blessing to the whole world in coming ages, but at present needed chastisement. The Japanese nation was living in winter, but spring was sure to follow.

Then he uttered a prophetic warning. "It will not be long before the great Mongols will send their myriad warships and attack this country. Then the whole people will surely abandon all the sanctuaries they used to revere and join in crying, 'O Master Nichiren, save us !' " [6]

He was right about the Mongol warships. From early times boats from China had come to Japan with treasures of various kinds for the imperial storehouses, and things like sulphur, arrows, pearls, herbs, straw mats and timber were traded in exchange. When the imperial treasury could no longer stand the strain of such trade, the Fujiwara took it over, and when their resources were dissipated it was Taira Kiyomori's turn. The lavish way in which he traded in Chinese goods wiped out the fortune of his family in one generation. The Kamakura shogunate, however, the thrifty northern farmers, refused to trade. They had seen the folly of over-spending. Homemade things were good enough for them. So Chinese boats stopped coming.

Some people, however, were not satisfied. Though they had little of value to take to trade with China, there were many things in China which they wanted, and buccaneering began. The coasts of Korea and China were continually pirated by little boats from Japan. When the Mongols came to power they wished to put an end to this illicit trade and establish more orderly relations.

It was about this time that the great Venetian traveler Marco Polo reported, "There is a very large island called Zepangu (which was the way he caught the name of Japan) fifteen hundred miles from the coast of China, where gold is so abundant that the riches of the King are incalculable and even the roof of his palace is covered with gold. The inhabitants, though living quite separate from other nations, are fair, handsome and of agreeable manner." [7] Marco Polo had never been to Japan, but when this description, fantastic as it was, reached Europe, it made men very eager to trade with the Orient and was one of the factors leading to the discovery of America.

To arrive at some agreement with the rulers of Japan the Mongols sent several groups of envoys. One of them arrived in Kyoto when the courtiers were preparing for an emperor's fiftieth birthday party. The message they brought from the great Mongol, Kublai Khan, concluded something like this : "We beg that hereafter you, O King, will establish friendly relations with us. Is it reasonable to refuse intercourse with each other ? It will lead to war, and who is there who likes such a state of things ? Think on this, O King." [8]

The courtiers suspended their birthday party preparations and drafted what they thought was a suitable reply. The Kamakura officials, however, refused to give it to the envoys and sent them back empty handed.

Not long after this a fleet of several hundred ships attacked two small islands off the mainland of Japan, capturing or killing the people and plundering whatever they could find of value. Then they sailed on to Kyushu. The news was rushed to Kamakura by riders on swift horses. A thrilling appeal was made to all armed men to put aside petty differences and rally in defense of the nation. Every man who could use bow and arrow and sword, and get a horse to take him there was urged to hasten to Kyushu. But the Mongols did not wait for these troops to arrive. The local Kyushu leaders had to meet them alone, with only their courage and their terrible swords to confront the poisoned arrows shot by Mongols seven hundred feet away, or the heavy stones hurled from a machine. At a distance the Japanese were helpless, but face to face with an adversary there was none who could withstand their spirited blades. When dusk came, the Mongols returned to their ships, intending no doubt to land again and continue fighting next day. But during the night a storm arose. And with the dawn, the Kyushu people discovered that the attacking fleet was far out to sea and headed for Korea.

The Kamakura government, however, was not misled. They thought that Kublai Khan would not be so easily thwarted in his ambitions. And they were right. Soon afterward more envoys were sent bidding the Japanese ruler to come and pay homage at the Mongol ruler's new court in Peking. This message infuriated the Hojo regents.

Ships filled with Samurai

They cut off the envoys' heads and betook themselves to great preparations for both offense and defense. They instructed officials in the coastal provinces of western Japan to get together helmsmen and sailors for a Japanese fleet, and they ordered the Kyushu landlords to build stone ramparts on their shores. For over five years they kept on preparing. Then another envoy came from the great Mongol. The government cut off his head and continued to strengthen their defenses.

Finally the second great fleet appeared, part of it made up of Koreans, and part of it of Chinese just recently conquered by the Mongols. Over four thousand boats, they say, there were altogether, some of them carrying a hundred men or more, and horses in addition. But this time the Japanese did not allow them to land so easily. They took out little boats to harass the fleet by surrounding single vessels and setting fire to them and attacking crews which tried to get ashore. For seven weeks the fighting continued along the shores of Kyushu. For seven weeks the resolute Japanese soldiers behind miles and miles of earthen embankments checked the advances of the Mongol marines. But losses were heavy on both sides.

Princes and courtiers in Kyoto spent all their time fasting and praying and having priests perform religious rites to bring about victory. The emperor sent his autographed prayer to the shrine of Hachiman in Kyushu. It read, "The enemy of the country must be vanquished."

"Throughout the length and breadth of the land could be heard the tapping and roll of temple drums, the tinkling of sacred bells, the rustle of the sleeves of vestal dancers and the litanies of priests. In thousands of temples wood fires were kept burning and the smoke of incense ascended perpetually." [9]

Seven weeks and three days the fighting continued fiercely. The reports which reached the capital spread panic. All work and business was suspended. Even courtiers suffered from a dearth of supplies. Then suddenly the sky grew dark, and again there arose a mighty wind of tornado proportions ; the Mongol squadrons were jammed together at the mouth of the harbor where they were lying. Vessels shattered to pieces. Men plunged into the water. The wreckage piled so high and solid that it formed a bridge from one shore to the other. The soldiers who went ashore were captured and put to death. Only a fraction of the ships and men escaped to the continent again.

Then what rejoicing there was all over the country! Then what a clamor the priests put up! The victory was theirs, in answer to their prayers. And they demanded suitable rewards. Both court and Bakufu were very generous with them, but still they clamored for more. And the fighting men, who had left their farms in the northeast and gone down to the defense of Kyushu, they also asked the Bakufu for recompense.

Nothing had been gained by the war, however; there were no spoils to divide. And there was still danger that the Mongols might return; because of repeated scares troops were kept in Kyushu for almost thirty years. Even if they had wished to, the Hojo regents would have found it very difficult to satisfy all of the claims presented to them. With the passing of the years, however, their standards had relaxed, their sense of responsibility had grown dull. Instead of being reared in the robust thrift and simplicity of his forbears, the eighth Hojo regent was brought up like an imperial prince. This caused great discontent among the thousands of fighting men who, though they had gone into debt in defense of the country, found no recompense or justice forthcoming from the Hojos. Their only hope, it seemed, lay in a civil war. Then if they were among the winners, there would be the estates of the losing side to take over and redistribute among themselves. It was not long before many of these malcontents, and monks too, had turned their backs on the decadent dictators and rallied to the support of the Emperor Go-Daigo, of whom more will be told in the next chapter.

These were the days of the sword. From earliest times, you remember, a sword had been one of the three sacred symbols of the emperor. But for generations in ancient times the use of metal swords had remained as the exclusive right of the ruling family. When not in use these early swords were kept in Shinto shrines to impress worshippers with the power of the imperial clan. In the Nara and Heian periods, nobles and officials came to share the privilege of wearing swords, but the swords they wore were nothing but bejewelled wooden things which served as decorations of rank. Swords which could stand the test of use were given only on special occasions such as the dispatching of expeditions to the north against the revolting Ainu or the sending of delegations to the Chinese court, and then they were bestowed with ceremony and only to the highest in command.

As the Fujiwaras left more and more responsibility in the hands of provincial officers, these latter were allowed to carry swords. And when Tairas and Minamotos came to guard the capital they provided themselves with swords on their own initiative. Even then, however, there was only one sword to a family, and the member to whom it was entrusted was regarded with highest respect. Combat was not on a large, impersonal scale. It was the hand-to-hand encounters of provincial swordsmen well aware of each

other's reputation that made possible the rule of the shoguns or military dictators.

With the establishment of the Bakufu at Kamakura,
sword-making became a prosperous industry and remained
so for seven centuries.[10] Because of their superb quality,
Japanese swords were in great demand in China and came
to be the chief item in export trade. The best Japanese
swords of the thirteenth century are the finest of any in the
world. A good one, they say, will cut a hair floating in the
air, or a pile of copper coins without being nicked.

To make a "noble blade," the swordsmith first of all had
to lead a pure and moral life. His craft was like a religion
to him. For each sword he started to make the smith went
through a period of prayer and fasting and used charms of
various kinds in his home and workroom to keep away evil
influences.

The first step was the forging. Several tiny strips of steel
were welded together to make a bar about six inches by two
inches, by half an inch. This was cut almost in half and
folded back on itself, then forged to its original size again.
Several bars like this were forged, and cut and folded, and
reforged twelve or eighteen times. Then all were welded
together and cut and folded and reforged half a dozen
times more before they were beaten out into a blade.

The second step was the tempering. In this process the
whole blade except the edge was covered with a clayish
mixture and heated in a bright charcoal fire until the back
reached red heat and the edge white. Then it was plunged
into water of a certain temperature. This made a very
hard, sharp edge and a resilient back.

The polishing and sharpening was the most difficult and complicated process. It took weeks and weeks of most perfectly controlled and painstaking labor. When it was completed and the maker's name was incised on the tang, the sword was ready for mounting. The hilt, fastened on with a simple little bamboo plug, was easily removed when occasion arose to show the smith's signature, but when the sword was being used, held absolutely firm. Marvelous little pieces of carved metal were bound to the hilt with sharkskin and silk cords to give a good grip and serve as ornamentation. The guards also were ornamented with gold and silver alloys in exquisite inlay designs. A master swordsmith's masterpiece was of enormous value. Good swords by lesser craftsmen sold at anywhere from a hundred up to five thousand dollars.

Since in addition to the exacting and costly process of making a sword, learning how to use one required years and years of devoted training, effort and discipline, it is small wonder that skilled swordsmen formed a distinct and distinguished class of society. Groups of them attached themselves to important landowners and were given regular salaries in property and rice in return for their readiness to use swords when needed. These swordsmen in the service of landlords came to be called samurai.

Centuries later it came to be the custom for each samurai, and for samurai only, to wear not one, but two swords in lacquer sheaths thrust through his belt. There were long swords for encounters, and short ones for cutting off the head of a defeated opponent, or for cutting open one's own stomach. A true samurai never hesitated to give his life in order to prove his sincerity or to defend his honor. Like the ancient Greeks, it is explained, the Japanese thought that the soul of man dwelt in his stomach. And ripping open the stomach was equivalent to saying, "I will show you my soul. See for yourself whether it is polluted or clean." [11]

Good swords themselves were supposed to have some hidden power or spirit akin to a soul in them. The gift of a good sword carried with it a sacred trust and inspiration, for the quality of the blade was thought of as reflecting the character of the owner, and owners sought to live up to the reputation of the sword handed down to them. Some swords had the reputation of preserving peace by their inner power without dealing death. It was a serious matter to unsheath a sword, for once it was unsheathed it had to be used effectively. Otherwise the sword was dishonored, and the owner, too, for showing such unsoldier-like haste in drawing it and hesitation in using it.

From the thirteenth century on, as samurai came to play an increasingly important part in political, social and economic affairs, they became increasingly more class conscious. As time went on there grew up among them a certain code of conduct, not written down as rules and regulations, but impressed deep in their minds and hearts. It was their way of life. They called it Bushido, the Way of the Warriors. Bushido had much in common with chivalry, but a great deal more which was peculiar to itself. Bushido is often spoken of as the "Soul of Japan." It is the basis of the most popular Japanese literature, and samurai are still the heroes of the majority of Japanese movies. A favorite feature on Japanese radio programs today is the chanting of heroic ballads repeating old stories of famous samurai, of how they lived and died. The following story of Akechi Mitsuharu, given here without its usual embellishments, is one which Japanese listeners especially delight in.

Besieged by a rival general, Mitsuharu set fire to his castle on Azuchi hill, and with less than two dozen men, all that remained of his six hundred samurai, attempted to escape to his other castle on the opposite shore of Lake Biwa. Confronted by the enemy en route, every one of his men fell, bravely fighting ; Mitsuharu himself was able to charge through the enemy on his horse and plunge into the lake. The sight of this single horseman, his coat of white silk twill painted with a dragon and clouds by a great artist of the day, the red and blue saddle and trappings of his mount moving close to the water, was so beautiful to behold that the enemy on the banks forgot themselves and cheered.

Landing on the further shore, Mitsuharu rode his horse to a shrine and there dismounted. Taking out a sheet of paper and a writing brush from the kit he carried in his girdle, the hero wrote, "The horse which swam across the lake with Mitsuharu on him," and tied the piece of paper to the horse's mane. He had no further need of his horse, but wishing to save its life, left it with its bridle fastened to the shrine and walked alone to his castle.

At dawn the next morning he appeared at the window of his watch tower shouting, "I have a word to say to the general of the advancing army, I, Akechi Mitsuharu. Will he come closer ?"

When the enemy came forward Mitsuharu went on, "My master fell in an ill-fated battle, and his wife and children are about to end their lives here. I shall set this castle on fire and die also, but rare treasures that once belonged to Lord Nobunaga are kept in this castle. We ourselves may perish as the fortunes of war decree, but these treasures in truth belong to the world at large and ought to be preserved for thousands of years to come. I will hand them over to you with a list. Pray take them to your master for safe keeping."

Having said this, by means of sashes he slowly lowered the treasures, wrapped in silk brocade bedding, into the hands of the enemy general.[12]

Certainly one cannot understand Japanese people today without some understanding of the principle, the education and the practice of the samurai.

Although it is often said that Bushido made Japan what it is today, it is equally true that Japan as it was in the thirteenth century was what made Bushido. It was not something new which appeared suddenly, but the natural outcome of the deep and widespread influences of Buddhism, Shinto and Chinese ethical teachings, and the economic and social conditions of the time. The newer sects of Buddhism were creating in people's minds a calm acceptance of whatever life had in store, and a not unfriendly feeling toward death. The Jodo sect taught that death is rebirth in paradise. And the Zen sect that life is a continual dying.[13]

Shinto taught pious reverence and gratitude toward one's own ancestors and especially for those of one's superiors. It is interesting to note in this connection that when worshippers went to ancestral shrines to pay their devotions, they were almost always confronted by a round mirror of polished metal. The mirror seemed to say, "To truly serve and reverence others, first of all you must know yourself. Look and see what ugliness and beauty, what evil and what good there is in you. Know thyself."

The ancient Chinese ethics emphasized loyalty in all relationships and propriety in behavior. Now the condition of Japan was such that men in power needed the support of many strong armed men, and men who had only their strong arms to defend them needed to band together under the protection of an influential landlord. Life was not easy for anyone ; the spirit of daring and bearing was often put to the test.

As a result of all these influences, Bushido developed among provincial troops in the Kamakura period. In the centuries that followed it took a stronger and stronger hold on the hearts of the people. It was their ideal. The spirit of Bushido still lives in many breasts today.

Samurai had no patience with vague moral theories and but little respect for knowledge unless it was of the kind men reveal in character. They were men of action and, without any explanation, executed what they thought was justice. If their lord needed something belonging to someone else, they would see how highly the owner really valued it by the defense he offered. "Let the strongest man win," they said. Another favorite maxim was, "To know and to act are one and the same."

Training in Bushido began in babyhood. If a child cried over a hurt, his mother would exclaim, "What a coward to cry for a little pain ! What will you do when your arm is cut off in battle, or when, for the sake of honor, you must rip your stomach open with your sword ?" [14] For discipline and experience young children were set all sorts of difficult tasks. They were sent far off to deliver a message among strangers. Often they were made to rise before the sun to do some chores, to go on a long errand barefoot in winter, or to visit execution grounds at night and leave some evidence that they had been among the heads exposed there.

A story is told of a famished little boy talking to his companion. "See the little sparrows open wide their yellow bills. How eagerly they eat the worms their mother brings, but for us when our stomach is empty, it is a disgrace to show hunger."

Samurai children were taught to endure suffering and control their faces, so as not to disturb anyone else by their expressions of pain, but they were also taught to be sensitive to the distress of others, and to have a sympathetic regard for others' feelings, even for blossoms and birds.

Cherry blossoms were great favorites with the samurai. Not showy in color or heavy in fragrance, not bearing thorns beneath its beauty, nor clinging to its stem after its beauty was gone, the cherry blossom appealed to them for its simplicity and modesty and its readiness to depart life while still in its prime.

Trained never to shed the blood of an opponent of unequal strength, or of unequal rank, samurai yet felt called upon not infrequently to sacrifice their own wives and children for the sake of the lord whom they served. There are many stories of loyal samurai who, when an enemy was trying to wipe out all the sons of their lord, if there was any resemblance between them, gave their own sons to the sword. And if their lord or one of their family had been treacherously killed by an enemy, they felt it a matter of principle and personal honor to wreak vengeance on the offender.   In such an event any sort of trickery was justified, for they were acting in accordance with their code and fulfilling the will of heaven.

CHAPTER IX

WANT AND CONFUSION
(FOURTEENTH THROUGH SIXTEENTH CENTURIES)

FROM 1300 to 1600 were three long centuries of change and confusion in Japan — an age of fighting farmers and merchant priests, of pirates and dilettanti ; an age when the lower classes of society came to the top ; an age when shoguns with foreign trade monopolies built gold and silver pavilions and emperors made their living by selling autographs.

The Hojos who had given Japan a hundred years of thrifty law and order, reasonably impartial taxes and prompt economical justice were undone by the Mongol invasion ; the priests had claimed the victory was theirs and had been generously rewarded. Then the southern landowners, who had fought for the defense of their own lands, claimed the victory was theirs, and resented the intrusion of the northerners. The northerners in turn with equal justice claimed they had left their lands in the north and spent everything they had in coming to the assistance of the south. All over the country people were dissatisfied and unsettled. They turned first to this side, then to that in the political struggles which ensued, fighting wherever and whenever they saw something to be gained.

At the beginning of the fourteenth century the imperial court, which had long been in the dim background of government affairs, thought to take advantage of the ill feeling toward the Hojos, and with the help of armed priests from Mount Hiei, Mount Koya and Nara, led a revolt against Kamakura, the capital of the dictators. The Hojos, no longer fortified with strong military leaders of their own clan, ordered an able warrior named Takauji from a district called Ashikaga in the north to put down the imperial uprising. Ashikaga Takauji's followers, descended from the Minamoto family, inherited resentment toward the Hojos for the way they had treated the illustrious Yoritomo's sons and appropriated his lands and power. Instead of attacking the emperor, therefore, they joined causes with him and, turning against the Hojos, soon brought about the surrender of the Kamakura government.

The emperor, Go-Daigo-Tenno, then thought he was through with military rulers and directed his efforts toward re-establishing the supremacy of the court. The estates which Takauji had helped him to win from the Hojos he awarded not to the soldiers who had fought to restore him to power, but to the priests, nuns, musicians and writers who had been his companions in less prosperous days.

Angered at this turn of events, Ashikaga Takauji set up his headquarters on the old site of Yoritomo's and began to rule the northeastern part of the country on his own responsibility. When the emperor sent troops to put him in his proper place, Takauji escaped from them and fled to Kyushu. There, many of his kinsmen had gone at the time of the Mongol invasion, and had remained to enjoy the

profits of seaport trade. With their support and the friends
he made by giving away lands, Takauji was able to return
to Kyoto and set up an emperor of his own choosing. His
was called the Northern Court. The Northern Court demanded from Go-Daigo-Tenno the imperial sword and
seal, emblems of the right to rule.

Unwilling to yield his position, Go-Daigo resorted to
stratagem and turned over only replicas. With the real
sword and seal still in his possession, he escaped from the
capital through a broken fence, and traveled in woman's
clothes to Yoshino near Isé, where he set up the Southern
Court. The next year, however, he died and Takauji was
appointed shogun by the emperor of the Northern Court.

Fighting still continued. Both courts had their sympathizers and supporters and both continued to exist about
sixty miles apart for about sixty years. The period from
1331–92 is known in Japanese history as the period of the
dual dynasties.

One of the most able and loyal men of this period was
a soldier, scholar and politician named Chikafusa. Chikafusa was Go-Daigo's friend. It was he who by feats of
arms had won possession of the Yoshino region and prepared for the Southern Court there. And after Go-Daigo's
death, he set out with a fleet of ships to go to the assistance
of Southern Court sympathizers residing in the Kwanto
district around Kamakura. Having been the center of administration for a hundred and fifty years, Kamakura, with
its harbor and propinquity to the fertile rice fields of the
Musashi plains, the broadest in Japan, was now a more
desirable location than Kyoto. Though most of his ships

were lost in a storm, and he never succeeded in taking the recently fallen capital of the Hojos, Chikafusa kept the Ashikagas so busily engaged in the Kwanto for several years that the Southern Court was allowed to enjoy some peace.

What has since proved to be Chikafusa's chief claim to fame, however, was the writing of a political thesis entitled "A History of the True Succession of the Divine Monarchs." This was designed to defend the imperial line against the ambitions of military dictators who would base the right to rule on might and merit, rather than on the divine descent from Amaterasu set forth in the Kojiki and Nihongi.

Great Yamato is a divine country [Chikafusa wrote]. It is only our land whose foundations were first laid by the divine ancestor. It alone has been transmitted by the sun goddess to a long line of her descendants. There is nothing of this kind in foreign countries.

It is the duty of every man born on the imperial soil to yield devoted loyalty to his sovereign, even to the sacrifice of his own life.

The principles of statesmanship are based on justice and mercy, in the dispensing of which firm action is requisite. Firm action is displayed first of all in the choice of men for official positions. Japan and China both agree that the basis of good government consists in the sovereign finding the right man and bestowing favor on him . . .[1]

Though by Chikafusa's time learning had become more popular in military circles, and all leaders kept priests in their employ as advisors and tutors in the art of managing people, little if any attention was paid to his scholarly essay. Sidelight on the position of the imperial household during this period is given by the fact that though there were four printing centers in the country in the Ashikaga period, at Kyoto, Nara, Mount Koya and the seaport city, Sakai, the History of the True Succession did not appear in print until more than three hundred years after it was written. Though in the nineteenth century, when the national integrity of Japan was critically threatened by the flood of Western influence, Chikafusa's thesis came to play a very important part in restoring the dignity of the imperial family, making the emperor the rallying center of all factions and saving the country from being parcelled out to foreign interests, during Chikafusa's lifetime it had practically no effect. The country was under the domination of Ashikaga shoguns and their Zen priest advisors.

Since the influence of Zen on Japanese culture was so profound it is rather interesting to trace its history. For centuries after it was introduced into China the Buddhist sect called Zen had remained protestant and obscure in the southeastern provinces, unable to make headway in the capital and urban centers. But when with the downfall of the T'ang Empire the Chinese were driven by the Mongols out of the northwestern part of the country, a new dynasty, the Sung, grew up around the mouth of the Yangtze River. This was the time when the Arabs were opening the sea-trade route along the southern littoral of Asia. The seaports of Canton, Amoy and Shanghai began to develop and replace inland cities as centers of civilization. The Chinese began to change from agrarian to mercantile interests. The Zen sect, long-established in this coastal region, became the official Buddhism of the Sung regime.

Zen had been introduced to Japan in Kwammu-Tenno's reign, when Kyoto was being built and Saicho's temple center was started on Hieizan. It continued to be practiced as an adjunct of other sects, but as in China did not flourish while rulers of the people were enjoying an easygoing, prosperous life. Zen emphasis was not on a merciful deity, but on self-control, meditation and the development of will power. Zen's time in Japan did not come until the Fujiwaras' long neglect of the provinces led to the rise of the practical military families.

Japan's first Zen temple was built in the early Kamakura period by a monk from Mount Hiei who had been converted to Zen on his second visit to China. When the carpenters were building his temple he let them sing his name in rhythmic unison, "Eisai, Eisai, Eisai, Eisai," to help them pull the heavy timbers, and in Japan today, if you see laborers raising a large post or beam you will also hear them singing, "Eisai, Eisai."

Contemporary with the decline of Kyoto and the establishment of the military dictators in Japan came increasing pressure on the Sung Dynasty in China from Jenghis Khan and his Mongol Tatars. In 1232 the Sung were forced to an alliance, and fifty years later Kublai Khan was ruler of all China. During these troubled times many important political figures from the Sung court, in the guise of Zen priests, sought refuge in Japan. The Hojo regency, lacking the cultural guidance which Kyoto with its many temples had enjoyed, was very ready to welcome these able refugees. Five monasteries were built for them in Kamakura and they were treated as government guests of honor. Their advice was sought and followed in both political and religious matters and especially concerning international relations.

Undoubtedly it was Sung-Zen hatred of the Mongols that prompted the Kamakura government's defiance of Kublai Khan's envoys. Zen influence also played a large part in the supplanting of the Hojos by the Ashikagas. The Hojos had refused to carry on foreign trade, but the Ashikagas in Kyushu found it very profitable. In their mercantile endeavors the Ashikagas discovered, however, that the Chinese studied by scholarly Japanese courtiers and priests of the older Buddhist sects was a very different language from that currently spoken. The Chinese of the courtiers and priests of the older sects was the form which had been learned prior to the cessation of official relations with China four centuries before; but Zen priests were familiar with the present-day spoken and written language and very well informed on current conditions in China. Their assistance seemed essential to foreign trade, and foreign trade seemed essential to restore the nation's treasuries.

It is said that when Ashikaga Takauji first heard opportunity knocking at his door he turned for counsel to a Shingon priest, who advised him to act under cover of imperial prestige and set up the northern branch of the imperial family, since he could not get his way with the southern. As the power of Takauji's leadership became apparent, however, Muso, the greatest Zen Master of the age, became interested in him. Having been successively in the employ of the Kamakura shogunate and Go-Daigo-

Tenno, Muso now became political and spiritual advisor to this promising Ashikaga general.

When Go-Daigo passed away and Takauji was busy organizing a new regime, the worldly wise Muso recommended that he build a temple in the capital in honor of the late emperor to whom he had never, to put it mildly, shown an abundance of respect. And Muso also recommended that a For-the-Peace-of-the-Nation Temple be established in the most strategic location of each province. The one in honor of Go-Daigo was called Tenryu-ji, Celestial Dragon Temple, and the furnishing of it was the occasion for beginning the regular overseas trading monopoly of which Takauji had dreamed since his stay in Kyushu.

The Mongol invasion doubtless had curtailed trade for a while. People in Kyoto in those days had nothing to spend and they could see little sense in trade. Only a few years before a courtier, turned hermit, had written, "We could do without anything from China except medicine. As for books they are spread all over this country and we could copy them. It is a foolish thing for ships from China to make the perilous journey over here crammed with cargoes of useless things." [2] But the Zen priests knew what profits there were in mercantile enterprise.

The boats in which they plied back and forth were called after the new temple Tenryu-ji Bune (bune or fune means boat). Since they were boats of only three to five thousand cubic feet, not much investment was involved. Going, they carried chiefly swords, sulphur, timber, fans, lacquer ware and an attractive stuff which looked like gold invented by the Japanese and called shinchu. Returning, they brought books, gold, silver and copper coins, scroll paintings, tea, silk, porcelain, pottery and other works of art. The profits on the round trip were sometimes as much as a hundred times the initial investment.

This overseas trade under the direction of Zen priests was the economic foundation of the Ashikaga shogunate. This it was that enabled Takauji and his successors who resided in Kyoto near the emperors to adopt their superior attitude toward the imperial family and to build gold and silver pavilions with gardens so beautiful that people called them "Flower Palaces." It was this that enabled them to retain their power in Japan until the middle of the sixteenth century, when piracy rivaling the Ashikaga mercantile monopoly became so prevalent that China finally closed her ports and refused to trade.

What with plagues and droughts, wars, fires and famines, life was scarcely worth living for the farmers and officials, dependent on the yield of the soil, who made up the bulk of the population. But for those who saw beyond the narrow confines of their own islands and extended their interest and efforts to foreign seas and ports, it must have been thrilling to be alive.

The all-conquering Mongols, who had struck terror in the hearts of people all the way from eastern Europe to the islands of the Pacific, had passed through their spring, summer, autumn and winter. While the Ashikagas were rising in Japan, a new dynasty called the Ming, Brilliant, was founded in China. The Mings were more familiar with graces and refinements than the Mongols had been, and more amicably inclined toward their island neighbor. They were practical and materialistic too, however. Their art consisted chiefly of architecture, porcelain and lacquer ware. Though an academy of painting was re-established by the Ming court, and there were artists in abundance, they seemed no longer to have the richness of materials nor the radiant quality of spirit which was shown in the work of a few centuries earlier. That the Ming policy toward Japan also had its practical side did not make their country any less attractive to adventurous Japanese. Piracy flourished and prospered.

As time went on, larger and safer boats plied back and forth at more frequent intervals. At one time certificates were issued by the shogunate which granted in return for a financial consideration the right to make a certain number of trips to China a year. These were the "tributary" ships; all others were "pirates." "Tributary" ships were chartered by temples, shrines and wealthy officials, and once one was chartered for the imperial court, but the court did not find it as easy as the temples and landlords did to collect merchandise to send. They had to hire a merchant to prepare a cargo for them and depend on him to pay a percentage on their investment when he returned. One great landlord, on the other hand, had permission from the shogunate to send fifty vessels a year, and to establish settlements for more than sixty Japanese in three different ports in Korea.

It is about the tributary ships that most records have been found, for they were officially sanctioned. Pirate ships no doubt operated in far greater numbers, but naturally did not preserve incriminating documents. The official ships were in charge of Zen priest envoys. They carried as part of their cargo gifts to be presented to the Ming court, and in addition articles for trade. The Chinese ruler sent presents in return for the shogun's offerings. Once ladies of the shogun's palace journeyed in palanquins the fifty miles from Kyoto to the port of Hyogo to welcome a tributary ship returning home. It must have been exciting to talk with the witty priests about their experiences in China, and on the sea. Then to examine and open the endless boxes, baskets, bundles and rolls, and find the gauze-like silks patterned with flowers and clouds, brought specially for the favorite of the shogun !

It is recorded that the Tara Maru, a tributary ship, on one voyage carried a chief envoy and party of eleven, twenty-four agents for temples and fourteen agents for landlords.[3] There were also on board eighteen owners of merchandise, three chief mariners, thirty-five ordinary passengers, five interpreters and servants, three clerks, fifty-two sailors, four actors, one horse breeder and four horses. In addition to the cargo for tribute and trade, provisions had to be taken along for a hundred and twenty-nine days, from January to May. These included rice, beans for the horses, oil, salt, soy, tea, fish, vinegar, half a bottle of rice wine per person per day and ten candles and ten bundles of charcoal per person for the voyage. Among the expenditures recorded for the trip are two kwan mon for a special festival celebrated at the first sight of Chinese land, ten kwan mon for festivals on the first day of every month and the five annual feasts, ten kwan mon for rice cakes and saké for sailors on New Year's Day, a three-kwan-mon fee for prayer, ten kwan mon for festivals and offerings of swords and sacred dances at various shrines on the coast of the Inland Sea, six hundred and eighty-eight kwan mon for food, four hundred and ninety for wages and other items totaling two thousand and sixty-five kwan mon.

One Zen priest envoy wrote in his diary for August 1 and 3, 1451, that the Chinese people

treated Japanese travelers as subjects of a tributary country and wanted to train them in the proper ceremonies to attend the birthday celebration of the Ming emperor. The Japanese, however, thought of nothing but trade and were annoyed at the idea of these formalities.

For August 25,

The village headman on hearing of the approach of our party of three hundred ran away and provided no lodging for us.

For October 9,

On seeing me composing poems the Chinese officials said that there were about five hundred countries paying tribute to the Ming court, but only the Japanese are able to read.[4]

Though the Ming sent several envoys to Japan who were always well received by the shogun, it was many years before they accomplished what they came for, and succeeded in getting an agreement from Yoshimitsu, the third Ashikaga shogun, to suppress the overseas activities of his countrymen. Perhaps it was the keen competition with other leaders in Japan that finally added to the persuasion of the Ming emperor's proposition, and led Yoshimitsu to send, with a delegation of Zen priests to the Ming court, a gift of a thousand ryo of gold, ten horses, a thousand leaves of silver, a hundred fans, three gold-foil folding screens, one suit of armor, ten lances, one sword, one ink stone and one ink-stone box. Thereafter he was hailed as the "King of Japan" and favored with a present of a thousand ryo of silver, fifteen thousand kwan of copper coin, ten hiki of brocade, fifty hiki of hemp cloth, twenty-eight hiki of blue cloth, three thousand hiki of woolen cloth. And at a maple viewing party in the capital in the early fifteenth century Yoshimitsu appeared in an elaborate Ming costume riding in a Ming palanquin.

As a soldier hero, and the proud husband of a court lady, Yoshimitsu had great influence in the palace. In 1392 he brought about the reconciliation of the northern and southern branches of the imperial family, rewarding them handsomely for appointing him chancellor. With the further honor and revenue from the Ming court, Yoshimitsu cut a very grand figure. Like the Ming emperor in Peking, he repaired old temples and built new ones in Kyoto. For himself he had erected a palace in a spacious park and, on the side of a lake in the park, a pleasure pavilion ornamented with gold leaf. Naturally endowed with personality and tact, he succeeded in calming agitated clan leaders and restoring peace to the country for several decades.

Yoshimitsu's favorite diversion was a sort of dramatic performance. From very early times, Yamato people had had "Noh." Noh were held in the rice fields in autumn to celebrate the harvest. Noh were held on the hillsides in spring when love was in the air. Noh were held at court on ceremonial occasions when orchestras were assembled and noble youths danced and sang. At first the word was used indiscriminately for exhibitions of talent.

Both courts and temples had trained troupes of musicians and dancers. In early Ashikaga times four troupes were especially well known. One of these was at Isé, and another among the old temples which remained at Nara. The common people were eager to get a glimpse of court and temple life, both of which for centuries had been kept a mystery from them. When public performances were put on, therefore, both rich and poor flocked to see them. When Yoshimitsu attended a program given by the Nara group, he was so impressed that he invited the actors to come and entertain at his court. One of them became a great favorite with the third Ashikaga shogun and was always with him. His name was Seami.

All Seami had to do was to please his loving patron. He wrote and performed several Noh especially for Yoshimitsu's court. These took on a rather different form from the Noh given on the temple grounds. They had fewer characters, and were more refined in every way. Seami's Noh combined beautiful music, exquisite costumes and the recitation of verse and fine-sounding speeches with a certain grace and perfection of pantomime which was supposed to touch the observer as profoundly and unpretentiously as a flower would.

The stories acted as Noh were not new; they were familiar ones for the most part, incidents from the old annals, Kojiki and Nihongi, bits of shrine and temple legends, episodes from real life in other days, from the tales of

Prince Genji and of the Heike. They were intended to express a real truth of life, not baldly or emphatically, but delicately, by means of idealistic symbols. The meaning was hidden beneath the surface with superb esthetic restraint. The chief characters were usually supposed to be not real persons, but their spirits. Often there were no properties on the stage, only a few pine trees painted on the back wall.

Seami never taught actors exactly what to do, but he told them to observe nature closely. When they were acting pieces about the gods, he said, they ought to have pine trees thoroughly in mind. When doing exotic scenes they ought to think of red maple and autumn leaves ; cherry blossoms were to be thought of while acting love scenes ; and winter forests while doing Noh based on tales of Heike. There were nine kinds of flowers, he wrote, in his notes about the Noh,[5] and actors should be familiar with them all. The lowest kind of flower was a rough and heavy kind like the tulip ; the supreme kind was the delicate wild orchid. In between came the strong but slender lily, the lotus, wide open, but still having style, the light blossom of the cherry and the solitary narcissus. Writers of Noh were sometimes described as "friends of the moon and flowers."

There are still several schools of Noh in Japan and each one gives a dozen or so performances during the year. Some of them still cherish and wear on very special occasions beautiful brocaded silk robes which have been handed down from great actors to their most gifted pupils for centuries. Their program usually includes a variety of Noh, half a

NOH STAGE

R PAVILION

EXCERPT FROM MORI SCROLL

SCREEN SHOWING ARRIVAL OF PORTUGUESE SHIP

THOUSAND MAT ROOM, HIDEYOSHI'S PALACE

dozen perhaps, interspersed with short, humorous folk plays
called Kyogen, foolish words.

Another popular pastime associated with Noh in Western minds was "tea ceremony." Tea has had an interesting
history in Japan. According to tradition it was first served
at a party which Shomu-Tenno (the emperor who "opened"
the eyes of the Nara Daibutsu) gave in his palace for a
hundred and twenty monks. Both Saicho and Kukai are
said to have brought tea seeds from China (where Zen
priests drank the beverage in order to keep awake through
long hours of meditation) and to have planted them in
Japan in the early ninth century. The son of Emperor
Kwammu (who founded Kyoto), having tasted the pale
green beverage in a monastery, was so delighted with it that
he issued a proclamation ordering the planting of tea in
various parts of the country. The greatest event in tea
history, however, occurred in Kamakura, when the son of
Minamoto Yoritomo and the able Hojo Masa became
ill from drinking too much saké and was cured by drinking
tea. The Zen priest-architect, Eisai, had just returned from
China with a fresh supply of tea and prescribed it as a cure
for his drunkenness. Eisai also wrote an essay, which came
to be a classic, describing the healthful influence of tea
drinking. He had brought new tea seeds with him from
overseas, and arranged for them to be planted and cared for
in a temple garden near Kyoto. The leaves from these
shrubs came to be the standard for judging the quality of
tea.

From its early use by Zen priests to keep them awake
through their meditations, and its later use as a sort of

medicine, tea drinking in the fifteenth century became the very fashionable diversion of society. Men in high positions upon occasion gave a small jar of tea leaves as reward to a follower who had performed some noteworthy service. Such a gift was greatly prized, and the recipient invited his best friends to come and share in tasting the tea with him.

In such gatherings the Zen priest Shuko saw interesting possibilities. With a well-cultivated taste for painting and for pottery, the two chief arts of Sung, he was a keen collector of Chinese imports. Shuko no doubt perceived that if a sort of ceremony were made of tasting tea it would be profitable in more ways than one. He encouraged the serving of tea with beautiful utensils in a small room spotlessly clean and surrounded by a miniature landscape garden. Passing their time in this way, men would perhaps develop a love of purity and repose of manner which would mean much to them, and greater appreciation for rare works of art would be developed also.

Shogun Yoshimasa of the Silver Pavilion, patron of Shuko and the arts was the first to take up this idea, and tea ceremonies came rapidly into vogue. Soldiers seemed to enjoy them as deeply as did men of gentler vocations. The greatest military ruler of the sixteenth century summoned all tea lovers of the country to bring their choicest teas and utensils to a party which lasted ten days. And then, in the seventeenth century when the country became unified and peaceful once more, tea became a nationwide institution and cultural discipline. Even powerful governors were very proud to become masters of the ceremony and poor people earnestly tried to imitate them.[6]

As the Ashikaga shogunate continued, conditions in the countryside of Japan went from bad to worse. Individuals participating in overseas trade were very wealthy and indulged themselves in all sorts of extravagances, but the masses who tried to squeeze a living from the soil were desperately poor. While the shogun was spending fortunes on gold screens for his palaces, on porcelain and painting, eighty thousand people in the capital within two months died of plague or famine. The streets and rivers were blocked with unburied dead.

Then the shogun ordered some temples to give doles, but continued to levy taxes several times a year. Small farmers found it impossible to raise even the tax rice, not to mention food for themselves, and so left their land. Since order and justice for the people were far removed from the thoughts of the shogun's officials, local chieftains found it greatly to their advantage to take large numbers of landless unemployed into their own service. And since estates were of little value without farmers to work them, wise landlords treated their peasants fairly enough to make them want to stay. Others built barriers and toll gates on their roads to prevent the free movement of peasants. In this way many families became quite independent of the shogunate.

Some sought to obtain official favor by making presents to one or more of the scores of court ladies with whom the shogun was surrounded, but these ladies were rather well occupied striving to obtain favor for themselves.

Rivalry within and between the great families became so intense that fighting broke out again in the capital; the imperial palaces and most of the important buildings were burned to the ground.

One shogun's wife made the best of this situation by taking the management of many public affairs into her own hands. She saw to the reinstallation of toll gates at the seven entrances to Kyoto on the pretense of rebuilding the imperial palace and then kept all the money herself. Struggles and fighting between great families continually increased and spread from the capital to the provinces. For over a century it went on. Not until about 1600 was peace finally restored.

The merchants and guilds called "za" added to the disorder of the country. From earliest times, in villages and ports, at temples and shrines, there had been merchants trying to sell their goods wherever people congregated. At first these merchants simply stood with their wares in large baskets and trays strapped to their bodies, or suspended on poles balanced over their shoulders. Then gradually markets had grown up in more populous centers where the merchants had a little sheltered space for doing business, which was called za, or seat (like a "seat" on the stock exchange). With Hojo orderliness and prosperity, many people had found it profitable to become merchants, and naturally the ones who sold the same kind of things were interested in each other. Some who sold oil at a certain shrine claimed that since they supplied the oil to keep the shrine lights always burning, the right to sell oil should be peculiarly theirs.

It was not until the Ashikaga period, however, when central authority was nil and everyone had to defend his own interests, that the zas came to be powerful organizations. Then in each large city the well-established salt dealers, for example, got together and formed a salt za. By paying a certain fee to the temple or government this group was given the exclusive right to sell salt in a definite area. Anyone else who tried to sell salt in their district was persecuted.

The privileges of the za were handed down from father to son. In Kyoto at this time there were zas of merchants selling silk, charcoal, rice, oil, fish, salt, timber, horses and many other things. There were also pawnbrokers and rice or money lenders. If any za thought another was infringing on its monopoly, a riot was started and the city was thrown into confusion. Some zas had rights in fairly large areas, and had to pass several toll gates in the course of delivering orders. If the tolls mounted high enough to make it worth while, the members of the za arrived armed en masse and tried to destroy the barrier. When they were successful they usually took charge of the barrier themselves and allowed their own members to pass through free, but collected taxes from all others, or forbade others to pass. Many of what were supposed to be public highways were usurped in this way and travel from one part of the country to another was both dangerous and expensive.

The elaborate entertainments and lavish spending of the shogun and of the officials and landlords who tried to keep pace with him filled the coffers of the za merchants with one hand but emptied them, for taxes, with the other. Gambling was a favorite pastime, and the pawnshops did a rushing business. When a group of samurai in the service of some great lord felt that too much of their equipment was being held for loans, they often attacked the warehouses, and by force rescued what they wanted. When a number of important officials and courtiers became too involved in debt, or when the populace were so hopelessly behind with taxes and obligated to the rice lenders that they rose up in active protest, an "act of benevolence" was declared and all accounts were cancelled.

Even the shoguns had great financial difficulties. They were described as very wealthy by contemporary writers, who marveled at the splendors of their gold and silver pavilions, but this in itself is evidence of how poor the rest of the people must have been. Kinkaku-ji and Ginkaku-ji may have seemed superb in comparison with other homes of the day, but they are simple indeed compared with such palaces as the Vatican in Rome, the Alhambra in southern Spain and the Ducal Palace in Venice, which date from about the same period.

Court nobles now had to turn their arts and accomplishments to practical use. They joined with the priests as educators and entertainers of the people, commercializing their knowledge of etiquette by producing textbooks, their skill in writing by becoming secretaries to rich merchants, and their musical talents by acting in Noh plays.

Emperors now lived in ruined mansions surrounded by nothing but a bamboo fence. Children made mud toys at their gates, and sometimes peeped behind the blind that screened the imperial apartments. There were no abdicated emperors, because of economic conditions. At one time an emperor's burial had to be postponed until sufficient funds could be found for the funeral ceremonies. Groups of traveling minstrels were sent out to collect small gifts for the imperial court ; emperors sold their autographs, and empresses wove little pouches of rice straw and string to exchange for rice.

An emperor who had no means for holding a ceremony when he succeeded to the throne left this advice to his son :

You have been brought up as if there was no one to be afraid of. Though it may be all right while you are a child to act as if you were of highest position, if you behave so later, people will jeer at you. You must spend much time learning how to act before the people. Do not criticize others. Do not be short in temper ; impatience will win you only contempt or hatred. Act always so as not to attract other's censure. These are my last words ; keep them as a guide all your life.[7]

The court ladies who had found life so free and easy and full of opportunities in Fujiwara days now could find but little security. Many of them entered nunneries at an early age, or retired to the temples where princesses resided. Others who clung loyally to their husbands were the pioneers of Japanese womanhood as it is known to the world today. They were called the "wives who carefully wash the hulls off rice" [8] and willingly served their husbands with true domestic virtue.

Many priests in these days acted very little differently from soldiers. The larger religious bodies like the more powerful landlords were continually struggling among themselves for first place in the capital. Throughout the provinces minor sects were constantly rising and falling, while major ones succeeded in establishing fortified strong-holds in many places. As colleagues of the shoguns the Zen sect perhaps had the more favorable position.

During the Hojo regency Zen influence had grown in Kamakura and spread in all directions, but it had not be-come a real power until the Ashikaga shoguns moved their headquarters back to Kyoto. Though the long-established orders of Mount Hiei strongly opposed an invasion of their sphere of interest they could not prevent it. Five Zen monasteries were established in the ancient capital which served as radiating centers for a new cultural development.

All art forms were refined and simplified. Zen artists did not indulge in elaborate decoration with lavish use of gold and color. Their materials were unpainted wood, black ink and white paper. In architecture they made the most of beautiful proportion and the arrangement of spaces, including in their design the surrounding scenery and creat-ing landscape gardens. Their temples gave a pleasant impression of economy which was distinctly esthetic ; they had an air of functional efficiency which other temples lacked. Their tea houses and pavilions seemed almost like the works of nature itself, so well did they harmonize with their environment. Instead of the richly colored and orna-mented sculpture of Fujiwara days when the deities Amida and Vairocana were supreme, Zen followers carved simple wooden portrait statues of men like themselves. In place of the gorgeous pigments and exquisite detail of the clas-sical Kyoto schools, Zen painters achieved their desired effects with a few clever strokes of black ink ; the fewer and simpler the strokes, the greater the art. As in the Noh, great truths were represented by impressionistic symbols.

Perhaps a still greater contribution than their guidance in either politics, economics or art, however, was made by Zen priests to Japan in the realm of popular education and character building. In the social upheaval and hardships of the Ashikaga period they set an example for courageous enterprise and inspired self-confidence. Learning and spirituality, they demonstrated, are useless if they do not lead to practical attainments. "Face nature and man, and learn." "Fear nothing, get results." "Wherever you go, be master." This they taught, along with reading and writing in their many schools. They would not blame environment for failure or wrongdoing. "Eels live in foul water," they said, "because they like it. The heart and environment are one. If your mind is clean and orderly, you will make your environment clean and orderly also. Do not be controlled; be master of every situation."

The line between cause and effect is often hard to draw. It may be that Zen teaching not only had an effect upon the spirit of the times, but was also in part a product of this spirit. The decline of imperial authority and the rise of a succession of military lords gave hope and confidence to many. Yamato farmers who for twelve centuries had seen only their own rice fields began to catch a larger vision. Yamato leaders who for eight centuries had thought chiefly of the supremacy of China had successfully withstood the Mongols. Chikafusa in his obscure essay had written, "Great Yamato is a divine country." The seeds of national consciousness were sown.

CHAPTER X

CATHOLICS AND CASTLES
(1550–1600)

WHEN things stick together it is usually the result of pressure, and when nations become unified it is more often due to external than to internal forces. The sixteenth century in Japan is often called the Age of Unification, and three great military heroes are usually given the credit for consolidating the score or more of jealously contending clans and temple strongholds into the semblance of a nation. But what really gave impetus to Nobunaga, Hideyoshi and Iyeyasu was the arrival in Japan of Portuguese traders and Jesuit missionaries.

Japan, it seems, was discovered by storm-driven Portuguese adventurers in the early 1540's and in September of that year a ship's crew of a hundred arrived on the large southern island, Kyushu. Strange demons the Japanese thought the Portuguese — with their great stature, and blue eyes in florid red-bearded faces. But when a Chinese in their company, by writing Chinese characters on the sand with a stick, explained to the headman of the village where they landed that they were southern barbarians engaged in trade, they were all given lodging in a Buddhist temple. They had one article with them which the Japanese regarded as a most extraordinary thing. The son of one of the welcoming natives later wrote, "It was about two or three feet long, straight, heavy and hollow. One end was closed and near this end was a small hole through which fire was to be lighted. Some mysterious medicine was put into it with a small round piece of lead, and when one lit the medicine through that hole the lead piece was discharged and hit everything. Light like lightning was seen, and noise like thunder heard ; bystanders closed their ears with their hands and flying birds and running beasts fell before them. One day my father asked the foreigners to teach him its use and he soon became so skillful that he could nearly hit a white object placed a hundred steps away. He then bought two pieces of these things, regardless of the high price asked, and kept them as the most precious treasures of his house." [1]

With conditions as they were in Japan, firearms were exceedingly desirable things to have, and local leaders from the various provinces of Kyushu vied with each other in trying to control the importation and production of them. First the lord of Satsuma seemed to have a monopoly on the traders and their cargoes — then the lord of Bungo attracted many of the Portuguese to his domains, but when another young lord offered still greater inducements, the boats all harbored in his port, Hirado. For many years Hirado was the center for foreign trade with Japan and in this trade firearms was the most important item. A few local blacksmiths went so far as to learn to make guns and powder themselves, and devised cannon of large pine trees, hollowed out, and bound with iron hoops. Within very few years after the introduction of firearms changes began to appear in both the social structure and the architecture of the country. Soldiers became more than ever a class by themselves and leaders had to devise new plans of fortification for their castles and strongholds.

In addition to firearms, such things as leather, glassware, woolen cloth and velvet, highly prized for collars, were included in the cargoes brought from Europe. Sugar, medicine, ceramic wares, cottons, silks and old Chinese coins were picked up by the Portuguese at various ports along their ocean route and traded in Japan for natural and fabricated products — gold, silver and especially copper, which afforded handsome profits.

The islanders also benefited materially from this trade, for the merchants spent freely while ashore and paid well for supplies and ship repairs. The apparently unlimited demand of the Portuguese for Japanese goods caused a marked rise in the price of everything native. The Japanese, unaware of the high value of copper in India and of the great profits to be made by converting copper into cannon, could not understand how the Portuguese could gain by their dealings. But the vision of achievement and power which native leaders caught from them inspired many changes in the country.[2]

Soon after the Portuguese traders, came the Jesuit missionaries — Father Xavier (later Saint Francis) arriving in Satsuma in 1549 was the first of these. Though it seemed to him that the Japanese language was invented by the devil to prevent his preaching, Father Xavier, after some success in Satsuma, proceeded to Hirado. From there he worked his way over to the main island of Japan and headed toward Kyoto. On the way he stopped at the court of the Ouchi clan, where, thanks to their wealth from mining, fishing and shipping trade with China, and a recently successful display of authority in the capital, this family and its followers were enjoying a rather gay and carefree life. They sneered at the poorly clad Jesuit for attacking their morals, and so he continued on his way, sometimes serving as baggage bearer for mounted merchants in order to make a living, and often sleeping in outhouses, or under the winter stars. His experiences in the capital were not encouraging either; it was a desolate place ruined by fires and fighting and deserted by courtiers. Since those who remained with the emperor would grant an imperial audience only in return for gold, Xavier in great disappointment retraced his steps to Hirado. There the merchants advised him that he should dress himself better if he wished to make an impression on upper-class Japanese. Acting upon their suggestions he took with him a clock and a harpsichord such as had never been seen there before and went again to the court of Ouchi, representing himself this time as an envoy from the Viceroy of India.

Now he created quite a sensation. The Ouchi chief was delighted with the presents and offered gold in return, but this Xavier refused, saying he would appreciate more the gift of freedom to preach in the Ouchi domain. To one accustomed to the grasping hands of Buddhist priests, this lack of greed must have been interesting, to say the least, and Xavier's request was answered with the gift of an old temple and some land for a church.[3]

The Japanese, who had always associated with religion and government a knowledge of the weather and the movement of heavenly bodies and regarded such knowledge with high esteem, were very much impressed with Xavier's discourses on astronomy.   He proved to them that the

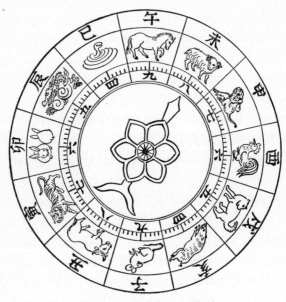

Face of Japanese Clock

world was round and explained comets, thunderbolts and showers.   They were, therefore, inclined to think that a person so wise in science could not be far wrong in religion.   Besides, this religion coming as it did, via India with shaven-headed priests, unintelligible rituals, rosaries, incense and images, to all of which they were accustomed, was thought by many Japanese to be merely a superior kind of Buddhism.   They were, however, skeptical of its teachings about a personal creator of the world, for they had never heard of anything like this from China, their fountain head of knowledge. They were also greatly distressed at the teaching that the beloved but heathen ancestors whom they worshipped were doomed to pass eternity in hell, but they did admire the missionaries who, though pelted and spat upon, merely wiped their faces and continued to preach. Seeing that the Fathers were admired also by the Portuguese traders whom they were eager to favor, many Japanese listened to the Christian doctrines with the same respectful attention they had given to new teachers from Korea or China. But when the Jesuits began to argue with the Buddhist priests that the Christian God and saints were the only true ones and that Buddhist deities and doctrines were mere fiction, trouble was in the wind.

After a stay of two and a half years in Japan, Xavier resolved to make China his chief goal and wrote, "If the Chinese adopt the Christian religion, the Japanese will also." [4] On leaving the country he took with him a keen young convert with the adopted name of Bernard. Though Xavier was lost in a shipwreck a year or so later, this youth, probably the first Japanese to set foot in Europe, finally reached Rome and Lisbon, and joining the Society of Jesus entered the College of Coimbra [5] and ended his days there.

In the course of the next thirty years the Jesuits met many ups and downs in Japan. One daimyo or feudal lord whom they converted turned the administration of his estates over to his son and devoted the rest of his life to preaching and charitable work among his vassals. Even when banished as the result of political complications he continued in exile to live as a Christian missionary. Some converts became fanatical, burning shrines and temples and ordering people to give up Buddhist altars in their homes. Others became Christians and made their vassals adopt the new faith also — only to keep in the good graces of the Portuguese merchants. Some Buddhists persuaded the emperor to sign a letter ordering the Jesuit in the capital to be driven out, but Nobunaga was the power of the throne, and the missionary in question, named Froez, managed to find favor with Nobunaga, and win the great hero's protection.

When Froez first saw Nobunaga, the latter was on the drawbridge of the new castle he was rearing, surrounded by a numerous court and seven thousand men under arms. Froez saluted Nobunaga in Japanese fashion but was requested to rise and cover himself, for the sun was hot. Nobunaga then inquired of the Father his age, how many years he had studied, how long he had been in Japan, and whether if the Japanese did not become Christians he would return to India. In reply to the last question, Froez declared, "If there were but one Christian in Japan I would remain to instruct and fortify him in the faith, but I am not yet reduced to that position, for there are a considerable number of believers in the empire." [6]

"But why have you no house or church in Kyoto?" Nobunaga went on, and Froez returned, "Your Highness, it is because of the Buddhist priests who have driven us out of those we had."

Though Nobunaga seemed to be favorably inclined

toward the well-bred and learned Jesuits, who approached important people in the capital with polished diplomacy, and guarded their safety against Buddhist intrigues, it was not until twelve years later that he bestowed upon them a site near his castle with timber and furnishings for a thirty-four-room house. The chief work of the Jesuits in this grand establishment was the training of twenty-five young noblemen in Portuguese, Latin, and Catholic doctrines, painting, drawing, carving and vocal and instrumental music. When Nobunaga paid them a visit, it is said he was delighted with their performances.

In 1580 the Jesuit's annual letter from Japan to the pope reported that Nobunaga had asked the missionary to show him on a globe the way he had come from Europe, had commented seriously that those who undertake such voyages must be great-minded men and with a smile had added : "Perhaps this gospel of yours is really some fine thing." [7]

In 1582 the annual letter reported that the number of Christians in Japan was a hundred and fifty thousand, of whom many were nobles ; a hundred and twenty-five thousand of these were on the island of Kyushu, while twenty-five thousand were scattered on the main island and altogether there were about two hundred churches. The visitor-general of the Jesuits in the East who made the survey for this report caused the Japanese much surprise on account of his great height and the negro slave which he had with him. They had never seen such a tall man or such a dark one before. At first sight of the negro, Nobunaga burst into laughter and tried to rub the black off ; then, because of his interest, the slave was given to him and remained with him until his death.

On the same boat which carried the visitor-general and his report to Europe it was decided that an embassy of four Japanese should be sent to bear friendly messages from three Christian lords in Kyushu to the pope in Rome, and Philip II of Spain.   (Portugal had passed under his rule in 1580.)

After almost two years of strenuous voyaging, according to a contemporary account, these envoys were welcomed at Lisbon in 1584 ; at Madrid they were received with great distinction by the king himself ; at Leghorn a de' Medici duke was waiting to attend them and escort them to the carnival at Pisa and thence via Florence to Rome, where Pope Gregory XIII (to whom we owe our calendar) provided for them a marvelous reception.   The procession formed to escort them to the Vatican was headed by the pope's Light Horse, followed by the Swiss Guard, the officers of the cardinals and the carriages of the ambassadors of Spain, France, Venice, and the Roman princes.   It also included the whole Roman nobility on horseback, pages with trumpets and cymbals, and officers of the palace all in red robes.   Then followed the Japanese on horseback in their national dress, three silken gowns of a light fabric one over the other, splendidly embroidered with fruits, leaves and birds.   In their girdles they wore the two swords, symbols of Japanese gentility.   Their heads, shaven, except the hair round the ears and neck, which was gathered into a queue bent upward, had no covering.   Their whole expres-

sion and manner, modest and amiable, but with a conscious
sentiment of nobility, was such as impressed the bystanders
very favorably. The appearance of these young men who
had essayed so many dangers and fatigues to pay their
homage to the Holy See drew tears and sobs from the audience, and the pope himself, when they prostrated themselves at his feet, hastened to raise them up and embraced
them many times.[8]

Upon the death of Gregory XIII a few days later, the
Japanese ambassadors assisted at the coronation of the new
pope, Sixtus V, and were given gold chains and medals and
shown many favors by him. They declined an invitation
from Henry III to visit France and started their return
voyage in 1586 after twenty-one months in Europe.

The year this embassy left Japan Nobunaga was assassinated. Having succeeded to his father's estates in Owari
province, east of Kyoto, in the same year that Xavier landed
in Satsuma, Nobunaga, though only sixteen, had soon
shown himself to be a man of inflexible will, resolved to
subdue all rival leaders and to create a new central government. In carrying out this purpose Nobunaga was the
nearest to an iconoclast that Japan has ever produced ; he
demolished Buddhist monasteries for materials with which
to rebuild the emperor's and the shogun's palaces, and
allowed no temple bell to ring lest it interfere with the gong
summoning his workmen. When its militant priests fought
against him, Nobunaga did not hesitate to order burned to
the ground even the great temple center on Mount Hiei
which dated from Saicho's day, with all its beautiful old
paintings and sculpture and its countless historical docu-

ments. He welcomed the Jesuit Fathers on more friendly terms than he did many of his own vassals and favored them more than the long established Buddhist priests, but he actually gave the newcomers only just enough to keep them hoping that he would give more. Though he did not live to accomplish his purpose, when Nobunaga was assassinated by the same good Buddhist retainer whom he had ordered to destroy Mount Hiei, he had under his control thirty-two of the sixty-eight provinces of Japan, and these compactly situated around the capital.

Nobunaga was succeeded by his general, Hideyoshi. Born the peasant son of a foot-soldier, Hideyoshi as a lad had been so wild that his parents could not train him. They sent him to a temple school, but he hated the sight of books, and, whenever he could manage it, armed his fellow students with bamboo rods and got them to fight under his generalship.⁹

"You priests are all a set of beggars," he told his teachers. "There is no reason why a brave child born in a world of commotion and strife should become a beggar."

At twelve, he beat and smashed with candlesticks the image of Amida before which he was directed to place an offering of food. Then he was expelled from the temple, and subsequently dismissed from thirty-eight jobs in succession. Uncannily quick-witted, resourceful, and a match for anyone in talking, he usually managed to get where he wished to go and to meet whom he wished to meet. Having picked Nobunaga as the most promising of many militant landlords, Hideyoshi quickly raised himself to a trusted

NOBUNAGA VISITING ARTIST MOTONOBU

NAGOYA CASTLE

HIDEYOSHI'S GARDEN AT GO-DAIGO TEMPLE

INTERIOR AND EXTERIOR VIEWS OF NIKKO SHRINE

position in this leader's service and helped to promote him to first place in the nation.

Hideyoshi is described by the historian Murdoch as the sort of man who endeavored not to kill two birds with one stone, but to disable many fowls with a single missile, catch them and use them to provide eggs for his own table. All of his outstanding achievements show this characteristic. He was not so much a destroyer as Nobunaga was, but rather a builder and organizer on a colossally daring scale.

In the brief span of ten years after the assassination of Nobunaga, Hideyoshi extended and consolidated his power over the whole of Japan. With heroic force and tactful negotiation he won the allegiance of all the great leaders of the country, initiated a national land survey for purposes of tax assessment and organized at Osaka a central administration noted for its efficiency. He conciliated the militant Buddhist clergy who had been Nobunaga's strongest enemies, and used them to help him win over the Kyushu clans. He disarmed all the civilians of the country by ordering them to turn over their swords and weapons for the building of great religious statues. With equal cleverness he invited all the chief daimyos of the country to his magnificent new palace for a royal reception and there, in the presence of the emperor, made them swear their loyalty to the Son of Heaven and to his chief minister, Hideyoshi, the Taiko. It was agreed that any who broke their oaths should be punished by their fellows. He also embarked upon the conquest of Korea and China.

While visiting the shrine of Yoritomo near Kamakura,

Hideyoshi is said to have patted the image of the first shogun familiarly on the back and remarked, "My friend, only you and I have been able to take all the power under heaven. You, however, were of illustrious descent, and not like me, sprung from peasants. But after conquering all the empire I intend to conquer China. What do you think of that?"

There are many interpretations of Hideyoshi's Korean expedition. Some say that he was afraid of the Kyushu daimyos because of their relations with the Portuguese and Spaniards, and wanted to test their loyalty, drain their resources and get them out of Japan. Some say he had to find active employment for all the soldiers of the country, and some that it was intended chiefly to satisfy his ego and immortalize his name. It is also said that this campaign was not the result of one man's ambition, but an attempt at colonization and trade expansion inspired by the example of the Portuguese and undertaken as a cooperative venture on a profit-sharing basis. Undoubtedly there is truth in each of these explanations, for Hideyoshi's projects were usually devised to accomplish many ends, but the fundamental fact that Japan was poor in natural resources must not be overlooked.

Agriculture was the mainstay of the nation, but when earthquakes, droughts, storms and pestilences destroyed the crops, or when unsettled conditions in the country gave farmers cause to take up arms, so that planting and harvesting was interfered with, there was always a great depression, from which the only escape was profitable overseas trade. In the midst of the disorders signaling the end of

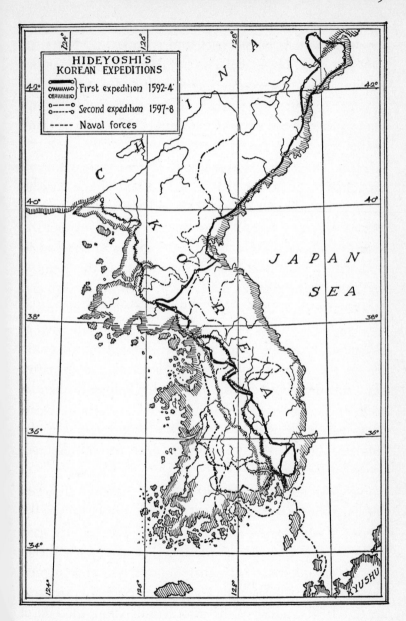

HIDEYOSHI'S
KOREAN EXPEDITIONS
⊶⊶⊶⊶⊶ First expedition 1592-4
○⊷⊷⊷⊷○ Second expedition 1597-8
----- Naval forces

the Fujiwara regime, Taira Kiyomori had come to power on a program of trade expansion. After the wholesale migration of farmers from northeastern to southwestern Japan when the Mongol invasion threatened, even the Hojo government, the most thrifty and economical one the country ever had, could not escape bankruptcy. Then, while the rest of the country remained in poverty, the Ashikaga shoguns with their Zen-priest trade advisers had made their way to gold and silver pavilions through mercantile adventures based on wider experience than Kiyomori had had at his disposal. But just as waves never wear their gleaming crests for long — as snow melts and flowers fade, so is it with the affairs of men. After Ashikaga Yoshimitsu's peak of prosperity came a gradual decline into the miserably disorganized state in which the first Portuguese found Japan.

Reared in the best farming part of the country, familiar with its possibilities and problems, Hideyoshi, when Nobunaga sent him down along the Inland Sea, saw clearly how limited were the opportunities of agriculture as compared with those the growing ports offered. Swiftly his imagination created a Japanese empire with vast continental resources and markets from which to draw wealth.

Though he was warned by the Korean king that the project of trying to conquer China was "like a bee trying to sting a tortoise through its shell" and though he was unable to persuade the Portuguese to sell or rent him two large vessels as he had hoped they would, Hideyoshi was not dissuaded from his purpose. The maritime daimyos were ordered to supply a number of ships in proportion to

their revenues, two ships for each hundred thousand koku
of rice. Every fishing village had to send ten sailors for
each hundred houses. Troops to the number of a hundred
and thirty thousand were carried overseas and, in Korea,
captured castle after castle in rapid succession. A very
short time was sufficient for the armies from Kyushu to
march the whole length of the peninsula and threaten the
Chinese border. Like their European brethren they were
none the worse soldiers for being Christian. But then

Sixteenth-century warship

Chinese troops came to help the Koreans. Supplies and
fresh troops for the Japanese armies sent out from home
had a more difficult time getting through. The Koreans,
reinforced by the Chinese, were now prepared for them
and shot fire-arrows into the small wooden Japanese boats ;
they also had a ship which looked like a tortoise covered
over with iron plates and with spikes at the water line. In
this they would pretend to retreat before a Japanese boat
until the latter was pursuing them at full speed ; then they
would suddenly turn their oarsmen round and ram the pur-
suers' boats with their spiked armor. With ships destroyed
and supplies cut off in this manner, the armies could not
hold out, and so a truce was declared.[10]

Hideyoshi had envoys present demands to the Chinese, asking among less significant things that permits for commercial intercourse be sent to Japan, and that half of Korea also be ceded to her. After long-drawn-out parleys in which the Taiko thought of himself as victor, the Chinese emperor, instead of agreeing to the Japanese leader's demands, sent an envoy to present him with a gold seal, gold headpiece and robe of state. The coming of the envoy raised Hideyoshi's hopes very high ; he expected to be appointed King of China. When at the elaborate ceremony of welcome held in Osaka Castle the envoy read his official message, however, it was only to appoint the Taiko King of Japan. This made the great one so furious that he issued orders for a new campaign. The same Kyushu generals went to Korea again, but this time met with less success, and in 1598 just before he died Hideyoshi ordered that they be recalled.

The prospects of the Jesuits under Hideyoshi had continued, now bright, now dim. On one occasion he had signed a paper granting them the right to preach throughout Japan and ordered a copy sent to Europe that it might be known there how greatly he favored Christianity. But after his experiences among the Christian daimyos of Kyushu whom the Buddhist priests helped him to bring into submission, Hideyoshi sent a set of questions to a Jesuit official.

Why and by what authority, Hideyoshi inquired, did he and his priests constrain Hideyoshi's subjects to become Christians ? Why did they overthrow temples and persecute Buddhist priests ? Why did they eat animals useful to man, such as cows and oxen? And why did they allow Portuguese merchants to buy Japanese and sell them as slaves in India?

When satisfactory answers to these questions were not forthcoming all Jesuits were ordered to leave Japan, but the order was not enforced and they carried on their work under cover. Three years later, in 1590, the four Japanese envoys, returning from their trip to Rome, brought with them maps, globes, clocks and watches, musical instruments and new kinds of armor and weapons which interested the islanders greatly. These young travelers attracted large crowds to see and hear them wherever they went, and they helped to make many converts among fashionable people. In Hideyoshi's own household a tea master and a consort became Christians. Courtiers who cared nothing for their religion began to wear Portuguese tunics, balloon trousers, long cloaks and high-crowned hats. They even carried rosaries and crucifixes and learned to recite Pater Nosters, so as to be in fashion. Bread, sponge cake and shrimps fried in batter (called as they were by the Portuguese "pan," "kastera," and "tempura") began to appear on the small lacquer trays and tables of the Japanese elite. Playing cards were also introduced, and those who used them in imitation of the Portuguese called them "karuta." Aesop's Fables were translated into Japanese by an ex-Zen monk, a leper and Jesuit convert, and this book was printed in the Latin alphabet by a mission printing press in 1593.

The same year that Hideyoshi had dispatched his first expedition to Korea, Spaniards of the Franciscan order had come to Japan from Manila and established themselves in

Kyoto to the great annoyance of the Jesuits. From that time on there was continual rivalry between these orders. In 1596 the San Felipe was shipwrecked on the coast of the island Shikoku. Thinking perhaps to frighten the Japanese into treating him well, the captain of this vessel pointed out all the Spanish and Portuguese possessions on a map and explained, "Our kings begin by sending into countries they wish to conquer, missionaries who induce the people to embrace our religion, and when they have made progress, troops are sent who combine with the Christians. Then our kings have little trouble in accomplishing the rest." [11]

This outspoken boast was quite in line with what Hideyoshi had long been suspecting, and so, for the sake of what he considered to be the safety and best interests of his country, he ordered that the missionaries be put to death. Twenty-three Franciscans and three Jesuits were crucified at Nagasaki in 1597. Of a hundred and twenty-five other Jesuits in Japan, eleven sailed away — the rest remained to work surreptitiously and without interference in Kyushu under the protection of influential converts.

In 1599 Hideyoshi died. Though he is justly famous as the greatest military hero in Japanese history, strangely enough, his most lasting influence was on art and architecture. The results of his patronage in these fields may still be enjoyed today.

From very early times Japanese clan leaders had built their so-called castles in easily guarded mountain passes and other naturally fortified places, usually surrounding them with ditches, embankments of earth and bundles of rice straw and bamboo. Nobunaga had introduced a new style of castle. He chose a site near Lake Biwa with excellent transportation facilities. Establishing there a well-protected settlement of officers and soldiers, he also encouraged merchants who did not belong to any za to come there and enjoy the privileges of free trade. Hideyoshi himself, in 1583, exchanged a piece of property in Kyoto for the best commercial site on the main island of Japan and started to build Osaka Castle. But it was not until his generals returned from their Korean expedition that this castle began to assume the proportions of a veritable walled city.

The Koreans had had some knowledge of wall building ever since the days of the Han Empire. During internal struggles and successive invasions of their peninsula by Sui and T'ang armies and the hordes of Kublai Khan they had good reason to put this knowledge to use. Then all the principal towns were surrounded with great stone ramparts and within the walls were built towers, not with sides rising several stories high under one roof, but with a number of single storied and roofed sections seemingly piled one atop the other. These were the models for the tremendous and beautiful castles which appeared in Japan toward the end of the sixteenth century.[12] It is often said that Japanese castles are the result of Portuguese influence, with the implication that they are copied from European architecture. They are the result of Portuguese influence, yes, but there is nothing Portuguese about them ; they are simply a natural reaction of Japanese feudal lords to the growing use of firearms and fire-throwing devices which came with the Portuguese. With graceful curves of wall and roof to lighten their serious solidity, they are a typically Japanese response to Portuguese advances.

For the building of Osaka Castle, Hideyoshi ordered materials to be brought from thirty provinces. A hundred boats a day plying the three rivers surrounding the castle carried the huge granite blocks for the walls and the stout timbers for the building. Sixty thousand men were employed three years in constructing its moat twenty feet deep, its enormous walls ten miles around, its nine-storied tower and grand halls. Newly worked mines in Sado and Kai produced abundant gold for decoration. On the outside, the roofs were covered with richly gilded tiles, and on the inside, ceilings, pillars, door frames and hardware all were plated with gold. Hideyoshi's bedroom was fifty-four feet square, and his bed, five by eight feet, had poppy-colored bedding and gold ornaments at the head. Near by usually stood the great black lacquer box containing the Taiko's armor and on this, when he was not wearing it, usually lay his sword.

In addition to his Osaka Castle, Hideyoshi had a "Palace of Assembled Pleasures," Jurakutei, in Kyoto. This also was surrounded by a stone wall, three thousand paces on each side, and the roof tiles were made to look "like jeweled tigers breathing in the wind and golden dragons intoning in the clouds." [13] When this palace was completed and Hideyoshi moved in from Osaka, several hundred gilded and silvered boats carried the procession up the River Yodo, and five hundred carriages with five thousand coolies transported them from the river to the palace

itself. Nobles and populace flocked to meet him and remained for days and days celebrating at his gates. In the
garden almost five thousand loads of earth were carried to
build an artificial mountain, and there too a dancing stage
was erected with music rooms to right and left where elaborate performances were given. The utmost skill of artists
of all kinds contributed to the Taiko's pleasure. When in
1588 the emperor set aside a century-old tradition and
came to Jurakutei in his ox-drawn carriage accompanied
by scores of courtiers to be the guest of Hideyoshi, he was
so delighted with the place and entertainment, it is said,
that he stayed five days instead of three.

The last decade of the sixteenth century found Kyoto in
high and exuberant spirits. Perhaps these were the best
years the capital ever had; certainly they were the best
since Michinaga's heyday around the year 1000, and the
three centuries to come were to bring it little to boast of.
Even with the Chinese and Korean situation on his mind
the Taiko gave one grand entertainment after another,
fetes in the melon garden, nation-wide tea ceremony celebrations, excursions to Mount Koya for visiting his mother's memorial temple, to Yoshino for viewing the cherry
blossoms, to Daigo Temple for disporting himself with his
friends in the beautiful gardens he had planned. At times
he had Noh performances every three or four days, and
being very enthusiastic about these had special plays composed in which he acted himself. Hideyoshi was fairly
generous with the court. He treated the farmers well who
tilled the fields near the capital. Foreign missionaries and
traders continually afforded new interests to citizens of

Kyoto ; merchants flourished there ; gold and silver mines began to supply new wealth, and artists had opportunities such as they had seldom enjoyed before.

The peasant son of a foot-soldier was drawing revenue from the whole country ; he had risen to the chief place in the nation and aspired to be King of China. Nothing was too magnificent or grandiose for him, nothing too rich or colorful. There were interior walls and doors of extravagantly spacious proportions to be painted in glorious and energetic designs. There were heroically splendid gates to be lacquered and carved with peacocks, tigers, lions and peony blossoms.

Eitoku and Sanraku were the foremost artists of the age. Their work is in stunning contrast to the Zen-style paintings of Sesshu, the greatest artist of the Ashikaga era. Sesshu was subtly spiritual and restrained in the use of color. Many of his masterpieces are but a few strokes of black ink on a piece of white silk or paper, serene harmonious strokes in some, explosive strokes in others, excitingly intersecting at right angles, but always his work seems to portray dignity maintained at desperate odds—the dignity of winter, of storm-cleft rocks and struggling gnarled old pines.

There are no odds in the arts of the late sixteenth and early seventeenth centuries. They are heroic in spirit, but they show the power and glory without the struggle and conquest, the blossoming forth of vigorous life without any counteracting forces. They are spring and summer, without autumn and winter. The subjects include Portuguese galleons in full sail, richly clad merchants in scenes teeming with life and exotic splendor ; maps of the whole world together with Chinese legendary figures; tigers in bamboo groves symbolizing heroic lords with associates bending to their will; all-powerful dragons with eyes that look in eight directions; monkeys which signify unconventional character and originality; life-size cherry trees in full bloom with birds flying through their branches.

In his early childhood Eitoku studied painting with his grandfather, the famous founder of a great school of Japanese painting. While still very young he excelled the work of his own father and was taken as official painter into the service of Nobunaga. A story says that Eitoku sometimes painted with a monstrous brush of straw, but however that may be his work is full of life and animation, done with bold and vigorous strokes and brilliant colors on backgrounds of gold leaf. Among his masterpieces is a pair of folding screens, each eight feet high by sixteen long, one painted with fabulous lions, the other with hawks on a pine tree.

The second great painter mentioned above as representative of the heroic period was Sanraku. As a boy Sanraku was made page to Hideyoshi and carried the general's cane when he went to supervise the building of Osaka Castle. One day while Hideyoshi was busy Sanraku began intently to draw a horse in the sand. Hideyoshi returning and observing the boy's concentration and talent asked him if he would like to be an artist. As a result of this incident, he came to be the adopted son and pupil of the great Eitoku. Sanraku reached the climax of his achievement in painting for Hideyoshi in his prime. Whole walls he covered with backgrounds of gold leaf and over them painted blossoming trees and flowers of all seasons, blooming together in luxuriant profusion, like joyful gardens of eternal paradise.

After the passing of Hideyoshi, the great artists who had served him were eagerly sought by powerful feudal lords and provincial nobles throughout the country. As they scattered from the capital to the castles of their new patrons, a keen appreciation for works of beauty developed far and wide. In another hundred years, even the common people had their cheap but artistic prints, their beautifully patterned silks and household wares of exquisitely decorated porcelain and lacquer.

When the Taiko came to the end of his days, he had only one child, a boy of seven years whom he loved very dearly. In order to preserve for this son, Hideyori, the supreme place he had won for himself, Hideyoshi appointed from among his trusted and able associates five senior ministers to govern the nation jointly until the lad should come of age.

It is recorded that upon his death bed Hideyoshi summoned to him Tokugawa Iyeyasu, the ablest and wealthiest of these five senior ministers and said, "After my death you alone will be able to keep the empire tranquil. I, therefore, bequeath the whole country to you and trust that you will expend all your strength in governing it. My son is still young. I beg that you will look after him." [14]

CHAPTER XI

PEACE AT ANY PRICE
(SEVENTEENTH CENTURY)

AFTER two centuries of almost continuous feudal strife for mastery of the capital climaxed by the Taiko's enormous overseas campaign, what Japan needed more than anything else in 1600 was peace. And peace Tokugawa Iyeyasu was determined to establish.

Like Nobunaga and Hideyoshi, his seniors by a few years, Iyeyasu was a son of the soil from the Mount Fuji region. Like them also he had risen to prominence and power through his own military prowess, sound judgment and tenacity of purpose. He had been a loyal ally of Nobunaga and after the latter's assassination had fought against Hideyoshi who was trying to take the control of the country away from Nobunaga's heirs. Recognizing Hideyoshi's real greatness, Iyeyasu later had submitted to him, but yet had shown himself sufficiently great to command the Taiko's honest respect. Hideyoshi had considered it a good bargain to give the Tokugawa leader, in exchange for five small provinces in central Japan, eight large ones in the northeast out of range of capital activities.

Iyeyasu loved and believed in the soil as the true foundation of national prosperity. Unlike the lords of the lands

in the southwest whose interest was largely in overseas
trade, he concentrated on developing mining and agriculture in the Kwanto. Consequently, when the Kyushu
daimyos, owners of fiefs yielding ten thousand or more
koku a year, returned from their unsuccessful overseas adventure with both troops and treasuries exhausted, Iyeyasu
was the lord of lands yielding about two and a half million
koku of rice each year. The koku was equal to approximately five bushels, and equivalent, it is estimated, to almost seven dollars.[1] Since Japan at this time was comprised of over two hundred individually owned estates,
some idea of Iyeyasu's relative importance is given by the
fact that the total annual yield of all these (including
Iyeyasu's) was only about nineteen million koku.

With his influence already strong when the Taiko passed
away, Iyeyasu did not overestimate his own power. He
was determined to give the country peace under Tokugawa
domination, but he did not press the issue. A popular folk
tale contrasts the characters of the three great heroes of
sixteenth-century Japan in verses supposedly written while
they were listening for the first cuckoo's song in spring.[2]
Nobunaga's poem went:

> The cuckoo —
> If it does not sing
> I'll put an end to it.

And Hideyoshi's:

> The cuckoo —
> If it does not sing
> I'll show it how.

The verse supposed to be typical of Iyeyasu is :

> The cuckoo —
> If it does not sing
> I'll wait until it does.

Among the maxims supposed to be favorites of Iyeyasu is this : "Life is like a long journey with a heavy load. Let thy steps be slow and steady, that thou stumble not." [3]

Nobunaga had become acting-shogun of Japan at thirty-five ; Hideyoshi had succeeded him at the age of forty-six — Iyeyasu was fifty-seven when his turn came, and he had had time to consider well the difficulties that threatened his ambitions. In the first place, there was China, which might be expected at any time to send an expedition in retaliation for Hideyoshi's invasion of Korea. Then, with their center in Osaka, were several other leaders only slightly less important than himself, who had ships and men all over the Far East and meddled in politics in the Philippines, Siam and India. The interests of this group were apt to conflict with those of the Tokugawas. Another difficult group was the imperial court in Kyoto, still made up largely of Fujiwaras which, though not very potent in practical affairs, was regarded with a sort of religious respect. Moreover, in Kyushu and flourishing centers such as Kyoto, Osaka and Sakai on the main island, there were the increasingly aggressive groups of Christians, both native and foreign, whose loyalty was directed to God, the pope and the holy fathers rather than to an old soldier like Iyeyasu. All four of these were potential sources of national disturbance and menaces to Iyeyasu's plans for peace.

Happily, the situation with China was smoothed over without great difficulty by the priests who under one ruler after another had served the government as advisers in foreign affairs. The most immediate opposition Iyeyasu had to face came from the rival leaders who were his colleagues in the regency appointed by Hideyoshi. As soon as the Taiko passed away Iyeyasu began to fortify his position by marrying his numerous sons and daughters to various prominent persons scattered throughout the country. An objection was raised at once by more loyal supporters of the Taiko's heir, Hideyori, and came to a head in the battle of Sekigahara. In this encounter Iyeyasu took long chances — the Osaka confederates had a hundred and thirty thousand men in the field against his eighty thousand, but by a coincidence of good luck and good management he won. This victory enabled Iyeyasu to obtain surrenders and oaths of allegiance from the majority of the nation's leaders, and after this one battle his foremost position came to be generally recognized. So impressive was this victory that even today in Japan the word Sekigahara is used proverbially for "a decisive struggle."

In 1603, by a new road which he had constructed from the Kwanto, the Tokugawa leader, with great show, marched into the capital ten thousand soldiers a day for seventeen days. Soon after this the emperor named him both Minister of the Right and Sei-i Tai Shogun and presented him with an ox-drawn chariot to ride in. When Iyeyasu appeared at the palace to render thanks for this appointment, it is said the emperor with his own hands proffered a cup of wine and expressed his gratification that wars no longer convulsed the nation and that the foundations of peace were laid.

Osaka sympathizers, however, were still a strong force to be reckoned with and Iyeyasu was content to let those who wished to, think that he was only holding in trust and consolidating the power of the Taiko to turn it over to Hideyori when he came to manhood. The same year that he was appointed shogun, Iyeyasu arranged a marriage contract between his granddaughter and this twelve-year-old boy, and took up his residence for a while in the palace which Hideyoshi had built near Kyoto.

With his own son he discussed the possibilities of setting up their shogunate in Osaka, but Tokugawa interests and Tokugawa strength were centered in the Kwanto. In the Kwanto, therefore, at Yedo castle, twenty miles farther from Kyoto than Minamoto Yoritomo's former capital, Kamakura, Iyeyasu soon established the administrative headquarters of his government. This "castle," if such it might be called, had been built by a poet soldier more than a century before and described by him in the verse :

My dwelling adjoins a fir tree plain ;
Hard by rolls the sea ;
The lofty peak of Fuji-san is seen from below the eaves.[4]

When first Iyeyasu saw Yedo (having been transferred there by Hideyoshi's maneuvers) the wooden walls were weather-stained, the thatched roofs leaked and the entrance steps were made of three planks from the hull of an old ship. A most trusted adviser, thinking it ill befitted the dignity of his lord, had suggested, "We may leave the interior for the present, but the entrance really ought to be rebuilt."

But Iyeyasu had laughingly called this an extravagant idea and replied, "Our retainers must be seen to before anything else." [5]

Then his thirty-two chief supporters had been assigned villages and fields roughly in the shape of a horseshoe surrounding Yedo. Each was recommended to build as quickly as possible a simple house for his family and come up to the castle for duty. While quarters were being prepared for them the more fortunate retainers enjoyed the comforts of lodging in a Buddhist temple; some stayed with farmers in the neighborhood, or raised temporary barracks, but others had to be satisfied with shelter several miles from the castle. Gradually houses had been built and the castle repaired, and a town had grown up which served as a center of government for the Tokugawa estates in the Kwanto.

When Iyeyasu was appointed shogun of the whole country, however, and chose Yedo as the seat of his government, great improvements were made. Landlords from Kyushu who only recently had acknowledged his supremacy were ordered by the new shogun to supply labor and materials to reconstruct the city and to build a really worthy castle. Hundreds of vessels which had been built for the Korean expedition were now used for transporting workmen and huge blocks of stone. Hills were leveled, moats dug and marshes filled in. A bridge built over a canal in Yedo at this time was called Nippon-bashi, Nippon Bridge, because, it is said, all Japan had a hand in making it.

When the daimyos from the southwest became exhausted from the enterprise those in the Kwanto were asked to take it up. There were miles and miles of canals and walls. The castle itself was three castles in one protected by a network of moats and stone ramparts. The white-plaster buildings were roofed with dark tiles and had gold ornaments on the ridges and corners. But though it suggested the power of Iyeyasu, it also, if compared with Osaka, gave evident proof of his thrift.

In 1605, to preclude the possibility of interruption of the Tokugawa peace program should he himself pass away, Iyeyasu had one of his many sons appointed shogun. This enabled the son to become well experienced and established in his position while the father was still alive to guide him. Though the aging hero moved to a castle in his favorite region farther west, Yedo remained the chief center of government in Japan and, with its name changed to Tokyo, still enjoys this honor today.

Iyeyasu paid frequent visits to Yedo, indulging on the way in hunting with hawks, a sport which was his life-long enthusiasm. Hawking he defended as an excellent means of keeping up horsemanship and other military disciplines in times of peace. It also afforded an opportunity, he said, for getting intimately acquainted with the country and country people. He often let his ladies ride along on such excursions, saying it gave them a good chance for exercise and a natural life such as they were unable to enjoy in their usual formal surroundings.

The Yedo government was designed to establish and perpetuate peace throughout the nation under Tokugawa supremacy. It was a centralized feudalism. Chief in command was the shogun and reporting to him were two groups of officials, the Tairo, Great Elderly Men who were superior soldiers, and the Roju, a group of political advisers chosen from among the well-tried supporters of the ruling family. From among the Roju was appointed one as governor of Kyoto, whose duty it was to watch the activities of the court and make sure that no reactionary movements started there. One was also appointed later as superintendent of Osaka Castle.

The Tairo and Roju met together to discuss and decide upon affairs of state, and under their supervision were five important offices : the shrine and temple administration ; chief executives of the treasury and of public utilities, buildings, communications, etc. ; the very important administrator of Tokugawa-controlled towns such as Yedo, Sakai and some Kyushu ports ; and the "great watchmen" or "spying elders" who were supposed to keep close watch on all happenings and to report their findings at meetings of the Roju. Under the administrator of towns were lesser municipal officials, each responsible for and kept informed by those from the next rank below. Among these were the representatives of the leading merchants, the landowners, the house owners or family heads, and of the five-family-units into which the population was divided. A similar system was instituted for the administration of rural domains under Tokugawa control.

The whole country never really came under the direct jurisdiction of the shogun. About one quarter of the total area of the country belonged to him, and this included

most places of political, commercial and industrial importance. But besides this there were many other fiefs whose
daimyos having sworn allegiance to Iyeyasu were allowed
independence in regulating the internal arrangements of
their domains in such matters as finance, justice, education
and industry. The shogunate reserved the right to declare
war and peace, to coin money and to make roads for the
whole country.

If a daimyo died without a direct male heir his estate became the property of the shogun, and if his allegiance
wavered there was constant danger of his being transferred
to a smaller domain. So long as he was faithful to Tokugawa interests, however, he was allowed to adopt heirs and
to rule his own followers and farmers without interference,
and was entitled to all the taxes that he could collect from
them.

In addition to his well-designed government organization for preserving peace, Iyeyasu devised a further pre-
caution. Along lines of communication and in the districts of greatest economic and military importance, such
as the broad and fertile rice fields of Owari at the foot of
Mount Fuji, in Mito which guarded Yedo from the north
and on the Kii peninsula which served as a barrier between
the Inland Sea district and the new capital, he established
members of his own family. In other important places
and between allies whose loyalty was open to possible suspicion he settled tried and trusted stalwarts from his ancestral province.

With the wealthy and powerful temples which had been
such a source of worry to Nobunaga, Iyeyasu also dealt in

accordance with his plan for peace. In some of them he caused divisions, and for others he founded and favored new counterbalancing centers. A new temple center to rival Mount Koya, for example, was established near Nippon-bashi ; one to rival Mount Hiei was granted a spacious site northeast of Yedo castle. The now-tourist-frequented Zojo-ji in Shiba Park was supported by the first Tokugawa shogun as a rival to Kyoto's influential and famous Chion-in. Iyeyasu himself, unlike his two predecessors, was a good Buddhist.

Though in dealing with the imperial court Iyeyasu watched cautiously, he was also generous and, superficially at least, respectful. Previous shoguns had shown the court only arrogance and neglect, but Iyeyasu turned over to it eight times as much tax rice as Hideyoshi had allowed and some money in addition. He also invited the feudal lords to help rebuild the imperial palace, and started the custom of paying an official visit to the emperor each year. The spectacular procession of the shogun and his followers on their way from Yedo to Kyoto could not fail to impress the populace with the dignity and splendor of their rulers.

The Christians, also, Iyeyasu treated with tolerance. He enforced the edict of Hideyoshi that no daimyo should turn to the new religion, but all others were allowed complete freedom of worship until 1614. The foreign priests he favored in proportion to the trade they brought. As early as 1598, in an interview with a Spanish priest from Manila, Iyeyasu made very attractive bids for merchants on their way from the Philippines to Mexico to stop and trade in Japan and teach his retainers how to develop their silver mines. The Jesuit Father who built the first church and held the first Mass in Yedo wrote a letter for Iyeyasu to the governor of the Philippines asking him to send ships for free trade in Kwanto ports and naval architects to build large vessels for the shogunate. But the Spaniards showed few signs of cooperation and their priests were continually making trouble with the Jesuits.

Just before the battle of Sekigahara an English pilot named Will Adams had reached Japan in a Dutch ship and been taken as a prisoner to Iyeyasu. One of the first questions he was asked was whether his country had wars. He had replied, "Yea, with the Spaniards and Portugals, being in peace with all other nations." [6] Then Adams showed Iyeyasu a compass and a map pointing out the route he had come by and Japan's position in relation to the rest of the world, and all in all made a very good impression on the shogun — a little too good an impression, perhaps, from Adams' point of view, for although he was given a regular income, estate, and a native wife, he was not allowed to return to his family in England. His advice on foreign relations and his service in shipbuilding were highly valued. One of the boats he built, with a Japanese crew aboard, was welcomed in New Spain (now California) ten years before the pilgrims landed on Plymouth Rock.

Adams was not cordial toward the Catholics. When some Spaniards came to chart the harbors of the Kwanto preparatory to trading there, he advised Iyeyasu that a country in Europe which attempted to survey another's coast would be considered hostile, and showed him on the

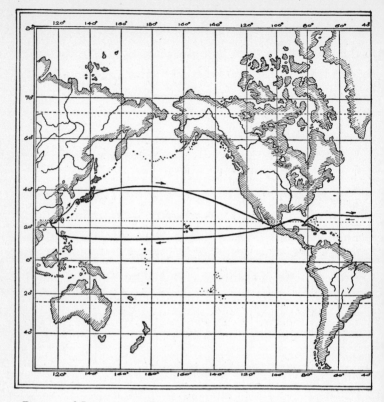

Routes of Japanese traders and envoys to and from Europe and

map all the conquests of the Portuguese and Spaniards in America, the Philippines and the East Indies. Adams' suggestions were given additional weight by the conduct of Catholic officials in the shogun's service and by the report of a man from the flourishing port of Sakai whom Iyeyasu sent to Europe to investigate the state of Catholicism in its homeland. Besides, a letter had been received from King James, of Great Britain, France and Ireland, suggesting

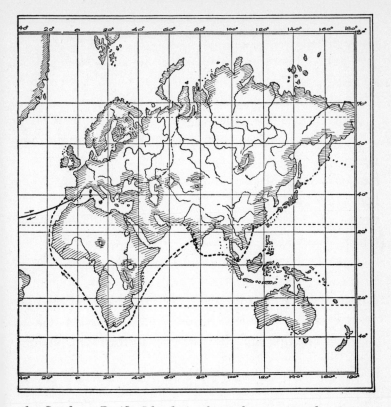

the Southern Pacific Islands in the early seventeenth century

friendly trade without benefit of clergy, and the shogun had signed an agreement granting freedom to visit any port in Japan and to build houses on tax-free land in Yedo. Thus, growing suspicion of the Spaniards and Portuguese and a wider range of commercial opportunities finally led the shogunate to order that Christianity be suppressed, that all churches be demolished, that all foreign priests leave the country and native Christians be exiled.

In the southwestern part of Japan, however, the Christians were stronger than the shogunate and the order was not obeyed. Several priests went to Osaka to solicit Hideyori's protection, suggesting that if he joined their followers miracles might be worked on his behalf.

Many others who for various reasons resented Tokugawa domination were prone to flock to Osaka and now Hideyoshi's extravagant castle became a great center of ill feeling and opposition toward the shogunate. The Taiko's heir, grown to manhood, gave evidence of becoming a son worthy of his father, one who would soon find it difficult to remain subservient to another. In the face of these circumstances Iyeyasu deemed it expedient for the sake of Tokugawa peace to destroy Osaka Castle. But though he surrounded it with a hundred and fifty thousand samurai, many of them with Dutch and English muskets and devices for shooting fireballs, the great fortress remained impregnable.

After several weeks with nothing gained, Iyeyasu arranged a truce and negotiated a treaty.

By this treaty Hideyori was granted full dignity and allowed to remain in his castle with all his samurai retainers. Iyeyasu even consented to supplement their salaries ; all he asked, to save his own face, was that part of the castle's defenses be destroyed. So as not to inconvenience Hideyori, Iyeyasu went so far as to supply the labor for doing this. The man who was ordered to superintend the destruction assembled a great crowd of workers and, before those within the castle realized what was going on, the outer walls were torn down, the outer moat filled up. When an objection was raised, it was found that the superintendent was away for his health and that the work could not be stopped without his orders. When complaint was made to Iyeyasu, he replied, "Peace has now been fortunately concluded. Let us not talk any more about moats and parapets." [7]

Then the Osaka partisans asked for allowances of rice for the samurai in the castle, and when Iyeyasu implied that they ought to be ashamed to accept a donation from one whom they had fought against, they realized how he had gotten the best of them.

The next year Iyeyasu besieged the castle again, and this time had little difficulty in bringing about its surrender. Hideyori, rather than give himself up, committed suicide.

By this conquest, having freed themselves from their only menacing opponents, the shogunate turned their attention again to their program for permanent peace.

In the country at this time were approximately two million samurai in the service of the Tokugawas and of the two or three hundred lesser feudal lords whose incomes were over ten thousand koku of rice a year. In addition to these were twenty-five to thirty million so-called common people. Rigid distinctions were drawn between the privileges of these three classes ; the commoners were further divided into farmers, artists and artisans, and merchants. Farmers ranked first, for they produced the necessities of life from the soil ; artists and artisans who created beautiful and useful things were a little lower in social status, while moneylenders, brokers and merchants, since they simply made profits on the labors of others, were relegated to the lowest class. Once a farmer always a farmer, once a merchant always a merchant, from generation to generation. The shogunate allowed neither intermarriage between classes nor the chance of working up from one class to another. The common people were also divided into groups of five families each, all the members of which were mutually responsible for the taxes and good behavior of their unit, and for reporting the misdemeanors of neighbor groups.

Soon after the fall of Osaka Castle the shogunate issued codes of laws regulating the activities of all classes of society from the imperial court down to the merchant, and even lower, to the slave class. These slaves, or eta, were segregated in special settlements and subsisted by performing such tasks as tanning, butchering and grave digging, which, being concerned with the handling of dead bodies, were regarded as vile.

Of the laws for the imperial court, perhaps the most significant were these : [8]

Not to study is to be ignorant of the doctrines of the ancient sages, and an ignorant ruler has never governed a nation peacefully.

A man lacking in ability must not be appointed to the office of regent or minister even though he belong to the Five Designated Families, and none but a member of these families may serve in such a position.

An adopted son shall always be chosen from the family of his adopter.

Reports shall be submitted to the emperor only by an official of the shogunate. Any other person who attempts to address the throne direct shall be sent into exile whatever his rank.

The laws for the military houses prescribed : [9]

Literature, arms, archery and horsemanship are systematically to be the favorite pursuits.

Drinking parties and gaming must be kept within due bounds.

Offenders against the law and persons guilty of rebellion or murder must not be harbored.

No social intercourse is permitted outside of one's own domain with the people of another domain.

Castles must not be repaired nor new structures started without permission ; such things going on in a neighboring domain should be reported without delay.

Marriages must not be contracted at private convenience.

When daimyos come to Yedo they must not be accompanied by more than twenty horsemen — only in rare cases may they dress in silk.

Samurai throughout the provinces are to practice frugality.

Laws for the common people, issued later, prescribed the minutest details of everyday life, such as the shaving of beards and the wearing of cotton clothing.

The average farmer with an income of seven or eight koku, worth about fifty dollars, a year was ordered not to build a house more than thirty feet long, nor to give more than one present on the birth of a child, a toy spear perhaps to a boy or a paper or clay doll to a girl. The amounts he could spend on a wedding outfit and a wedding feast were also specified, together with many other items.

To keep the people satisfied with their new regime the shogunate instituted an official system of education.

When troops were gathered in Kyushu for the Korean expedition, Iyeyasu had met a young Fujiwara with a very impressive knowledge of Chinese philosophy. As it happened, this Fujiwara, Seika, was the first real scholar with whom Iyeyasu had ever talked, and his Chu Hsi philosophy fitted in well with Iyeyasu's conservative ideas. According to it there were in nature two forces, one static and one dynamic, and these took the form of the five elements — wood, fire, metal, water and earth. Each of these elements was associated with a special virtue — benevolence with wood, righteousness with fire, propriety and politeness with metal, wisdom and intelligence with water, and faithful dutifulness with earth. The seed of these virtues was supposed to be in each individual, and persons who by self-culture brought all these virtues to full flower were thought to make the ideal leaders and rulers of men.

This doctrine further emphasized right relationships, loyalty between lord and subject, filial piety between father and son, love between wife and husband, obedience between elder and younger brothers and sisters and kindliness among friends. It taught people to maintain these proper relationships at all costs ; not to try to overstep their position, but to be content and satisfied with their lot in life. According to the Chu Hsi teachings, great honor came only from upholding one's principles even unto death.

It seemed to go so perfectly with Iyeyasu's peace plan that schools were established in Yedo as soon as possible for teaching this philosophy and all promising young officials were required to attend them. It was not long before similar schools sprang up all over the country, and for two hundred and fifty years Chu Hsi philosophy was the basis of all official instruction. In these schools the samurai learned something also of the liberal arts, military disci-

plines, Japanese history and poetry. Under the third Tokugawa shogun, when peace was well established in the country, a plan was devised for teaching military discipline with
the idea not of killing others, but of being so skillful as to
win a point without endangering life. Then fencing came
to be taught with bamboo poles, and swords were forced
out of practical use. Less thought was given to the quality of blades and more to the ornamentation of the sheath
and hilt, and the sword became again, as it was in Heian
days, a decorative symbol of class superiority.

The common people had never been allowed to wear
swords. In schools for them no military training was
given ; only penmanship, reading and use of the abacus
were taught. But when the thousands of samurai with
very little money and very little to do began to accost common people truculently in the towns or on country roads,
some means of self defense was a matter of life or death.
For common men to fight back against samurai was criminal, but there was no law against their being pliant, and
they soon began to master the method of defense known
as jujitsu. The principle of jujitsu is not to overpower another, but by yielding before his force to let an attacker
lose his balance and throw himself.[10]

Iyeyasu died in 1616. Though his heirs inherited neither his breadth of mind nor his strength of character, they
did contrive to perpetuate for over two hundred years his
policy of peace. The methods they used were supervision
and suppression of the people, and isolation.

It was an important feature of the Tokugawa government that everyone was watched, from the emperor him-

self down to the meanest merchant, and everyone was encouraged to report the irregularities of others. Persons who did irregular things were punished.

That a closer watch might be kept on the doings of the daimyos, they were all ordered, no matter where their estates were located, to build and maintain in Yedo a residence suitable to their rank, to leave their wives there all the time like hostages, and to live there themselves, for a while at least, every two years. This helped enormously to promote the building and commercial prosperity of the shogun's capital, and also served effectively the purpose of checking any unforeseen reaction. When any daimyo appeared to be increasing in wealth more rapidly than seemed desirable to the shogunate, this fact was noted, and the privilege of undertaking some expensive public work was conferred upon him.

The project of erecting a mausoleum and shrine at Nikko to honor the memory of Iyeyasu was begun in 1623 and carried on for twelve years. All the lords of the country were required to contribute valuable materials, the artists to contribute their best skill and most heroic designs. The architectural forms of palace, Shinto shrine and Buddhist temple were all combined in this glorious achievement. The gold leaf used, it is said, if spread out in one piece, would cover nearly six acres, and the timbers placed end to end would reach over three hundred miles.[11] There is a popular saying in Japan, "Do not use the word magnificent until you have seen Nikko." The sayings of the daimyos whose fortunes were depleted by this extravagant undertaking were not recorded. Some idea of the pressure brought to bear on them, however, is evidenced by the fact that one of their number who had nothing else to offer uprooted over eighteen thousand cryptomeria trees from the forests of his province and supplied the labor for transporting them and transplanting them around this shrine.

As part of their program of supervision and suppression of subversive activities the Tokugawas ordered the Catholic missionaries to leave the country, and forbade them to preach their gospel, but the Christians somehow managed to carry on. This defiance of their authority provoked the shogunate greatly, and after Iyeyasu's death, several Christians, both foreign and native, were martyred for their faith. As usual, persecution intensified rather than diminished zeal. The babies of Japanese Christians were nursed only once a day so that their innocent hungry cries might rise up to God together with the prayers of their elders on behalf of the believers. Though all Spaniards and Portuguese supposedly were driven out of the country, in 1637 a revolt occurred in Kyushu. Some thirty thousand men, women and children, downtrodden and discontented peasants, fought under banners inscribed with red crosses, and shouted "Jesus," "Maria" and "Saint Iago" (the patron saint of Spain) as their battle cries. Their resistance and endurance struck terror in the Tokugawa generals sent to quell them, but finally they were driven into an old castle and surrounded. A letter shot out of the castle on an arrow to their besiegers explained their motives:

We have done this not with the hope of taking lands and houses but simply because Christianity has been prohibited by the shogun. Should we continue to live as Christians and

these laws be not repealed we must incur all sorts of punishments, and perhaps, our bodies being weak and sensitive, sin
against the Lord of Heaven. These things fill us with grief
beyond endurance; hence our present condition.[12]

Imprisoned in their castle for two months, still they
would not surrender. Finally the shogunate called upon
the non-religious Dutch merchants to turn their shipboard
cannon against the stronghold of the rebels. But not until
food and ammunition alike were completely exhausted was
it overwhelmed. Then the shogunate, unwilling to take
further chances with Spanish or Portuguese converts, resolved to adopt the "Closed Door" policy, and prohibited
all intercourse except that with the Dutch and Chinese in
the port of Nagasaki. This prohibition remained in effect
until 1854.

CHAPTER XII

THE GOLDEN AGE OF THE BOURGEOISIE
(1675–1725)

FROM the days of the early settlers the headquarters of
the chief clan leaders had been the centers of the nation. Close to their dwellings loyal followers had settled,
shrines had been established and markets had been held on
special days. In "Closed Door" Japan were two hundred
or more such centers of varying sizes and degrees of prosperity. By far the most flourishing of these were Osaka
and Yedo, the castle towns of the two great national leaders, Hideyoshi and Iyeyasu.

After the siege of 1615 the citizens of Osaka had quickly
restored their city. Only ten years later, according to official records, it had a population of almost three hundred
thousand, with twenty-eight mansions occupied by feudal
lords, two hundred government officials, one thousand
three hundred and four rice brokers, a hundred and thirty-
two bridges, two hundred and eleven hotels and inns, fifty
bookstores, two hundred and seventy-seven druggists, five
execution grounds, forty-one brothels, three hundred and
thirteen Buddhist temples, eleven Shinto shrines, two hundred and fifty-six tea houses, seven hundred and six brew-
eries, twenty-four bath houses, six hundred and sixty-seven

pawnshops and five thousand four hundred and sixty-three fishing boats, ferries and other small ships plying the Inland Sea.[1]   And like Yedo, the political center of the country, Osaka, the great commercial and industrial center, has continued to increase in national importance up to the present day.

This port as far back as the sixth century, when Prince Shotoku, the Father of Japanese Culture, was regent, had been a harbor where newcomers from the continent had been welcomed and where, after worshipping the sea god, envoys had been dispatched overseas.   Its cosmopolitan tradition stretched over a thousand years, but renewed impetus had been given its adventurous citizens by the inspiration of Portuguese and Spanish traders.   Some had managed to get ships of their own in which they could sail the high seas, while others had hired passage to foreign ports where opportunity beckoned.   All were prompted by their own initiative, carried on their business independent of superior authority, and enjoyed the profits themselves.   Hideyoshi had encouraged this sort of enterprise, and kindred spirits from all over the southwestern part of the country had looked to his castle as their capital.   How many of them were engaged in this unlicensed maritime trade may be guessed from the fact that when Iyeyasu was anxious to enlist the cooperation of Spanish shipowners in Manila he had tried to make a favorable impression on them by capturing and executing two hundred Japanese pirates, apparently a small fraction of the total number.

Since this uncontrolled trade was not only unprofitable, but also a potential source of trouble for the Tokugawas, they tried to put an end to it. When the Tokugawa government became effective in Osaka the mercantile population had to invent new business interests. Some of them scattered to castle towns throughout the country where they could put their profiteering experience into practice, but many remained and put up a sort of united front against too close supervision and control by the shogunate. A few obtained licenses from the Yedo officials and went to buy goods from the storehouses in Nagasaki where now the Hollanders alone were permitted to import and export. But before long Osaka, with its central location and excellent transportation facilities, had become the rice market of the nation.

Daimyos in general had very little money ; their income was in rice, which the peasants from their estates brought in ox cart after ox cart, all hulled and packed in big straw bags, to the granary of their lord. Rice was still the most important medium of exchange and the standard of value, but the Dutch traders were not interested in rice ; it was of little value compared to its bulk and it was grown more abundantly in Java and the Indies where the Dutch had their bases than in Japan. They wanted gold, silver and copper. The daimyos, on the other hand, wanted to be able to buy the white raw silk of superior quality which the Dutch traders brought from China, and they were also eager to possess some of the medicines, glass mirrors, telescopes, clocks and other curiosities from Europe. Osaka citizens were quick to see possibilities of profit in this situation.

There was a family called Yodoya which had opened a

produce exchange in front of their own house when Hide-yoshi's samurai had first started to swell the population of the city. During the Taiko's regime this family had risen to prominence and wealth by their extraordinary ability in transporting, distributing and fixing the price of rice. With numerous other brokers, they went on from speculation in this commodity to speculation in gold and silver, developed a network of swift communications throughout the country and continued to prosper marvelously even under the Tokugawas, until it was realized that they were drawing wealth from all the provinces — more than the Tokugawas themselves could claim. Such a state of affairs could not long be endured. The Yodoya house, the most conspicuous of these multi-millionaires, was ordered confiscated by the fifth Tokugawa shogun on the charge that its members were living in luxury ill-befitting their social rank. A complete list of their possessions would fill pages and pages, but a few are enumerated here to give an idea of what constituted a wealthy merchant at the end of the seventeenth century.

In Osaka alone they owned four hundred and twelve houses and, scattered through surrounding provinces, over three hundred houses, farms, fields and woodlands, and seven hundred and thirty storehouses containing beans and rice. They owned almost three hundred large junks for carrying on their business, and among countless other things : one hundred and fifty folding screens covered with gold leaf ; five hundred and fifty flowered carpets from the Loochoo islands ; ninety-six sliding doors made of crystal ; over three hundred hens, chicks, sparrows, doves and ma-

caws made of solid gold for purposes of ornament ; ten
dishes and twenty rosaries of coral ; rubies, pearls, agates and
amber in untold numbers ; seventy-five tons of quicksilver ;
seven hundred and forty-three paintings ; five thousand
rolls of velvet, two thousand of poppy-colored Chinese brocade, ten thousand of black Chinese silk ; a hundred and
seventy telescopes and spectacles ; a checker board of solid
gold ; thirty-five tons of cinnabar, seventy-seven pounds of
the highly prized ginseng root supposed to prolong life,
and numberless swords and teacups of great value. All in
all, their estate was estimated at a hundred and twenty-
two million ryo, about two thousand tons, of gold.[2]

A popular saying of the time went something like this :
"August Yedo is the city of the samurai, and Kyoto the
city of fine ladies ; Osaka alone is the city of the merchants
who are daring, self-respecting, faithful to promises, yielding to no threat, broad-minded and brightly dressed." [3]
But Yedo was not without its wealthy merchants either.
Since all the daimyos were required to maintain mansions
there, it afforded an excellent market for both the necessities and luxuries of life. Purveyors to government officials
lived in grander style than many feudal lords themselves,
and were escorted through the city by a procession of servants. Stores on the principal thoroughfares had open gates
like palaces and were continually crowded with samurai
and their attendants. One Yedo merchant with a flair for
advertising got all the entertainment girls singing a song
about the boat load of oranges with which he started his
fortune and, after a great fire swept the city, became very
wealthy selling lumber. Silkworm dealers from six north-

eastern provinces held a convention in Yedo in 1672 to discuss methods for promoting their business, and some years later began to publish a yearbook on sericulture. In Yedo, as well as Osaka, the Genroku period from 1688 to 1703 was a time of great commercial prosperity.

With prosperity, as always, came gaiety and a demand for entertainment. The samurai were ordered to be frugal, and the salaries of rice which they received for keeping themselves in readiness to defend their lords were not adequate for much expensive celebration, but many of them had little idea of paying for things. They considered themselves superior to the common merchants and acted as if they were conferring a favor by borrowing money. They boasted of their ignorance of money matters and made promissory notes that read, for example, "In the event of my failure to repay the loan, I shall not object to being publicly ridiculed," or "Should I fail to discharge my obligation at the fixed time, I should be considered as no man." [4]

Had not the samurai brought peace to the nation and made prosperity possible ? Then let them be treated with respect. But the merchants, while they aimed to copy the costumes, accomplishments and household decorations of the samurai, still could not repress some annoyance at their swaggering attitude, and often repeated the taunt, "Though the samurai has not eaten, he acts as if he were full." Though continually professing an idealistic interest in Chinese scholarship and military discipline, many samurai could not stifle a secret desire to enjoy the realistic amusements of the carnal bourgeoisie, and the two classes came in frequent contact. Especially in Osaka was this true, for many of Hideyoshi's samurai had been forced by circumstances to give up their soldierly pursuits and had turned to trading for a livelihood. To Osaka also, before the doors of their native land were closed, had returned many Japanese who had traveled abroad and lived in Korea, China, Siam, the Philippines, Java and the busiest ports of the Southern Seas. These home-coming adventurers had seen life in great variety and were accustomed to freedom and excitement. Wealthy merchants, talented samurai and these men of worldly experience naturally mingled together and, out of the association, developed what is frequently called the Genroku Renaissance.[5]

Toward the end of the seventeenth century all the arts took on new life. Literature, music, the theater, painting, applied design and poetry all blossomed profusely, with brilliant new blooms which appealed to the common people and won their enthusiastic patronage. Three outstanding figures in this movement were Saikaku, the realistic novelist, Chikamatsu, the romantic dramatist, and Basho, the symbolic poet. Each in his field created a new type of art for the common people to rival the ancient forms which the samurai held as classic. Saikaku wrote novels with common men as heroes to rival the time-honored Heian court tales of princely amours. Chikamatsu created a new type of drama which far outshone the aristocratic Noh performances in popularity, and Basho created a new poetry whose spiritual quality had far wider appeal than the formal verses the samurai practiced writing.

Saikaku was sophisticated to the nth degree and held

nothing sacred. Defying all traditions and conventions, he identified himself with the gay pleasure-quarter, and in brutally frank and vivid terms extolled the joys of the flesh. "Why offer money to Buddha?" he wrote; "is not a land of women, paradise? Give your money to women."[6] Women and money were his theme. His most famous work was a tale somewhat like the Genji Monogatari with a common man instead of the Shining Prince as hero. This "Middle Aged Gentleman of Passion" is done in a style which, though much less refined than hers, has a curt brilliance like the "Pillow Book" of the Heian court-lady Sei. All of Saikaku's writings, novels, short stories and sketches of contemporary life and manners, being both realistic and humorous and done in the everyday pleasure-quarter vernacular, were very popular with the common people and did not fail to appeal to the samurai either. Because of the startling and perverting nature of their revelations, however, the shogunate had them suppressed. On his deathbed at fifty-two, following the ancient custom of all men of distinction, Saikaku wrote a poem of passing:

The moon of this floating world,
I have looked upon two years too long.

In Prince Shotoku's day music was supposed to bring harmony to men's hearts and make them easy to govern, but Genroku music did something very different. Much of it was plaintive and wailing, exciting lovers to despair and even to suicide. Whereas the favorite instrument of courtier and samurai was the stately thirteen-stringed koto, the bourgeois instrument was the samisen, a sort of three-stringed banjo introduced from the Loochoo islands where children used them for toys. A popular form of entertainment in the early days of middle-class prosperity had been a recitation of some old romance accompanied by a strumming of open chords and descriptive phrases, but this soon developed into a more dramatic form.[7]

In 1603 a temple dancer eloped with her lover and started the show business in a dry river bed in Kyoto. In simple little acts she took men's parts and he took women's and they created such a sensation that she was invited up to Yedo to perform for the shogun and the daimyos. Other troupes appeared in imitation of this one and were acclaimed with equal enthusiasm by the common people. Officials called them Kabuki, off balance, leaning to one side, not quite right. Kabuki stood for eccentricity and dissipation, and by many were thought to be no more than publicity stunts for commercialized vice. The son of a samurai writes in his autobiography :

During a summer festival there would sometimes be a series of plays lasting seven days together when traveling actors set up a temporary stage in the temple yard. Then there would always be a proclamation that the samurai of our clan should not even go beyond the stone wall of the temple. Many went anyhow, with their faces wrapped in towels, wearing only a short sword so they would look like common people. These disguised samurai broke over the bamboo fence of the theatre, whereas the real common people paid their fees. If the management tried to stop the intruders they uttered a menacing roar and strode on to take the best seats.[8]

Because of their demoralizing influence, the shogunate banned all actresses from the stage. Young boys took the

Outdoor theater with musicians at left, dancers on stage, and the audience at right, including two Samurai with faces covered

place of the girls, and Kabuki went on ; and so did the demoralizing influence. Then young actors too were banned,
and only mature men were allowed to act. Without the
charms and beauty of youth to aid them it became necessary to improve both the plays and the acting in order to
attract an audience. It was then that the real art of the
Japanese theater started, and costumes and scenery became
increasingly gorgeous.

Some theaters had puppets instead of men. Here the
play itself was most important, and for such a theater in
Osaka, Chikamatsu began to write. Though a product of
the same age, he was not as irreverent a man as Saikaku.
Chikamatsu knew how to enjoy his emotions, but he understood his duties as well. His plays were usually based
on the conflict between two motives, "Giri" and "Ninjo"
they were called, duty and sentiment, loyalty and self-
indulgence, conservatism and liberalism, the chief conflict
of society in his day. Some of his plays dealt with historical subjects and others were written almost in a single
night, after a love suicide or a similar piece of news which
everyone was discussing. Chikamatsu realized that everyday life was full of dramatic situations and touched com-
monplace events with his creative genius. No matter how
weak his characters, they have their strong moments which
command respect—no matter how strong, they have some
endearing human weakness. Samurai, officials, wealthy
merchants, and common folk suffering from poverty and
government regulations, all are given liberal treatment.
Chikamatsu neither praised nor blamed ; he helped people
to see the hearts and minds of others with understanding

sympathy, and the way he did this had a lasting effect on the social ideals of both samurai and merchant. His poem of passing, however, suggests that he did not take himself too seriously :

Last words ?
Well, well, I hope the cherry will bloom as ever after I am gone.

About fifty of Chikamatsu's five-act plays are still available for the modern reader,[9] and many of them are still produced in the theaters. In the earlier ones there is frequent use of long narrative parts in alternating five and seven syllable lines to be chanted by the chorus at the side of the stage ; but as Chikamatsu became more experienced in technique, and as puppets of greater and greater accomplishment were devised, dialogue came to play a more important part. Puppets were made about two-thirds of life size and fitted so cleverly with machinery that they could roll their eyes, raise their brows, open and close their mouths, move their fingers and even manipulate a fan.

In Yedo living actors who wrote their own plays had been more popular than the puppets, but now they too began to act the dramas written for puppets. Plays based on historic subjects showing the loyalty and devotion of a retainer to his lord found greater favor in the shogun's capital than those dealing with love suicide. There wisdom, benevolence and courage constituted the ideal character and the samurai were supposed to specialize in these virtues. The common citizens of Yedo, however, being noted for their scrappy dispositions, were especially delighted by comedies in which merchants were shown putting something over on samurai.

The theaters in which the Kabuki were presented also came to be highly developed in the Genroku period. Two or three story structures they were with elaborate stage, pit and galleries. The first-class boxes were hung with split bamboo curtains and surrounded by gold screens so that the wealthy merchants could enjoy the entertainment in elegant seclusion. The principal approach to the stage was not from the side or back but by a long, narrow platform built aisle-like through the pit. This might serve as the verandah of a house, a street in a town scene, or a road in the country, and it afforded the spectators a chance to look closely at the actors. Instead of drawing a curtain for changes of scenery, they had a revolving stage and passed from one scene to the next in full view.

The audience came to the theater in the morning, laden with lunch boxes and saké bottles, and stayed all day, eating, drinking and walking around as their natures directed.

Besides the theaters there were the pleasure boats on the canals and rivers of Osaka. Rich merchants owned their own luxuriously appointed ones and engaged caterers, musicians and dancing girls to provide entertainment on them. Poor people hired less pretentious public boats, took along their own food and drink and did their own singing and dancing.

This picturesque, romantic diversion became so popular that the word which was used to describe the reckless gaiety of life in the pleasure-quarters was "Ukiyo," floating world,[10] a delightfully carefree drifting on the tide, where no bonds or restrictions could hold one back, where within narrow confines, each man could order life to his own satisfaction.

In former days artists had painted only for temples, palaces or castles, but the colorful and spectacular Ukiyo offered such an abundance of attractive subjects, and the prosperous merchants such a ready market, that a new type of art developed, called Ukiyo-e, pictures of the floating world. At first they were painted in colors, not realistically but by each artist subjectively according to his own taste. Moronobu was one of the early artists to do this. When the demand for such pictures became greater, artists began to cut their drawings on blocks of wood and to print large numbers of copies. These prints could be sold very cheaply and people liked to have them as reminders of a favorite actor or beauty in the pleasure-quarter, or as helps to experiencing thrills which they could afford only in imagination. It was from penny prints which traveling friends brought as presents from a visit to the city that country people got their notions of urban life.

The earliest prints were done only in heavy black lines on white paper, but the addition at first of two colors, rose-red and green, and then of others made them so much more desirable that eventually an exquisite variety of color and detail was used. Books of pictures which told stories without words of events in the lives of professional entertainers were also printed from wood blocks. Very often these prints and story books were obscene and not infrequently they profaned sacred subjects. The name of the old saint Daruma who had sat in meditation so long that he lost the use of his feet, was given to pleasure-quarter ladies who rarely left their silken cushions, and the Bodhisatva Fugen, usually shown in Buddhist paintings riding an elephant and reading a sutra, was travestied by famous beauties dreaming over love letters.

The pleasure-quarters were made to resemble as closely as possible the Heian palaces of seven centuries before. The ladies in them wore voluminous robes of gorgeous silks, and cherished gifts of beautiful accessories. For this purpose, as well as for decoration in homes of Yedo officials, daimyos and wealthy merchants, the applied arts blossomed with a multitude of blooms during the Genroku period.[11] Korin and his brother Kenzan are known all over the world for the marvelous designs they created for gold-lacquer writing boxes, small ornamental screens, precious textiles and other domestic furnishings. Both were brought up in Kyoto, and their work is welcome evidence of the continuing and genuine refinement of life in the ancient imperial capital. Many of the silks of the Genroku period were also made in the city of fine ladies, and some are still preserved in museums and private collections. Their exquisitely woven patterns and subtly harmonized colors are beautiful beyond description.

As one can find nothing vulgar or flamboyant in the work of Korin and Kenzan, neither is there anything in the writing of Basho to offend the most gentle soul. He stands in striking contrast to Saikaku and Chikamatsu, the other two members of the famous literary trio of the Genroku period. The noisy brilliance and venality of the floating world were profoundly distressing to him. He longed to create some purifying influence. Sitting alone in midnight stillness pondering the problem, Basho heard a sound, the splash of a frog jumping into a pond. A sudden flash of insight came to him ; he would make a fresh sound in the stagnant old pond of poetry.

The oldest collection of Japanese poetry dates from the Nara age and contains many long poems, together with the thirty-one syllable tanka. The latter form came to be used almost exclusively by Heian court versifiers, and the spontaneous expression of earlier days deteriorated into stilted and stylized composition. For pastime, nobles had held contests in which those participating were challenged with the first three lines of a tanka and required to supply two concluding lines at once. From the thirteenth century on three lines alone, of five, seven and five syllables respectively, came to be used occasionally as a complete form. Such poems are called "haiku."

By Basho's day many people were writing haiku, in which frail sentiments were expressed with an attempt at rhetorical dexterity. Someone described these haiku as "slobber," but Basho, adopting the same brief form, filled it with profound and sublime meaning. Not only did he himself become the greatest Japanese poet of all time, but he initiated a great popular movement of haiku writing ; over a million names are included in anthologies of haiku today.

The supreme art of haiku writing in the Basho manner consists not so much in what is said as in what is suggested. Basho was a mystic. He spent month after month wandering through the country listening for the voice of nature

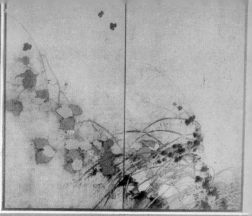

PAIR OF SCREENS

TEA JAR

LACQUER BOX

HANGING SCROLL, PINE TREE IN SNOW

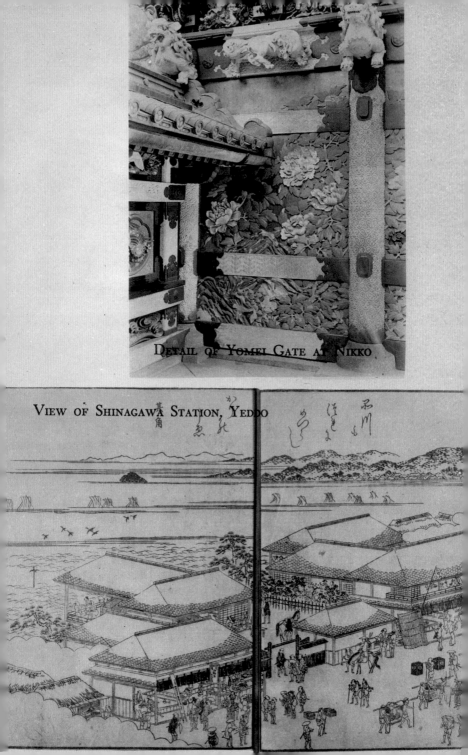

DETAIL OF YOMEI GATE AT NIKKO

VIEW OF SHINAGAWA STATION, YEDDO

and adoring her works. The seventeen-syllable notes on his deepest experiences contain the essential facts for making the experience live again and for showing kindred spirits the way to gratifying truths.

One day when he and a pupil were going through the fields, looking at the darting dragon flies, the pupil made the verse :

> Red dragon flies !
> Take off their wings
> And they are pepperpods !

"No," said Basho, "this is not haiku. If you wish to make a haiku on that subject you must say :

> Red pepperpods !
> Add wings to them,
> And they are dragon flies ! [12]

There is another story about Basho which shows how modest he was and also in how much favor haiku were held by even the lowliest people.

On one of his many rambles, the story goes, Basho came upon a group of rustics out enjoying the light of a full moon, drinking saké and composing haiku. As soon as they noticed him the rustics thought it would be fun to ask the wanderer to join them — and Basho could not very well refuse. One of the number spoke up and said, "Everybody here is bound to compose a verse about the full moon. You must compose something too." Basho apologized and said he was a humble man from a country place, and begged to be excused.

"No, no," they said, "we can't excuse you. Good or bad you must compose one verse at least."

"Well then, I will give you one," agreed Basho, and began

'Twas the new moon . . .

"The new moon ! Stupid fellow, this is the full moon," one of the rustics exclaimed, but the others bade him let the guest go on, as it should be very amusing.

Then Basho continued :

'Twas the new moon,
Since then I have waited
And lo ! Tonight !

The whole party was amazed at his aptness and asked the stranger's name. When he told them they were greatly excited and sent for all their friends to come and join a party in his honor.[13]

Basho's last haiku was :

On a journey, ill —
And my dreams o'er withered fields
Are wandering still.[14]

And still his poems are learned by heart and repeated on suitable occasions in all sorts of Japanese households.

The effect of the haiku movement was sobering and wholesome. People began to take somewhat less interest in the gay pleasure-quarter and to find more enjoyment in the country. A tremendous eruption of Mount Fuji which

occurred in 1707 also startled the people into an appreciation of the awful power of nature in contrast to the "floating world." This eruption, which was Fuji-san's last, buried Yedo, seventy-five miles distant, under six inches of
ashes and terrified the people with darkness and thunder-
ing noises. It seemed like an ominous expression of a
deity's mighty wrath.

From the days of the Ainu who gave it the name "fire"
or "bursting forth," Fuji-san had been famous in Japanese
poetry and lore. Towering almost two and a half miles
above the surrounding lakes and plain, in clear weather it
was visible a hundred miles away, and held in awe because
of its outward pure serenity as well as for its inner volcanic
fire. As early as Iyeyasu's time there had been sects of the
native Shinto cult which emphasized the spiritual and
physical value of mountain climbing, and as travel between
Yedo and Kyoto increased, Fuji-san's perfect cone became
an increasingly familiar and inspiring sight. In the late
Tokugawa period people began to come from all over the
country in white robes, with little bells jingling from their
girdles and climbing sticks in their hands, to make pilgrimages to the top. Climbing Fuji-san came to be a popular religious practice, as it still is today,[15] and an austere
discipline to balance wanton tendencies.

CHAPTER XIII

WHEN PERRY CAME
(MIDDLE NINETEENTH CENTURY)

SINCE 1635 no Japanese had been allowed to leave his native land and only a few Hollanders and Chinese had been allowed to enter it. Though during the two centuries of isolation there were usually a half dozen or more Europeans residing in Japan to carry on the trade of the Dutch East India Company, they were confined to the tiny island, Deshima, which lay in Nagasaki harbor and was only two hundred thirty-six paces long by eighty-two paces wide. Most of these traders had little interest in Japan beyond "their ledgers, their guilders and their schnapps," and for this reason enjoyed but slight esteem among the natives.[1] Local families, however, acted as their cooks and servants, providing them with food, drink and household wares, and in this way becoming familiar with their ways.

Furthermore, the shogunate, which had a monopoly on all foreign trade, maintained a staff of interpreters and commissioners, sometimes two hundred or more, who had frequent dealings with the foreigners and came to be fairly well informed not only in the Dutch language, but also in anatomy, medicine, natural history, botany, horsebreeding

and astronomy as taught in Europe, and in the newly discovered wonders of electricity. When men of high caliber
like Kaempfer, Thunberg, Titsingh and Siebold were resi-

Plan showing Nagasaki harbor with Deshima and its bridge
to the mainland just left of center

dent at Deshima the tiny island became a great center of
learning.[2] Provincial governors sent their brightest young
men to Nagasaki to study Dutch sciences so that the prestige of their native places might be enhanced. Some official

students opened schools of Dutch learning in Yedo. The eighth Tokugawa shogun established a great library of foreign books there,[3] encouraged the cultivation of tobacco and sweet potatoes as supplementary crops to rice, had an observatory with a telescope erected in Yedo and a rain gauge and sundial set up in his palace park.

Several Japanese artists went to Nagasaki to study Western techniques of oil painting, map making and copperplate engraving. In this way they added not only to Japanese knowledge of Western subjects, but also to the accuracy of Western maps of the Japanese islands and surrounding territories. Some of them specialized in "Nagasaki prints" by means of which their fellow countrymen, even in remote districts, were able to get some idea of the appearance of the Hollanders' ships, houses, customs and costumes.[4]

Politically minded students read Dutch news letters and other sources of information about contemporary conditions in Europe, America and China. They learned of the American and the French Revolutions, the Napoleonic Wars, the imperialistic expansion of England in India and Malaysia, of Russia in Siberia and Alaska. They learned of the shame and loss which even their great neighbor China suffered before the guns of the British navy, and of the constantly increasing activity of Americans in the Pacific area. When these students, a few hundred perhaps, thought of the state of affairs in their own country they became very serious and restless.

In 1814 the English seized the Dutch possessions in Java and Sir Stamford Raffles, the English governor, sent representatives of the English East India Company to Nagasaki to ask for trading rights such as the Dutch had. The mission did not gain its point, but it reported, "The Japanese are a nervous, vigorous people whose bodily and mental powers assimilate much nearer to those of Europe than what is attributed to Asiatics in general."

Other English ships which tried to put into Japanese ports about this time, and several attempts by Russians to establish relations with the Japanese, did not retard the latter's eagerness for a knowledge of world affairs. Dutch agents, stranded on Deshima with nothing to trade, on account of the trouble their ships were having with the English, were gladly supported by the Japanese in return for preparing a Dutch-Japanese dictionary and teaching what they knew of international movements. A few Japanese at this time also began to study Russian and English, but these students of Western ways were but a little leaven in a very large lump.

About thirty million people it is estimated there were in Closed Door Japan, eighty per cent of them farmers, seven per cent samurai, three per cent merchants, two per cent artisans and eight per cent officials, priests, actors, outcasts, etc.[5] The bulk of the population was scattered throughout the folds of the mountain ranges in small valleys and plains where sweet potatoes, rice and other cereals and mulberry bushes could be grown, where timber could be cut from the forested slopes and small fish caught in the swift flowing streams, but where few progressive ideas were allowed to penetrate.

The average family had about two acres under cultivation, not all in one piece perhaps, but in little patches here

and there within easy walking distance of one of the sixty
thousand villages in which farmers' homes were clustered.
If farmers could have used for themselves all the produce
of their lands they might (except in times of drought, in-
sect plague, severe storm, earthquake or volcanic eruption)
have lived quite comfortably, for the country was at peace ;
they were for the most part hard-working people and their
wants were simple. Unfortunately, however, they not infrequently were driven by officials to raise more and more
rice for taxes to pay the salaries of the unproductive samurai
and other expenses of superiors and government, and their
own shares of the harvest were scarcely enough to keep
them alive. The farmers' wives dried and salted fish, and
pickled vegetables to store on the kitchen shelf. Often
they helped along the family income by raising silkworms
in spring and summer and weaving the spun silk into cloth
in the winter. Sometimes the children helped them make
sandals or mats from rice straw, or lanterns, baskets and
umbrellas of bamboo which could be exchanged for food
or other domestic necessities.

But when, as sometimes happened in spite of their best
efforts, the farmers became desperate and the officials took
no measures for their relief, whole villages would rise up in
an angry mob, carrying their sickles and long-bladed hoes
for weapons and straw mats for banners, beating drums,
blowing horns, ringing bells and shouting their resentment
and demands. As they approached the castle where their
feudal lord or local officials resided, the samurai outside the
walls would run into the courtyards and bar the heavy
gates. Then, after a while, representatives would be sent

out to negotiate with the farmers concerning their demands. The ringleaders of the rioters were always severely punished, sometimes even crucified, but usually their efforts brought relief for a while.

Artisans and merchants had their troubles too. They swarmed in the few large cities each of whose populations numbered nearly half a million, where hastily built wooden houses with open-front shops were crowded close together and fires frequently broke out. Their businesses were strictly regulated and they had constantly to be on their guard against losses from dealings with samurai, whose tastes were high and salaries low. Like the farmers, most of them limited the number of their children for economic reasons, to two or three; but though they thus deprived themselves of the ready pleasure which poor Japanese today seem to find in their many babies, they had plenty of diversion as compared with country people.

The chief excitement in the villages was afforded by the eagerly anticipated first nightingale to return in spring, an evening's gossip in the light of a full moon, the festivals of local shrines and temples or occasional wandering acrobats and story tellers. In the cities, however, interesting things were always happening and life was very much more free and easy. Farmers liked to break away from their fields whenever they could manage it and go to the city to become tradesmen or day laborers, and their daughters found domestic service in large city houses much more attractive than the grueling routine of the farm. Such desertion of the land by peasants was not at all approved by the government and rigid measures were devised to prevent it. Nevertheless, the city censuses continued to show increases in population.

The first accurate geographical knowledge of their country came to the Japanese when one of their able students of Western science, after eighteen years of extensive travel and conscientious measurement by the methods of both astronomy and land surveying, produced an accurate large-scale map of the whole country. This gave men in authority their first true picture of the coast lines of the various islands, the courses of roads and rivers, the contours of mountains and the circumferences of lakes. By 1850 communication facilities between important centers, considering the difficult topography of the country, were fairly well developed.

Roads and transportation had been greatly improved when the daimyos from all the provinces were required to pay regular visits to Yedo. There were five main highways all starting from Nippon-bashi in Yedo. The two most traveled, the Eastern Sea Road and the Central Mountain Road connected Yedo with Osaka and Kyoto. The other three ran to Nikko, northeastern Japan and the great silk-growing district northwest of Mount Fuji. With a hundred and forty-six daimyos and their long retinues of banner and baggage bearers traveling back and forth from Yedo at frequent intervals, the Eastern Sea Road was very colorful and lively. The great print artist, Hiroshige, took delight in picturing the fifty-three stations where travelers might stop to get fresh horses for the next lap of the journey.[7]

Because of the many narrow mountain passes and the

many rivers which had to be crossed, there was little wheel traffic along these main highways. Daimyos and very important people were carried in sedan chairs on the shoulders of their servants, while lesser passengers and baggage were carried on horseback. At rivers one sometimes found bridges of boats tied together or ferries to take one across, but wading or riding across on the shoulders of a porter was not at all unusual. For food and rest along the way inns were provided. There travelers were given small charcoal fires to warm themselves if it was cold, a large tub of hot water was available for bathing and thin mattresses, three feet by six, were spread on the straw mat floor for them to sleep upon. There was a rule that they should stay only one night at each inn.

At intervals on the roads barriers were established where travelers had to pass between six in the morning and six in the evening and show some evidence that they had good reason to be making a journey. A significant number of those who passed the barriers were pilgrims visiting famous temples and traveling salesmen for quack medicines. Actors had only to perform to prove their profession, villagers usually had passports from their village head. For anyone taking a side route to avoid these barriers, the penalty was crucifixion.

The fastest travelers on the Eastern Sea Road were the official express messengers. They always ran in pairs, one carrying a small lacquer box containing the documents or money being sent and the other carrying a lantern marked "Official Business." They had the right of way. All other traffic stood aside to let them pass, and by a relay system they were able to cover the distance between Yedo and Osaka sometimes in as few as fifty hours. Other common carriers for tradespeople made three trips a month between the two cities, taking on the average eight days for the journey. For an extra fee they could do it in five days.

Bulky goods and produce in large quantities were generally transported by boat, and usually sent first to Osaka, then redistributed from there to other parts of the country. Many daimyos maintained warehouses in Osaka and sent the local products of their districts there to be sold. Salt fish and seaweed were brought from northern Japan, silk and lacquer from Kyoto, saké from the island of Shikoku, bleached textiles from Nara, the old temple capital, cotton cloth from Kawachi, candles from a section two hundred miles north of Yedo and rapeseed oil for lighting from central Japan. The three districts which exported rice in large quantities were central Kyushu and the northeastern and northwestern provinces of the main island. Some idea of the business between Osaka and Yedo may be had from the fact that there were over twenty thousand small boats plying back and forth between these two cities. Boats chartered for official use flew white flags with red discs in the center and the name of the ship underneath.[8]

Japanese homes of the middle nineteenth century were much the same as Japanese homes today. The chief differences today are electric lighting and American-style clothes for school children of all ages, both of which are now in use almost everywhere in the country. There are many Western-style houses in urban districts nowadays, but they are by no means in the majority even in the cities.

The outside of Japanese homes in the last days of the Tokugawas varied somewhat in accordance with local conditions of climate, occupation and available materials as, to be sure, the inside did too, but there were several characteristics common to them all. Country houses almost invariably were only one story high, the walls were built of unpainted wood and rough clay with bits of twigs and straw in it, and the acutely sloping roofs were covered with heavy straw thatch. In cold and windy districts stones were laid on top of the thatch and firewood, dried vegetables and other winter supplies were piled or hung close to the walls under the wide eaves. The homes of more prosperous country folk sometimes had roofs of gray tile and a coat of lighter plaster over the clay walls. They also had the added privacy of a fence or wall which ordinary farmers did not enjoy.[9]

But whether the house belonged to a rich family or a poor one, and whether it was in the city or country, its floor was raised about two feet off the ground and covered with padded straw matting, and the front of it had not a small door with a lock and key but a very wide opening which could be closed by paper-covered lattices sliding in grooves, or by light panels of wood at night and in bad weather.

In entering a typical middle-class house one did not withdraw from nature and the outside world ; rather the world outside the door was seen as part of the dwelling ; the moon and grasses and singing insects were its decorations. The interior with its natural wood ceilings and pillars, its straw-covered floor, and only one hanging-scroll landscape painting and a few flowers to ornament it, was simply a refined and sheltered corner of nature itself. The quality of household materials varied with the economic condition of the family, but the quantity displayed at any one time was invariably the same. The desired effect was not one of accumulated possessions, but rather one of long and fond use and perfect harmonizing of unassertive elements. Glaring and conspicuous furnishings were carefully avoided by housewives of good taste.

In addition to their natural simplicity and modesty, Japanese homes also showed an amazing adaptability and economy. In fact, that refinement which is generally thought of as typically Japanese esthetic taste is undoubtedly due in large measure to the prevailing poverty of the country and the people. Built with the least possible labor from readily available materials, their houses were designed to give great flexibility. Any room might become sitting room, bedroom or dining room, and any number of persons could be accommodated, for chairs and beds were simply cushions spread on the floor when needed and piled up in the closet at other times. Dining tables were individual lacquer trays likewise placed on the floor. Heating was by small charcoal fires in jardiniere-like containers carried where needed. Water was sometimes led into the house from a stream through bamboo pipes but more often was drawn from a well. Lighting in Tokugawa times was by candle and oil lamp. Instead of bowl and pitcher bathing arrangements, Japanese from very early times have had special bathrooms where a large quantity of water was heated in a tub with an attached stove and where they could splash freely. They were more free in their nightly bath than at any other time of the day ; then only could they indulge in the luxury of being purely themselves and doing just as they pleased without giving thought to formalities.

Tokugawa education for both boys and girls discouraged all sense of individuality. According to the teaching of the Buddhist temple schools the less one was a willful individual and the more one lost oneself in the harmony of the universe, the better. In the official Confucian schools boys were taught chiefly the importance of conventionally prescribed modes of behavior for maintaining right relationships. They were never a unit in themselves, but always a part of some larger unit which demanded their loyalty — the family, the school, the town. So long as they acted for the good of the larger unit they were respectable members of society, but if they rebelled against existing conditions they would bring disgrace upon their superiors, and rather than do this it was often considered proper to commit suicide. In the private schools where girls went for instruction from the daughters of well-known men educators the textbook was "The Great Teaching for Women," [10] which expounded chiefly the virtues of sweet obedience to parents, husband and ruler, controlled speech, gentleness, amicability under all circumstances, constancy, faithfulness without jealousy, and also frugality and thrift.

The religion of the people was closely associated with this same lack of individualism, the same sense of being part of a larger unit, of being bound in personal relationship with the great spirits of the universe, of the past and of the future. They were not so much concerned with sin or saving souls as with living everyday lives worthy of their

ancestry, knowing reality and being able to face with serenity any experience which life might bring. This knowledge
and power was to be achieved by intuition rather than
through theological exposition, sermons or lengthy prayers.
The profoundest Buddhist teachings were expressed in seventeen-syllable poems — no words can explain what water is,
you must stick your finger in it — or in paintings of a few
brush strokes, clouds across the moon, a man in a tiny boat
on an expansive sea, a patch of green grass emerging from
melting snow. The true spirit of Shinto was not to be
found in books but to be breathed in the fragrance of the
century-old evergreens that surrounded and towered over
every shrine.

Christianity had been almost completely stamped out in
the early seventeenth century, and the Dutch, who were allowed to continue trading on the island of Deshima, had
carefully avoided religious controversy. Still the Jesuits
and Franciscans left their influence. They had shaken the
confidence of Japan in India and China, on whom she had
been culturally dependent for over a thousand years. The
saints of India and the sages of China were no longer to be
as faithfully relied upon. Obviously, the saints of the
southern barbarians were also powerful and good, and their
teachers had shown up many of the inadequacies of Chinese science and learning. When the nation's doors were
closed, many Japanese thinkers, therefore, turned their attention away from Chinese and Buddhist studies and directed their efforts toward the study of their native cult and
literature.

Tokugawa Mitsukuni, a grandson of Iyeyasu's and the

head of the Mito branch of the family, had read in the introduction to a forty-volume history of Japan, written by the famous Education Commissioner Hayashi who was his teacher at an official Confucian school, the theory that the remote ancestors of the imperial family were not deities but flesh-and-blood descendants of southern Chinese adventurers who, very early, had found their way to Japan. This idea was so offensive to Mitsukuni that he resolved to keep this book in obscurity and to make up for it by writing another which would avoid any disputation over ancestry by simply beginning with the victorious first emperor, Jimmu-Tenno, but which would justify loyalty to the imperial house of Japan. Though many of his family and friends tried to discourage him he persisted in setting aside eighty thousand koku of rice a year to pay for his undertaking, and with hundreds of assistants made a nation-wide search for historical documents and other materials from shrines, temples and all possible sources. Not even the outline of the "Dai Nihon-shi" was completed during his lifetime, and it was more than a century after his death that the first part, one hundred volumes, was actually published, but the work continued to be carried on, and in 1905 was finally completed. Hayashi's history, still kept in manuscript was published in 1921.

To help in his colossal historic enterprise Mitsukuni urged a Buddhist priest well-versed in Sanskrit to carry on a study of that earliest collection of Japanese poems called Manyoshu. During the five unsettled centuries since the fall of the Heian court this anthology was forgotten and there was no one in early Tokugawa times who could

read the archaic style in which it was written. But once interest in it was revived, scholars went on further back in
Japanese writings to the Kojiki, the first history completed
in the early days of Nara. And there they discovered or
thought they discovered the true character and psychology
of their ancestors, and the way they lived before they began to copy Chinese and Buddhist ways.

The man who did the most important work in this field
was named Motoori. Motoori was a merchant's son, but
since his father had lost a fortune his mother thought the
boy should follow a different career, and so she sent him to
Kyoto to study medicine. There he made many friends
among young Fujiwaras and other courtiers, who though
very reduced in circumstances still continued to live in the
ancient capital and to carry on their classical traditions.
And when Motoori returned to his native place to practice
he had more customers for his literary knowledge than for
his medicine. Instead of a great doctor, Motoori became
the greatest scholar of Japanese literature, carrying the
torch of thorough and conscientious research into the darkness that shrouded the early culture of Japan.[11]

Just as at the Nikko memorial to Iyeyasu one comes first
upon the brilliant splendor of the shrine and then after a
long climb up mossy stone steps overshadowed by cryptomerias comes finally to the simple tomb where lie the great
hero's remains, so Motoori came first upon the brilliant
splendor of the Genji Monogatari and other Heian court
literature, but after thirty years of painstaking study arrived at the simple stories of the early emperors as told in
the candid, unembroidered style of the Kojiki. If the fact

was that an emperor while out hunting was chased by a wild boar and saved his life only by climbing a tree, then the Kojiki stated that the emperor saved his life only by climbing a tree. According to the Nihongi, however, which was written a few years later with a flourish of Chinese literature to impress the Chinese court, the emperor ordered a follower to kill the boar, but seeing the follower afraid to shoot an arrow himself kicked the animal to death and would have killed the follower had not the empress objected, whereupon he forgave the follower and rejoiced in the kindness of his wife.

The results of his studies of the Kojiki, Motoori wrote out in his own superb hand, and one of his students volunteered to cut the whole work, just as it was written, on cherry wood blocks so that it might be printed and made available for other scholars. This attracted great attention in intellectual circles and there was a movement to return to the natural and real, to direct action unhampered by bombastic Chinese moralizing, to the "Yamato heart" which was good by nature.

After Motoori's day, as a result of the fiery teachings of one of his followers, who spoke and wrote in simple terms which everyone could understand, this movement assumed a religious and political aspect and was known as Neo-Shinto. Neo-Shinto extolled the virtues of the imperial family and emphasized the desirability of making the divine emperor, whom military rulers, from the twelfth century on, had forced into the dim background, once more the actual ruler, the center of authority and enlightenment. This movement, coupled with the discontent of an oppressed and suppressed populace, and the eagerness of the Dutch scholars to burst the bonds of isolation, constituted a strong internal threat to the Tokugawa regime.

Then Commodore Perry steamed into Yedo Bay with four United States gunboats prepared for action. Beacon fires spread the alarm from hill to hill, and people ran to and fro in great confusion. Petty officials came in little boats and warned the intruders to leave at once, but instead of withdrawing, the American commodore approached still closer to the capital of the shogun and insisted that someone of suitable rank be sent to receive the letter which he brought from President Fillmore.

Realizing full well the weakness of both their finances and their coast defenses, the shogunate used every scheme they could devise to evade a direct response ; Perry, however, maintained an attitude of polite but positively unyielding formality, and at last a special pavilion was constructed for a meeting. At the appointed time, with five thousand samurai and several local officials ranged in ranks to watch the proceedings, the commodore stepped ashore attended by three hundred marines and a private guard of two huge and handsome negroes. In profound silence the governor of Uraga received the vellum letter in its box of rosewood with gold fittings, and the ceremony concluded without a word being spoken. Soon after, Perry, promising to return again in the spring with a larger squadron for a favorable reply to the President's request for "friendship, commerce, a supply of coal and provisions and protection for shipwrecked people," steamed out of Yedo Bay.[12]

Then the shogunate, which had never before deigned to

consult any but the most important daimyos, distributed copies of a translation of President Fillmore's letter to all the daimyos and invited their opinions. The daimyos went home and discussed the matter with their samurai. Those who had studied with the Hollanders in Deshima recommended the opening of Japanese ports, but the large majority thought back to the aggressiveness of the Spanish

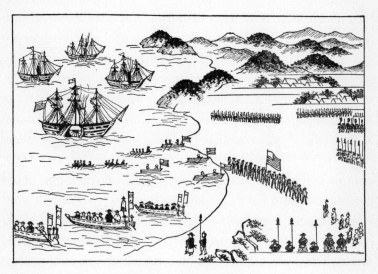

Perry's landing at Uraga

and Portuguese and the trouble they had caused and decided that it was better to keep "barbarians" out of Japan.

With "thank money" from Yedo and Osaka merchants, the shogunate started a cannon foundry and a ship-building program to prepare themselves against the return of the United States fleet, realizing full well, however, the futility of their efforts. But it also occurred to them that by expanding foreign trade and keeping a government monopoly on all transactions they might be able to strengthen their economic position. Since the copper mines which had supplied their chief medium of exchange were almost exhausted, they studied various methods of carrying on trade. The visit of several Russian boats to Nagasaki during Perry's absence only helped to convince them of the inevitable.

Perry returned in February 1854, with ten ships instead of four, armed with two hundred and fifty guns, came ashore with a brass band and great parade and made presents to the highest officials of whiskey and champagne, standard literary works, rifles, revolvers, clocks, perfume, a sewing machine, a telegraph and a toy locomotive. The telegraph was a great marvel; officials in their best kimonos strained their necks and eyes to detect something going on in the wires. With frightened laughter dignified men rode on top of the toy locomotive and railroad car as it went round and round its circular track. The pictures of the United States' war with Mexico in two books which they received struck real terror into the hearts of the rulers of Japan, which had had over two hundred years of peace. Remembering the two monstrous negroes who had served as Perry's guard, however, they must have enjoyed being able to send with the presents they gave in return two enormous wrestlers, an almost unbelievable variety of Japanese, weighing three or four hundred pounds.

After a month of negotiations a treaty was at last drawn up and signed, with copies of it in four languages, English, Dutch, Japanese and Chinese. It provided for :

peace and friendship between the two countries,
the opening of Shimoda and Hakodate to American ships and
the supplying of necessary provisions by Japanese officers,
relief of shipwrecked people,
the freedom of Americans in the ports, subject to just laws,
careful deliberation in transacting business,
trade in local ports subject to local regulations,
a "most favored nation" clause,
the residence of United States consuls at Shimoda,
the exchange of ratifications within eighteen months.

Perry's men and Japanese wrestlers

Satisfied with the results of his carefully planned expedition, Perry proceeded to inspect the port of Shimoda to the west of Yedo Bay and to make a trip up to Hakodate, the chief port of the northern island Hokkaido, in the region frequented by New Bedford whalers. Before returning to the United States he also steamed down to the Loochoo islands and arranged with the daimyo of Satsuma in western Kyushu for an open port there.

The Satsuma fief was rather out of range of shogunate activities and its leaders had continued to carry on a certain amount of trade and to exert a certain political control over Loochoo even during the Tokugawa isolation. This made them oppose any expansion of the shogunate's trade monopoly and join with other daimyos, who for various reasons were against opening the country to barbarians, not because they wished to keep the country closed, but in order to embarrass the Tokugawas and further their own position as leaders of the nation.

When Townsend Harris, the first United States consul to Japan, arrived in Shimoda in 1856 it was a sorry place. Most of the buildings had just been destroyed in an earthquake, and he had to put up in a few rooms in an old temple ; the annual ceremony of "stamping on the cross" which had been kept up for over two centuries to prevent any revival of Christianity had just been officially discontinued, but the teaching of "the pernicious doctrine" was still strictly forbidden, and people were urged to have no intercourse whatsoever with foreigners. The common people who constituted over eighty per cent of the population had nothing to say in the matter. They continued patiently to cultivate their little patches of rice and tend their little shops, but daimyos and samurai, especially from the southwestern seacoasts of Japan, kept charging the shogunate with incompetence and cowardice and took up the slogan "Sonno joi," "Honor the emperor, expel the barbarians."

For two years Consul-General Harris tried in vain to negotiate a treaty allowing the United States unrestricted trade in Japan. He told how the world had been changed by the introduction of steam ; how Japan, if she did not do so voluntarily, would be forced to abandon her exclusion policy ; how by simply permitting her people to exercise their ingenuity and industry she might soon become a great and powerful nation ; how a moderate tax on commerce would soon give her a large revenue by which she might support a respectable navy ; that it was better to yield to a consul-general than to an armed fleet as China had had to do, and so on.[13]

Finally Harris discovered that the shogunate was delaying the signing of the treaty until they could get the approval of the emperor at Kyoto. This was the first inkling he had had of the existence of a ruler other than the shogun, and it put a different light on the situation. The moment the emperor's approval was received the daimyos would withdraw their opposition, shogunate officials assured him. And when Harris inquired what they would do if the emperor refused his consent, they answered promptly and decisively that the government had determined not to receive any objections from the emperor.

In this, however, they had not calculated well. All the shogun's rivals and enemies had rallied around the emperor and drafted a document, the purport of which was that the imperial mind was gravely concerned over the transactions with the United States, for they constituted a dire menace to the prestige of the nation and involved dangers of a most serious nature which jeopardized permanent peace.

This was the beginning of the end for the Tokugawa shogunate. They could postpone but they could not prevent the signing of trade treaties with Western nations. Harris's demands were repeated by British, French and Russian officials, all clamoring for similar rights, with gunboats to render their demands more effective. The ports of Yokohama, Nagasaki and Hakodate were opened for trade with these countries in 1859 in accordance with treaties which the shogunate signed.

CHAPTER XIV

THE SECOND GREAT CHANGE
(LATE NINETEENTH CENTURY)

YOKOHAMA in 1859 was a swampy little village of about a hundred houses, except for one hilly strip, cut off from the mainland at high tide. Because of its resemblance to Deshima the foreigners with new trade treaties objected to being settled there, but the shogunate went ahead with the construction of a causeway and the preparation of the ground for building. Soon shops and storehouses, stone jetties, warehouses and a custom house were ready for occupancy and the newcomers could do nothing but move in. In less than two years the foreign population included fifty-five British, thirty-eight Americans, twenty Dutch, eleven French and two Portuguese — one hundred and twenty-six in all ; in five years it had increased to six thousand, had three British bankers, several foreign doctors and civil engineers.[1]

Imports consisted largely of sugar, woollens, cottons and liquor. For exports the Japanese were rather hard put to it ; they had so little that foreigners wanted and could so ill afford to lose any of their copper, gold and silver. They offered, however, copper, isinglass, vegetable wax, tea, tobacco, fish and oil. And though in the flourishing days of Nagasaki they had always imported silk, when they found

how the foreigners valued it they began to produce it themselves and developed the silk trade into one of their greatest sources of revenue.

Approximately eighty acres is said to have been the area
of the foreign settlement in 1865, but already it included
five hotels and a Catholic chapel, a social club and sports
field, twenty-four grog shops, bowling and billiard parlors,
a milliner, French baker, livery stable and sea-bathing establishment.   There was a volunteer fire brigade with three
engines, a race track and a park on the bluff, where a missionary had planted American geraniums and where army
and navy bands gave public concerts.

The settlement's first newspaper appeared November 23,
1861, and was called Japan Herald.   A single sheet
folded to make four pages, it carried nothing but adver-
tisements on the front.   O. H. Baker, Ship and Family
Chandler, carried the largest of these in Volume 1, Number 1, and begged to inform the inhabitants of Yokohama
that he kept constantly on hand to offer at the lowest re-
muncrative prices everything from hats and caps to boots
and shoes, and from soap to "American solidified milk."
"Lea and Perrins' " celebrated "Worcestershire Sauce" was
given a prominent place inside, along with carefully detailed reports of the prices of imports and exports in both
the Yokohama and Nagasaki markets, an account of a fire
which destroyed several hundred houses in the native quarter of the city and the "Latest European News."   Under
this head appeared the following :

The Secessionist President, Jefferson Davis, is reported to be
dead.

Garibaldi is reported to have declined the Commander-in-chiefship of the Federal Government of America. The Federal Government is preparing to send a large force down the Mississippi from Missouri.

In consequence of the state of the cotton market the Lancashire manufactories are now generally working short time.

Baron Ricasoli is said to have proposed compensation to the pope for the surrender of his temporal authority.

Spain, with France and England, has determined on a military intervention in Mexico.

A project of marriage is reported between the Prince of Wales and a Danish princess.

On another page we read, "The next outward mail leaves Shanghai on Monday next. The following on the 7th December arriving at London via Marseilles January 26th." Three columns of notifications from the British consul-general gave warning to British subjects that they were not to ride or drive in such a way as to endanger others, not to discharge firearms except at designated places, nor go in pursuit of game without written permission. Neither were British subjects to intrude into Japanese establishments without invitation, or to assault or offer any violence to Japanese officials. Furthermore, notice was given that since it was neither safe nor expedient in the present state of the country to stray into villages and towns at a distance and pass the night away from the settlement, such practice was a serious cause of anxiety to the shogunate authorities and should not be indulged in.

The attitudes of various classes of Japanese toward foreign diplomats and traders differed widely. Townsend Harris, for example, wrote in his diary in 1856, "The people are of genial disposition and are evidently inclined toward intercourse with foreigners, but the despotic rule of the country and the terror they have of their so-called inflexible laws forbids them to express their wishes." He saw in the common people such cleanliness, simplicity and honesty, frugality and contentment as he had seen in no other country. And when later, by his own dignified conduct, he had gained the respect of government officials and was received by them in Yedo he found that most careful preparations had been made for his visit. The road to the shogun's capital, though lined with curious spectators all along the way, was kept free of other traffic and especially swept for his procession. As was their custom when some great dignitary of their own country passed, the watching crowds instead of shouting madly kept reverent silence and bowed heads. The quarters prepared for his entertainment within the castle walls, though they had never held such furniture before, were provided with chairs, tables and a bed copied from Harris's own. Even a bathroom and water closet, such as he was accustomed to, were provided for the American consul so that he might be entirely comfortable and favorably impressed by his hosts. Their nervousness, inexperience in Western ways, and consequent vacillation and delaying continually annoyed him, however, and their polite efforts to avoid yielding to all of his requests and yet not give offense he frequently condemned as lying.

When traders began to come in numbers many complained at first because Japanese merchants were so hesitant to do business by themselves without referring to the officials who had been in charge of all dealings during the isolation. But soon their complaint was that the Japanese had their eyes as wide open to trade and commerce and making cent for cent as any other nation, and would buy no wooden nutmegs.

The group that made real trouble were the conservative samurai. The earthquake which destroyed fifteen thousand houses soon after Perry's departure they said, was, like the epidemic which cost so many lives after the introduction of Buddhism in the sixth century, chastening by the deities of the land. They looked upon the foreigners as invaders who had begun by taking a few ports and would soon over-run the country. Though swordsmanship had gone very much out of fashion in Tokugawa times, a number of samurai revived the ancient art and felt they were doing the nation a great service by using it not only on the barbarians but also on their own leaders who, they felt, were weakly betraying them. Dozens of assaults and assassinations were perpetrated by these overzealous patriots, and enormous sums in consequence were paid as indemnities by the government. A group of them, ordered to rip open their stomachs for having killed some French sailors, expressed in several poems the satisfaction they found in sacrificing their own lives for the sake of their country. Perhaps they should not be blamed for feeling as they did, for even Townsend Harris just after hoisting the first consular flag ever seen in the empire wrote in his diary, "Grim reflections, ominous of change, undoubted beginning of the end. Query, if for real good of Japan?"

The island nation was in a grave situation indeed. Two

centuries of peace had weakened its military defenses, skill and spirit almost to the point of extinction, and now it was threatened by navies representing the fruits of two centuries of continual conflict and conquest. Two centuries of isolation had done nothing to develop assurance or ability in international diplomacy in the Japanese, and here they were faced by diplomats of world experience clamoring for treaties. Two centuries of feudalism had withered the budding sense of national unity, weakened the hold of the shogunate and unaccustomed people to change, and now the very strongest of the Western nations, as different from Japan in every way as they could possibly be, were challenging Japan as a nation. No other people had ever survived such a test. But the Japanese combined in their nature the triple characteristics of sun and sea and mountain.[2]

One of the most representative leaders in the Second Great Change and the one who probably did more than any other individual in making Japan what it is today was Fukuzawa Yukichi. His autobiography embodies so well the changes which took place in Japan during this transition period that it is quoted here at considerable length.[3] Fukuzawa's theme was : "Young men, poverty and ignorance are hobbling your country ; master Western science, make money, free her." This was a complete change from the attitude of the old samurai who were inclined to spurn moneymaking as beneath their dignity and who valued honor and name above all else. "Independence and self respect" was the motto of his life. When Perry came to Japan, Fukuzawa Yukichi was a poor country boy of nineteen, but versatile and virile. From hearing the talk of the samurai about the need for national defense he resolved to go to Nagasaki and study the science of Western gunnery. To study Western science seriously, his brother told him, one must be able to read the books published in Holland with letters printed sideways, and this he resolved to do. The next time his brother had business in Nagasaki he went along and began his study of the ABC's. They seemed very odd looking indeed and it took a full three days to learn the twenty-six letters.

After staying for some time in Nagasaki in a gunnery expert's home and doing all sorts of odd jobs in return for his food and lodging, circumstances took him to Osaka and there he began to study with a doctor named Ogata who had a school in his home.

No other group of students in Japan at that time could compare with us in energy and hard work. For a whole year I had not used a pillow to sleep on but had been studying without regard to day or night, rest or relaxation. I would be reading all day and when night came I did not think of going to bed. When tired I would lean over my little desk or stretch out on the floor, resting my head on the raised alcove floor. All my friends lived in this way. When we happened to have some wine at suppertime I would drink it and go to sleep. I would wake up about ten o'clock and, sitting at my little desk, read on through the night. In the early morning hours when I heard the commotions of boiling rice in the kitchen I took that for a signal to fall asleep again. Just in time for breakfast I would wake up and go out to the bath house for a morning plunge. Then on coming back I would fall to at my morning rice and to reading again.

The only Dutch texts the school owned were a few on medicine and physical sciences, in all about ten volumes. Each student was therefore obliged to copy every word of the one precious copy. If a student copied ten pages of a dictionary a day he could earn more than his cost of living.

There were then no steel pens in use in Japan and our only paper was the ordinary coarse Japanese kind, meant for brush writing. Some students used to rub this paper with a porcelain bowl to smooth it first and then copy Western writing with a fine brush, but most of us soon learned to size the paper with alum coating and then to use the quill pen. There were several stores that sold birds' quills, usually of cranes or ducks, cut about three inches long, quite cheap. Fishermen were said to use them for catching bonito. When shaved down the quills served for pens very well. For ink — no foreign ink had been brought in — we rubbed the native ink blocks with water and kept the liquid in a pot or sometimes we soaked a piece of cotton in it for ease in carrying.

As this was the only way to have foreign texts we became quite skilled in writing while some friend read the original. Though we were all really good friends, the older ones helping the new students by explaining texts and answering questions, we never helped each other with class preparations. No one ever thought of being so cowardly as to take help in preparing his required work, no matter how difficult. Then each student had to depend on his own ability with the grammars and the one big dictionary the school possessed.

Of course, at that time there were no examples of industrial machinery. A steam engine could not be seen in the whole of Japan, nor any apparatus for chemical experiments, but when we learned something of chemistry and machinery we wanted to try it out. We managed to make chloric acid to use in plating iron with tin when no tin craftsman in Japan could plate anything but copper or bronze with tin by using pine pitch. We tried to make iodine from seaweed and worked till we were black with smoke, but without success. Then we tried ammonium chloride. We learned that horse hoof would serve the purpose. So we bought some fragments of it from a tortoise-shell ware store ; it was sometimes used for fertilizer.

We covered the hoof with a layer of clay in an earthenware jar and put it over a fire. A smelly vapor came out which we condensed in an earthenware pipe. Our experiment was going very well and the condensed vapor was dripping freely, but the stench was terrible. Our clothes became so saturated with the smell that when we went to the bath house in the evening the street dogs howled at us. Then we tried the experiment naked, but our skins absorbed the smell. We endured it without complaint but the neighbors objected and the servants wailed that they could not eat their dinner on account of the sickening gas.

One day a new text in physical science recently translated from English to Dutch was loaned to us for two days. All that we knew about electricity then had been gleaned from fragmentary mention in Dutch readers. But here was a full explanation based on the experiments of Faraday even with the diagram of an electric cell. We decided to copy the chapter on electricity — one hundred and fifty pages with diagrams. When the time came to return it we all handled the book affectionately in turn and gave it a sad leave taking as if we were parting with a parent. When we heard it had cost eighty ryo ($80.) [4] we were dumbfounded. Ogata's students soon became the best informed men on electricity in the entire country.

In Yedo there were constant demands for Western knowledge from government offices and feudal nobility, and anyone able to read and translate foreign books was rewarded. Osaka, however, was a city of merchants devoted to internal commerce, who looked down with contempt on students of Dutch. There was no living in it for us, but we knew that we alone possessed the key to knowledge of the great European civilization. However ill fed or poorly clothed we were, we knew we had something beyond the reach of princes. We were proud of our hard work.

Of course we were all for free intercourse with Western countries, but there were few among us who took really serious interest in that problem. The only subject that bore our con-

stant attack was Chinese medicine ; and we thus came to dislike everything that had any connection with Chinese culture.
Our general opinion was that we should rid our country of the
influences of the Chinese altogether.   We ridiculed students
of Chinese medicine whenever we met them.   "Look at
them," one of us would begin, "they think they are learning
something ; they listen to those crazy lectures of their master,
but he simply repeats the same old mouldy theories handed
down for how many centuries !"

In 1858 Fukuzawa left Osaka and went up to Yedo, and
the next year the port of Yokohama was opened to foreign
trade.

When I went to Yokohama for sight seeing I found to my
great disappointment that I could not talk with the merchants
nor read any of the signboards.   I had been striving with all
my powers for many years to learn Dutch and now English
seemed sure to be the language of the future.   So I determined to study English, but there were no teachers.

He therefore bought a book of Dutch-English conversa-
tion and after a while managed to get an English dictionary and one friend to study with him.   They tried to meet
all the shipwrecked fishermen they heard about who had
been picked up by foreign ships, and asked them to pronounce English words.   Soon they realized that English
was not wholly different from Dutch and that their knowledge of Dutch could be applied to English.

In 1859 on the advice of Townsend Harris it was decided that a Japanese embassy should be sent to Washington and that they would go on an American ship, but the
shogunate also wanted to send an escort ship across the

Pacific, manned entirely by Japanese officers and crew. A Japanese ship was therefore dispatched from Yedo in January, 1860, ahead of the envoy's steamer, and on this Fukuzawa managed to take passage.

For a whole month we saw nothing but waves and clouds and one sailboat said to be carrying Chinese workmen to America. It was like being in jail and having earthquakes day and night.

But after five weeks they landed in California, and thousands lined the shores to see these strange newcomers.

There were many confusing and embarrassing moments, for we were quite ignorant of the customs and habits of American life. When we were taken to a hotel we noticed all over the floors carpets and rugs such as only wealthy Japanese could buy from importers' shops at so much a square inch to make purses and tobacco pouches with. It was astounding to see a whole room covered with it — and our hosts in the shoes they had worn on the street walking on this costly fabric. We followed them in our hemp sandals.

Before leaving Japan I was an independent soul, a carefree student fearing nothing, but on arriving in America I suddenly became shy, self-conscious and blushing. The contrast was funny even to myself.

One evening we were invited to a dancing party. When we arrived we saw ladies and gentlemen hopping about the room together and could not quite make out what they were doing. It struck us as terribly funny but we knew it would be rude to laugh.

At one dinner given for us a whole pig was brought onto the table roasted — head, legs, tail and all. We at once thought of a fairy tale of a cruel witch who indulged in gruesome feasts. Still, it tasted very good ! On taking leave our host and hostess kindly offered us horses to ride home on. This pleased us, for a chance to ride horseback again was a relief. We touched whip to the horses and trotted back to our quarters. The Americans stood and watched us with evident surprise.

I was impressed by the enormous waste of iron everywhere. In garbage piles, on the seashore, old tin cans, empty cans, broken tools. Why, in Yedo after a fire there would be hundreds of poor people looking for nails in the charred wood, so valuable was metal in Japan. And we had to pay fifty cents for twenty or thirty oysters — in Japan they would have cost only a cent or two.

One day I asked a gentleman where the descendants of George Washington might be. He replied, "I think there is a woman who is directly descended from Washington. I don't know where she is, but I think I heard she was married." This was a great shock. I could not help feeling that the family of Washington should be treated with great reverence.

When he got back to Japan, Fukuzawa found that the shogun's chancellor who had signed the trade treaties with the foreign powers had been assassinated, and the cry, "Expel the barbarians" was everywhere.

Nevertheless, he brought out a dictionary of English which was to serve as a foundation for a series of later books, and when in 1862, while America was involved in Civil War, the British offered to take an official Japanese embassy to Europe by way of Singapore and Suez, he was appointed to go along as interpreter. With the allowance given him for expenses he bought many books in London, the first English books to be imported into Japan and the first to which Japanese students had free access.

The anti-foreign samurai, however, made things as difficult as possible for such students; they thought that scholars who read foreign books and taught foreign culture were traitors, trying to mislead the people and make way for the Westerners to exploit Japan. But clamoring and persecuting samurai, notwithstanding, the shogunate officials were in direct contact with the foreign powers, and were obliged to carry on intercourse willy-nilly. And the Satsuma leaders, after a disastrous encounter with British warships, entertained profound respect for the technical development of the West. Facing facts realistically, they became very willing to learn from England, and imported three English sugar factories, a foundry and machine shop and a cotton mill with English engineers to teach them methods of operation. They also added to their Loochoo trading fleet several European-style boats.

Most leaders came to feel that perhaps, after all, intercourse with the West would not be such a bad thing if only they could manage to preserve their national integrity. This, however, they realized could never be done so long as there were factions within the country itself. Only by presenting a strongly united front to the demands of Western nations could Japan hope to survive. Tokugawas and anti-Tokugawas both began to feel that the logic of the situation required the restoration of the imperial dignity. The prestige of the imperial house in ancient times owed much to the fact that it alone was officially recognized by the Chinese court. Though shoguns had later been authorized to take over the internal administration of the country they had had very little to do with overseas affairs. Both Ashikaga Yoshimitsu and Hideyoshi, it is true, in consequence of their relations with China, had been designated "King of Japan," but the Tokugawa shogunate had never felt easy about assuming the responsibility for foreign diplomacy.

In 1867 the old emperor who did not want foreigners stepping on the Land of the Gods died, and his fifteen-year-old son succeeded to the throne with the support and ready advice of four southwestern seacoast daimyos.[5]   Soon afterward the shogun tendered his resignation :

"My ancestor received more confidence and favor from the court than any of his predecessors, and his descendants have succeeded him for more than two hundred years. Though I fill the same office, almost all the acts of the administration are far from perfect, and I confess it with shame that the present unsatisfactory condition of affairs is due to my short-comings and incompetence. Now that foreign intercourse becomes daily more extensive, unless the government is di-rected from one central authority, the foundations of the state will fall to pieces. If, however, the old order of things be changed and the administrative authority be restored to the imperial court, and if national deliberations be conducted on an extensive scale, and if the empire be supported by the ef-forts of the whole people, then the empire will be able to maintain its rank and dignity among the nations of the earth. Although I have allowed all the feudal lords to state their views without reservation, yet it is, I believe, my highest duty to realize the national ideal by giving up entirely my rule over the land." [6]

There were repercussions of this for several months. The shogun himself was ready to fight when, after peace-fully resigning, he found that he was treated as an enemy of the imperial house by the four southwestern seacoast daimyos, and that they stepped right into the place which he had vacated. His loyal supporters were not willing to give in easily either. The commander of the Tokugawa navy even attempted to set up a new government on the northern island, Hokkaido, in defiance of the new powers behind the throne. But the new leaders were well prepared and qualified for their position.

Because of their geographic location they had always been in closer touch with foreigners than the northeastern daimyos had been; first with the Korean countries and China, then with the Portuguese, Spaniards and Dutch, and now with the English. When the sixteenth-century hero, Hideyoshi, had managed to subdue them by employing Buddhist spies, the Satsuma clan had angrily resolved to do away with all Buddhist centers of idle, extravagant priests and the effect of this had been healthy, in the economic sense at least. While in many other parts of the country samurai had been detached from the land and formed a great body of decadent unemployed, in the southwestern provinces they had worked as farmers and kept up their military discipline even in the years of peace, for they belonged to the "outside daimyos" and never knew when they might want to defend themselves against Tokugawa encroachments. The education and well-being of the people generally had also been carefully watched. As a result, the leaders of Satsuma, Choshu, Hizen and Tosa were able to carry on the Second Great Change with remarkably little friction.

The new regime was designated Meiji, Enlightened Government. Even before the enthronement ceremonies for the youthful sovereign were held he had given audience to foreign envoys and issued an edict granting foreigners full protection with capital punishment for offenders. This was liberalism, sudden and extreme. The idea of the "Son of Heaven" face to face with common Westerners was shocking even for many of the Satsuma clan to think of, but it was quite in line with the philosophy which one of their number had boldly proclaimed for the new government.

"Since the middle ages," he said, and paid with his life for saying it, "our Emperor has lived behind a screen and never trod the earth. Nothing of what went on outside his screen ever penetrated the sacred ear. The imperial residence was profoundly secluded and, naturally, unlike the outer world. Only a few court nobles were allowed to approach the throne, a practice most opposed to the principles of heaven. While it is the first duty of man to respect his superior, if he reveres that superior too highly he neglects his duty, while a breach is created between the Sovereign and his subjects who are unable to convey their wants to him. This vicious practice has been common in all ages. But now let pompous etiquette be set aside and simplicity become our first object." [7]

Economic considerations undoubtedly did much to make this philosophy an acceptable platform, for the imperial court, a few days before the announcement of the new regime, it is stated, had only twenty to thirty days' stock of rice and very little money. In accordance with the aims of the new regime, the enthronement ceremony [8] itself, which had been based on Chinese customs of the T'ang Dynasty and in use for a thousand years, was now reformed. Chi-

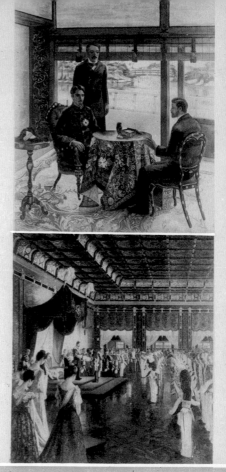

MEIJI MEMORIAL HALL MURALS

PERIAL PROCESSION TO DIET BUILDING, 1937

ROOM IN MODERN JAPANESE INN

CHILDREN ON SCHOOL PLAYGROUND, TOKYO

nese costumes and decorations were abandoned, and Shinto ritual offerings were substituted for the burning of incense. A great globe map of the world was prominently displayed.

Kyoto also was involved in the great change. It was considered to be too out of the way a place for the Meiji capital. Osaka was proposed as a substitute because most of the nation's wealth was concentrated there, and the cooperation of the rich merchants was much desired. The boy emperor was taken to Osaka on a visit and given a chance to review the warships of various clans lined up two miles off shore. But since foreign governments were accustomed to think of Yedo as the center of power, and since Yedo's neighboring port, Yokohama, was flourishing so rapidly, the Tokugawa properties in these two cities were confiscated and the imperial residence was moved to Yedo. Its name was then changed to Tokyo which means Eastern Capital.

The imperial cortege left for Tokyo on the Great Eastern Sea Road accompanied by three thousand officials. On this journey, which required twenty-two days, the emperor had the first opportunity of his life to observe the regular activities and living conditions of farmers and common people. He enjoyed stopping the procession and watching the farmers harvesting their rice.

Just before the New Year he was taken back to Kyoto for his wedding ceremony. An imperial messenger delivered a dress and sword as imperial wedding gifts to the selected lady on the appointed day, and she proceeded to the palace in an ox-drawn cart. There seated on a platform she was honored with a repast provided by the court, and by secretary conveyed her respects to her future consort. A special messenger then proceeded to the emperor's presence and announced the installation of the empress and the ceremony was ended.

On his second journey to Tokyo the emperor stopped to pay his respects at the Isé Shrine dedicated to his divine ancestress Amaterasu. This was also an innovation prompted by his Neo-Shinto supporters to impress upon the people reverence for the founder of the imperial house. Popularization of the emperor was not to be carried too far. It was the theory of divine descent that had preserved for him the throne and which would continue to bind the Japanese nation together as a family. A strong Shinto revival was therefore promoted, while Buddhist priests were stripped of their privileges and Buddhist temples throughout the country were ransacked and desecrated. Statues small enough to carry were stolen by marauders for the valuable metal in them, and gold leaf was scraped off wherever it was found.

The new government was designed to give the nation the strength of unity. What unity had been achieved thus far, however, was more sentimental than real. There were still two hundred and seventy-six daimyos with as many separate fiefs. Each daimyo commanded his own samurai, and several of them had navies; each exercised the right of legislation over his own domains and regulated the collection and expenditure of revenues according to his own ideas. Not more than one sixth of the land of Japan had reverted to imperial control as a result of the shogunate's downfall. To make the government really effective some means had to be devised for giving the sovereign supreme command of all armaments, armies and navies, for investing him with authority to promulgate laws for the whole land, and, most important perhaps of all, for creating a central treasury.

By 1869 the four southwestern seacoast daimyos had most of the offices of the new government filled by their own men, and most of the policies were entirely of their own making. The Tokugawas had been allowed to retain three of their ancestral estates, but for some time were given no part in public affairs.

Though a really stable government was not achieved until two decades later, immediate steps were taken for the centralization of power. First a group of the strongest daimyos voluntarily offered to return their feudal rights to the court and all but seventeen of the rest followed suit.[9] (This was not unlike the reform for which Fujiwara Kamatari and Prince Naka had set an example by giving up their own lands in 645.) These and the Tokugawa fiefs were converted into seventy-two prefectures and the daimyos were rewarded for their cooperation with positions in the new government and with government bonds which were negotiable as capital for undertaking new businesses and industrial enterprises.

The method of dealing with the land and farmers was very simple indeed. Though theoretically it was claimed that all the land belonged to the emperor, those who were working and living on the land were allowed to remain where they were in return for a tax in money based on the land valuation. They were allowed to buy or sell, will or

inherit and move about as they pleased. What did most
to win the loyal support of the farmers for the new government, however, was the granting of uniform laws to all
classes of people and the adoption of the principle of universal conscription. To be on an equal footing with the
old samurai was a great thing for common farmers and artisans ; and it was a great thing for the new government to
have the staunch support of this great mass of the population.

Timber and mining lands, and those unfit for cultivation, remained as the private property of the imperial
household and an important permanent source of revenue
for them. Urban properties, which had belonged to the
Tokugawas in the ports and Yedo, were sold to whoever
had courage and money to buy them, in order to raise immediate funds for the new government.

Instead of the regular rice stipends which they had received from their feudal lords, samurai were granted annual pensions payable in bonds as long as the government
felt they could afford it ; after that the samurai had to
shift for themselves. This was harsh treatment indeed,
for many who had had little experience in handling money
failed miserably when they tried to go into business.
Others who had held responsible executive positions on
the estates of their feudal lords eventually made great suc-
cesses in banking, shipping, communications and industry.
Since finance had never been a strong point with the
samurai, prospective success or failure in this matter did
not mean so much to them, but the fact that the government had taken away their right to wear two swords and

their exclusive privilege of defending the country was a source of considerable disturbance for several years to come.

During the process of political and social readjustment, the advisers of the young emperor deemed it wise to have some definite assurance themselves, and to give the other feudal daimyos some indication of the direction in which the new government was heading. All were therefore summoned to an assembly. The "Charter Oath" proclaimed on this occasion to enlist the confidence and co-operation of the entire nation in the program of the Second Great Change has been translated as follows :

An assembly widely convoked shall be established, and all affairs of state shall be decided by impartial discussion and in the light of public opinion.

The civil and military powers shall be centered in a single whole, and, in order that the national mind may be satisfied, equal opportunity shall be assured to all classes.

The whole nation from the upper to the lower classes of the people shall be united and shall strive for the progress and welfare of the country.

All outworn customs shall be abandoned and justice and righteousness shall regulate all actions.

Intelligence and learning shall be sought for throughout the world, in order to strengthen the foundations of the empire.[10]

CHAPTER XV

ON THE WAY TO WORLD POWER
(1868–1919)

ENRICHMENT and strengthening of the nation ! Enrichment and strengthening of the nation ! This was the clarion call and the resolute ambition of the new government leaders.[1] This was the goal toward which they worked with inexhaustible energy. In their travels through Europe and America they had been really convinced of the superiority of the West in material civilization. There was no more doubt of that in their minds than there was of their own superiority in the spiritual realm. And they suffered, these island people, from a sensitivity that made it most difficult for them to endure being looked down upon.

The most striking superiority of Western nations was in their armies and navies, but closer study revealed the marvels of industrial development and the benefits of public education. Nothing daunted by the herculean nature of their task, the new government determined to build up a national defense inferior to none, and an independent self-respecting citizen body. This entailed a complete remodeling of national discipline and education, a tremendous social revolution carried on by peaceful means.

In 1871 the young emperor issued an edict which ran,

"My country is now undergoing a complete change from old to new ideas which I sincerely desire ; therefore, I call upon all the wise and strong-minded to appear and become good guides to the government. During youthtime it is positively necessary to view foreign countries so as to become enlightened as to the ideas of the world. Girls as well as boys should be allowed to go abroad ; and my country will be benefited by their knowledge so acquired. Women have had no position socially because it was considered that they were without understanding, but if educated and intelligent they should have due respect." [2] At the government's expense five girls were sent the following year to study in America ; the eldest was fifteen but the youngest one was eight. Two studied at Vassar, the youngest, many years later, graduated from Bryn Mawr and returned to Tokyo to establish the Institute of English Learning for girls, now called in her honor Tsuda College.

Soon hundreds of students were flocking to the United States and Europe. Rutgers College in New Jersey alone had over three hundred in a short span of years because of its connections with the Dutch Reformed missionaries. A few were specially admitted to Annapolis. Law students went to Cornell, Ann Arbor, Harvard and Yale. Philadelphia, with its railroad and locomotive companies and nearby bridge works and State Geographical Survey was a favorite center for young engineers. Students of agriculture were scattered throughout the country. There were about seven hundred altogether in 1887, and thirteen of these were girls. Many received Masters' and Doctors' degrees. German universities, it was felt, gave better intel-

lectual training, but they lacked the moral and religious influence of the American, and were not so practical and
wide-awake.

In 1871 also the government instituted a Department of
Education, and the following year a national system of
compulsory education was introduced. The country was
divided into educational unit areas, and an elementary
school was built in each. At first four years' schooling was
required for each child, but soon this was increased to six.
There was some room for choice in the matter of textbooks
used, but the curriculum of the elementary schools was uniform everywhere and greatly facilitated the molding of the
many scattered clans into a united nation.

For training the army of teachers required by these new
schools many normal schools were established, most of
them for men, but a few for women.[3] Middle schools, special schools, foreign-language schools, technical schools and
universities were provided for those who wished to continue their education beyond the compulsory level. To
hasten the process of reform, experts and scholars from
Europe and America were invited to come to Japan as advisers to the different departments of the government and
as professors in the universities.

Frenchmen were requested to assist in preparing a criminal code and in teaching army strategy and tactics; Eng-
lishmen, to help build railways and lighthouses and develop
telegraphy. Italian sculptors and painters were asked to
introduce Western art; Germans, to train doctors and army
officers and to help put into effect local government systems. Americans served in establishing the educational

and postal systems, in carrying out agricultural reforms and colonization projects.

The northern island, Hokkaido, became a sort of frontier to which adventurous spirits turned with all their new ideas. Homesteads were granted to those who would settle there, and many samurai were conscripted to go there and work on farms. An agricultural college was opened with an American as its director, and various crops and breeds of cattle were imported from the United States. This island was not so cut up by rivers and mountains and by dense population as the rest were, and so larger scale farming was possible. Corn and potatoes were grown in quantity ; apples and tomatoes and sugar beets yielded very successful crops. Fish canning and the making of fish oil soon developed as profitable industries along with the manufacture of paper. The first railroad in Japan was also built in Hokkaido from some coal mines to a seaport forty-five miles distant. A Pennsylvania Railroad engineer was in charge of the construction and the engines were imported from the Baldwin Locomotive Works in Philadelphia.

More important than these, however, were the industrial developments which the government, by providing land and bonds for capital, had promoted on the other islands. Western methods of extracting and refining ores were put in practice in the copper, gold and silver mines. To supply the needs of extensive foundries and shipbuilding yards, coal and iron mines were opened, and steel industry started. Cotton spinning, silk reeling and textile mills and pottery factories were promoted. Steamers and stage lines were operated between several places, and railroads were

being built.   Yokohama and Tokyo were connected by telegraph, and newspapers were published in several cities.   Almost a million people were employed in manufacturing, a
million and a half in commerce, before the end of the first
decade of Meiji.   The total annual value of exports and
imports during the same period had risen approximately
from thirty million to sixty million yen.

While the chief interest in learning was utilitarian, purer
scholarship also developed rapidly under Western teachers.
In feudal days it had been considered shamefully disloyal
not to uphold everything one's master taught, but now
scientific equipment and techniques were introduced and
Japanese students for the first time began to search for
truth for truth's sake.   The search extended especially
through the fields of biology, medicine, botany, astronomy,
geology and history.   Tokugawa scholars had studied history just as they wrote in a vertical column from the top to
the bottom, from the present of their own country down to
its remote past, but Meiji scholars wrote like Westerners
in horizontal lines and they extended their studies into all
corners of the world, comparing their own historical documents, stone age pottery and skulls with those of other
countries.

General Ulysses S. Grant visited Japan in 1879 during a
trip around the world and reported to fellow Americans,
"This is a most beautiful country and a most interesting
people.   The progress they have made in their changed
civilization within twelve years is almost incredible.   This
is marvelous, when the treatment these people and all Eastern peoples receive at the hands of the average foreigners

residing among them is considered. I have never been so struck with the heartlessness of nations, as well as individuals, as since coming to the East." [4]

The ambitious and able young samurai from the southwestern seacoast regions who had been instrumental in founding the new regime, however, had by no means reached their goal. The financial burdens involved in converting a disunited feudal country into a modern nation were enormous. The cost of building a completely new school system, training and equipping a new army and navy and subsidizing the development of industries, railroads and shipping, had imposed a great strain on everyone. There were many who had little enthusiasm for the new government. Particularly difficult in this respect were the unemployed samurai of other than Satcho (Satsuma and Choshu) clans who had been given no opportunities by the new leaders. The Restoration of the Emperor had done nothing to restore the power which had long been passing from their hands. The vulgar merchants' money controlled their destiny. Instead of the "impartial discussion," "equal opportunity," "justice and righteousness" which the Charter Oath had led them to expect of the new government, they found a dictatorship very similar to that they had known before. Only the name was changed from Tokugawa to Satcho. They even had the same embarrassing trade treaties of 1858, granting to foreigners extraterritorial rights and control of Japanese tariffs.

The new government sent an embassy to the United States and Europe to arrange with Western powers for the revision of these treaties but met with no success. There was a split within the government itself ; Saigo Takamori, the great hero-general of the Satsuma clan, firmly believed that the nation could best be put in order by mobilizing an expedition to convince Korea of her error in failing to recognize the Meiji government. His rivals were equally determined that peace must be preserved in order to carry out the reforms of the Second Great Change. A compromise had to be made. Saigo led an expedition to Formosa to subdue savage tribes which had slain some Japanese traders. After putting them into subjection, Saigo tried to annex a part of the island, but the Chinese government protested. England came to Saigo's side in negotiations and it was decided that China should pay Japan an indemnity of fifty thousand pounds. This served to strengthen Saigo's position with the discontented samurai at home. His rivals, therefore, instituted a senate to include and reconcile some of the leaders of other clans and provided for an annual meeting of prefectural governors.

Two years later, however, a rebellion broke out in Kyushu. Discontented samurai from many parts of Japan had gathered around Saigo. They were supposed to be the best-trained soldiers of the country with generations of military tradition behind them. They presented a grim challenge to the new imperial army ; but after seven months of hard fighting were finally suppressed. This increased the confidence of the government in the ultimate success of their reforms, but it caused a crisis in government economics.

With the large increase in quantity of imports a small increase in tariff would have facilitated greatly the financing of the young home industries, but the foreigners still stuck to their treaties and refused Japan the right to raise the duty on their products. Prefectural councils then were created to assist in local financial administration and collection of taxes. Rich merchants and industrial development notwithstanding, the country was intrinsically poor ; the loyal, hard-working farmers were still the greatest asset in the national accounts. Industries which the government had been supporting were now transferred to the private ownership of wealthy families who had made possible the founding of the Meiji regime. And authorization was given for the establishment of the Bank of Japan with the right to issue paper money and do business directly with the imperial treasury. In the solution of this economic crisis lay the foundation of the system of state control of finance peculiar to Japan.[5]

Opposition to the control of the nation by a few clans, however, next manifested itself in the formation of political parties and rampant press criticism. The government was brought to announce the following Imperial decree : "My family has been in uninterrupted possession of the government of this country for over twenty-five hundred years. I have completely restored the imperial power which suffered diminution in the middle ages, and have reunited the whole empire. It is my wish to give my people a system of constitutional government which shall be accepted and protected by my successors. But the time is not yet ripe for the introduction of such a system. European civilization must first be more widely spread and more firmly rooted. But I promise that in the twenty-third year of

Meiji, 1890, a parliament shall be opened.   Let the officials and the people prepare for it." [6]

The emperor's closest and ablest adviser, Ito,[7] who as a boy had stowed away to England in search of the secret of Western power, now made another extended trip to Europe, this time to study carefully the political institutions of the West and their suitability for adoption by the Satcho leaders.   Bismarck, then the chief figure in Europe, had started with conditions not unlike those obtaining in Japan, and had built up a united nation with far-reaching international influence.   With its faint suggestion also of the Fujiwara court in its prime the great soldier-chancellor's bureaucracy seemed to have much to recommend it.

Upon Ito's return the official apparatus of the central government was thoroughly overhauled.   A Cabinet with nine departments was established, each department being responsible directly to the emperor who appointed the minister in charge.   These departments were :

Home Office	Board of Agriculture and
War Office	Trade
Board of Education	Treasury
Foreign Office	Department of Justice
Admiralty	Board of Communications
	and Public Works

A Privy Council was also formed of men who had previously rendered distinguished service and were now to be considered as the emperor's specially appointed advisers for life.   And a Supreme War Council was instituted. When this reorganization was complete the long awaited Constitution was promulgated.   It began :

"The Empire of Japan shall be reigned over and governed by a line of emperors unbroken for ages eternal.

"The emperor is sacred and inviolable."

In comment Ito explained, "As the supreme right is one and indivisible the legislative power remains in the hands of the sovereign and is not bestowed on the peoples." And also, "All laws, imperial ordinances and imperial rescripts, of whatever kind, that relate to the affairs of state require the counter-signature of a minister of state." [8]

A popular assembly called the Imperial Diet was provided for, but since it was the function of the Cabinet to initiate, determine and carry out the general schemes and politics of the government, and since as the chief executive administrative organ of the state this Cabinet exercised all powers, executive, legislative and judicial, which were vested in the crown by the Constitution, it is obvious that the people had made little headway against the Satcho domination. The issuance of all administrative and emergency ordinances, the making of treaties, the making or unmaking of war all were virtually controlled by the Cabinet in the name of the emperor. The chief and practically sole function of the Diet was to discuss the budget presented by the Cabinet. If the Diet did not consent to the budget the Cabinet could resign, or it could dissolve the Diet. If the Cabinet resigned the emperor appointed a new one in accordance with the advice of the Privy Council. The emperor himself could not say, "I object to such a large budget," he could only trust the judgment of the ministers whom he appointed; they, not he, were responsible for all official acts. Thus the emperor was indeed "inviolable," as the Constitution proclaimed, for he "could do no wrong", and the Satcho advisors, as lifelong members of the Privy Council, might appear to have been better intrenched than ever in their position of influence.

In fairness it should be pointed out, however, that there was great danger of the populace, uneducated in the ways of politics, being swayed by any sort of irresponsible eloquence ; and at this stage of its development the nation could not afford to have a government going back and forth like a football from one team to another. For the improvement of relations with Western nations it was absolutely necessary that a stable government be maintained. Had the Satcho regime been firmly established and had it enjoyed the support of the people as a whole it need not have been fortified with such precautions ; the very nature of the Constitution was an indication of the people's strength, and also of the centrifugal force of Western influence. If the little island empire was to be enriched and strengthened, if it was to become an independent and self-respecting nation (and what good was there in existing without independence and self-respect?), the people could not be flying off on Western tangents, they would have to concentrate and centralize all of their energies and limited resources in a unified program for improving both economic and cultural conditions.

Japan's first general election took place from July 1 to 3, 1890. Every man who paid a land tax of fifteen yen or over was allowed to vote. Just what the newly won legal instrument was going to do for the people was not quite clear. It was an intricate thing and decidedly foreign to

Japanese ways of thinking. It was something a modern nation ought to have and now the people had it, but what they were really interested in was a reduction of the land tax and a revision of the trade treaties. Several diets were dissolved and a Cabinet had to resign due to impasses on these issues, but in 1894 England at last conceded treaty revision and the other nations soon followed her lead. In the same year the new army and navy were able to prove their worth in a contest with China whose supine attitude toward the West and lack of interest in international trade irked Japan excessively.

As a result of the Sino-Japanese War, China ceded to Japan the Liaotung Peninsula and the islands of Formosa and the Pescadores. She also agreed to the complete independence of Korea and the opening of the Yangtze for navigation. Then Japan had a disappointing experience with European diplomacy. Russia, Germany and France, in the name of "the peace of the Far East," made Japan renounce her claims to any territory on the continent and, together with Britain, proceeded to establish themselves in strategic places in North China and Manchuria. This continued foreign aggression finally aroused bitter feeling in Peking, and the Boxer uprising occurred. Japan, being nearest, was able to send the first relief to the besieged legations, and her troops gave an excellent impression of efficiency, discipline and good behavior. The outcome of this was the Anglo-Japanese Alliance in accordance with which recognition was given to "the independence of China and Korea, the special interests of Great Britain in China, and of Japan both in China and in a peculiar degree, politically as well as commercially and industrially, in Korea, and the rights of both parties to take such measures as may be indispensable to safeguard those interests either against the aggressive action of any other power or in the case of disturbances in either country." [9]

According to Sir Charles Eliot, "One result of the Boxer troubles was that Russia remained in military occupation of Manchuria and this created a position most dangerous for Japan's interests. Japan undoubtedly desired peace, and while realizing that war might be inevitable, did her best to avoid or postpone it. She acted in concert with Great Britain and the United States, and Russia was induced to sign a treaty pledging herself to withdraw her troops from Manchuria in three installments. Russia did not withdraw her troops from Manchuria at the dates fixed, and the Japanese Government opened direct negotiations at St. Petersburg. They proposed that Russia and Japan should each recognize the other's status in Manchuria and Korea respectively ; that both powers should respect the territorial integrity of China and Korea and be parties to an engagement that all nations should have equal commercial and industrial opportunities in Korea and Manchuria. The negotiations lasted for five and a half months, but Russia proved unyielding and unconciliatory." In the war which followed, the Japanese army and navy achieved a series of brilliant victories and piled up an enormous national debt. Both Japan and Russia, therefore, were very willing to accept President Theodore Roosevelt's mediation. By the peace treaty signed in Portsmouth, New Hampshire, in 1905, Japan acquired supremacy in (and subsequent annexation of) Korea, a lease for the Liaotung Peninsula and the South Manchuria railway, together with mining and other pertinent rights, and the southern half of the island, Sakhalin, where there were oil fields.

Though, as a result of this Russo-Japanese War, Japan's international standing was further improved, internally the condition of the government was serious. The people who had fought and paid for the war with the lives of their dear ones and their taxes rioted against the civil leaders for agreeing to terms of peace which provided no indemnity to liquidate the costs of the war. The development of trade and industry depended on borrowed capital. The newly acquired territories were still liabilities rather than assets and required the creating and maintaining of larger armies. The government was required to yield more and more to popular demands. In 1918 the precedent was set for commoners to become premiers, suffrage was greatly extended, and the government, in spite of the Constitution, closely approximated European political institutions.

But before this the World War had broken out. Japan joined the Allies and was called upon to take action at once against the German leased territory in Shantung and her island possessions in the Pacific. Having succeeded in capturing all these by the end of 1914, Japan next assumed the responsibility of convoying the Australian troops and providing Allies' vessels in the Mediterranean with protection against German submarines. She did not send troops to Europe, but joined with England, France and the United States in the Siberian expedition of 1918. As in the United States, shipping and industry boomed tremendously during the war, and Japan enjoyed unprecedented economic prosperity. It was her financial salvation.

Now Japan felt that she had done well. In one brief half century of strenuous effort she had transformed herself from a bankrupt feudal state to a modern nation almost twice its original size. The explanation of this miracle was to be found in her well-organized educational system and the diligent, hard-working students devoted to the progress of the nation. Even elementary school students were familiar with the heroes of the West, the history of Western governments and scientific inventions. Where religious influence lagged, moral instruction was strong. And in the universities, scholars and experts were developed whose knowledge was not confined to their own hemisphere but extended to the whole world. Japan felt she had earned the right to propose at the Paris Peace Conference in 1919 that the principle of racial equality be admitted, that the League of Nations grant to all nationals of the member states equal and just treatment in every respect with no distinction either in law or fact on account of race or nationality. There were six dissenting votes out of seventeen, however, and Japan had to give up this cherished ideal. Still, she was now a member of the League of Nations and one of the great powers of the world. The terms of the Versailles Treaty gave her a mandate over the Caroline and Marshall islands and certain rights in Shantung.

CHAPTER XVI

UNEASY JAPAN
(1919–1937)

DURING the World War and the Versailles peace negotiations, most of the important nations of the world, for the first time in history, came face to face with each other. The leaders of poor nations were vividly impressed with the manner in which their more powerful neighbors had provided for themselves and became more conscious than ever of their own limitations. During this period also the people of various countries had their first direct experience with colossal industrial and financial enterprises. They began to realize that beyond the "millions" of which they had only vague concepts were the "billions" of which great men spoke with ease. It was all very disconcerting. Those who had little, thought themselves equally deserving with those who had much, and protested in the name of social justice. Those who had much, thinking their winnings well earned and not more than adequate for their own needs, resented the grasping attitude of their poorer neighbors. They said that people ought to live together in peace and not disturb each other. But those who had little, continued to worry both themselves and those who had much, until the whole world was seething in uneasiness.

Japan was especially susceptible to this uneasiness for three reasons, her peculiar national character, her relations with the West, and her economic position.

The Japanese have always been extremely sensitive. The early adventurers who brought bronze swords and mirrors to stone-age settlers seem to have been well aware not only of their own cultural superiority to the more primitive inhabitants of the islands, but also of their own deficiencies and limitations as compared with continental peoples. This awareness they bestowed on their descendants who reacted strongly to all progressive influences from abroad, not with a defeatist attitude as might have been expected under such enormous odds but with inherent passion for heroic attainment. Time and again the Japanese have found at their doors foreigners whose powers it seemed impossible to equal. Time and again their fortitude and diligence have surmounted the greatest difficulties.

When in the days of Prince Shotoku, men of Yamato encountered foreign Buddhist priests of very superior attainments and political ambitions, they learned to read and write themselves and developed their own scholars and politicians. When the great T'ang Empire loomed in all its glory threatening eclipse of the Heian court, the Heian court set up its own bureaucratic government and outlived the T'ang by two hundred years. From the encounter with the Mongol armada, Ashikaga leaders turned their minds to profitable overseas trade. Spanish ship captains, who pointed with pride to maps of their widespread possessions, served as inspiration for Japanese expansion through the seacoasts and islands of the southwestern Pacific. And when from the long Tokugawa isolation Japan opened her door and came face to face with the West, she was painfully conscious of her limitations, but her old proud spirit survived.

Like the Chinese script and institutions which she had adopted at the time of her First Great Change, modern Western civilization was little suited to Japanese conditions. Western civilization was based on free competition between men and on the control of nature ; the Japanese, on the other hand, for generations had been accustomed to the control of men by feudal lords and free competition with earthquakes, swift-flowing streams and rocky mountain slopes. Western civilization was sustained by large scale industry and commerce, but Japan, unfortunately, was poor in natural resources. Still, the West offered a stimulating challenge which the Japanese by nature could not ignore, and having accepted could not lay down.

Japan's relations with the West is the second of the reasons given above for her present uneasiness. From the Western point of view when Japan was discovered she was "quaint."[1] After the Russo-Japanese War she was "amazing," but Westerners did not take her representative very seriously when he declared at the Portsmouth Conference, "As a matter of necessity Japan must become a great power on the Asiatic continent."

To become a great power on the Asiatic continent, however, was Japan's chief ambition. The West had all the rest of the world in which to exert its influence and compete for economic advantage ; eastern Asia it seemed might rightfully be her special province. She had succeeded fairly well in mastering the techniques of the West, and she had much more in common with the Chinese than Europeans had. With this ambition in view, after acquiring rights to the South Manchuria railroad and annexing Korea,[2] Japan set about extending her influence in China by negotiation.

When the Chinese Republic was in the making its guiding spirit, Sun Yat Sen, spent much time in Japan, and its President, Yuan Shi Kai, a more practical politician but also under Japanese influence, signed an agreement to : grant special privileges to Japan in Shantung, Manchuria and eastern Mongolia ; engage Japanese advisers ; concede land for Japanese shrines, schools and hospitals ; introduce Japanese advisers into the Chinese police force ; buy about half of their war munitions from Japan ; concede three railway lines in the Yangtze valley and the right of priority to Japanese capital in Chinese railways, ports and mines. Included among the demands [3] was one for the right to carry on Japanese religious propaganda.

Western attention temporarily was concentrated on the World War in Europe. Yuan Shi Kai died a few months later, and his successors would not accept the arrangements he had made with Japan. They preferred to ask help from strangers, rather than lose face before this upstart member of their own family, and joined the Allies in 1917 in time to get a seat in the Hall of Mirrors at Versailles.

Russia, in the throes of revolution, concluded her separate peace with Germany before the other Allies, and the new Soviet regime, the avowed enemy of imperialist colonial policy, was soon making overtures to China for treaties on terms of full equality. Many Chinese leaders were susceptible to those Soviet advances; Communism became rampant in China. Huge Russia with her slow but steady movement toward the Pacific had for a century been a source of uneasiness to Japan. But Soviet Russia added to the old economic threat a new one of revolution and destruction of the family system, the foundation of Japanese national polity. Japan could not tolerate the extension of Soviet influence in China; she tried to overbalance it with her own.

When, its war concluded, the West turned its attention to the new World Power, Japan seemed "presumptuous," and they decided something ought to be done about it. They called a conference in Washington in 1922 and persuaded Japan to sign the "Nine Power Treaty." This treaty pledged nine interested powers to:

respect the independence and territorial and administrative integrity of China;

provide the fullest opportunity to China to develop a stable government;

maintain equal opportunity for the commerce and industry of all nations throughout the territory of China;

refrain from taking advantage of conditions in China to seek special rights which would curtail the rights of other states.

Western interests seemed properly safeguarded; Japan seemed properly restrained.

But then, as if the Japanese were not satisfied with modifying the map of eastern Asia and disturbing the delicately balanced spheres of Western influence there, Japanese farmers in California worked very hard and prospered, and factories in Japan turned out large quantities of cheap goods which began to appear in all the markets of the world. Many Westerners were happy to buy rubber-soled shoes and rayon shirts at prices they could afford, but those engaged in the making and selling of such things at higher prices were not happy at all. To take care of this situation immigration and tariff barriers were set up against the Japanese.

As Western ideas of Japan changed, Japanese ideas of the West changed also. A close-up view of conditions in the West was rather disillusioning. The costly efforts of Western educators, clergy and politicians to develop a healthy social and economic order seemed not entirely successful.[4] Western diplomatic methods, in which at Versailles and Washington Japan had her first real schooling, inspired in her a sense of insecurity rather than respect. The United States, back in the early years of Meiji, had refunded its share in an indemnity claimed by Western nations and had shown much-appreciated generosity at the time of the great earthquake in 1923, but with the Exclusion Act in 1924 its attitude seemed very much changed.

The old Tokugawa idea that it was safer to keep Western nations out of Japanese affairs began to gain ground; Japan had studied the whole West rather thoroughly, but the West, it seemed, had never been interested in really knowing Japan; they regarded her only superficially with some romantic emotion but with little understanding of her character or her problems. Furthermore, the Japanese thought Westerners were unpleasantly legalistic — they acted as if man were made for laws and treaties rather than the other way around. They emphasized rights, and touched very lightly on duties. In Europe, it seemed to the Japanese, most calamities were caused by men, whereas in their own country they were caused by nature and no one was to blame. Earthquakes and typhoons were no respecters of rights, but Japanese children and adults for generations had been disciplined in duty. They preferred to think in terms of character rather than laws, to deal with each case on its own merits, and make changes in agreements as situations changed. It seemed not only undignified but also impractical to take so many matters to court and public hearing as the West did ; according to the Japanese way of thinking, most differences were better settled by the persons immediately concerned through the mediation of friends or sympathetic parties rather than by professional lawyers.

More important still, perhaps, was the realization that Western ways were extremely expensive.[5] Piped water, sewage systems and central heating were costly to install and potential sources of great danger in time of earthquake. Telephone lines were also expensive and dangerous in a country visited by at least one typhoon each year. Automobiles required roads and gasoline — gasoline had to be imported and roads had to be carved out of the farmers' rice fields. Western clothes for men, with their tight collars and sleeves and trousers, were less comfortable than kimonos but more convenient for business and, therefore, quite generally adopted, but Western clothes for ladies which had to be fitted to the individual, which continually

changed in style and required suitable hats, gloves, shoes and
handbags were much too costly for most men's wives.   In
the Western diet meat, milk and butter played a prominent
part, but Japan could afford little pasture land for grazing
cows or goats.   There were the additional problems of
Western conveniences depriving many people of opportunities for earning, and destroying the individual's stamina.

Japan's change of feeling toward the West was eloquently
stated in a lecture by Mr. Tsurumi at Williamstown in
1924 :

Japan is discovering that Western civilization, dominated
by the machine and the passion for comfort, offers no solution
to the great problems of inherent permanent national stability,
serenity of spirit, and man's greatest achievement, the conquest of himself.   Triumphant man may not be revealed in
the end adorned in a top hat and attached to a telephone.
Asia has a civilization of her own.   To restore and develop the
best in that civilization is a fine work worthy of the noblest
endeavors.

Japan's greatest uneasiness, however, was due to her economic situation.   This had always been a matter for concern, but comparison with the great powers of the West
accentuated her limitations.   Japan, for example, had a
population one half that of the United States to be maintained on a group of islands about the same size as the
single state of California.   Though the traditional mainstay of the nation was agriculture, only about fifteen per
cent of the country was arable, and this, supplemented by
the products of sea and river, had barely supported the
static thirty-million population of the Tokugawa era.   It

afforded no excess for expansion. Attempts at trade in previous periods of history had depleted the country's mines to a point of imminent exhaustion. Though half of the country was covered with forests, much of the timber was practically inaccessible. Her chief resources were well-bred silkworms, the potential hydro-electric power of her rivers, and the energy and skill of her loyal people.

With these resources, industries had been developed and enormously expanded, but almost all the raw cotton basic to her largest manufacturing enterprise, and almost all the rayon pulp basic to her third largest industry had to be imported and transported thousands of miles.[6] Manufactured exports for several years had mounted by leaps and bounds, but this could not be expected to continue. Inevitably a saturation point in world markets would be reached.

Japan's success in trade competition depended on her ability to maintain low prices. These were made possible by several factors, chief of which, perhaps, was the extraordinary capacity of her people for organization and cooperation. Also, Japan had entered the industrial world after techniques and machines were fairly well developed, and her factories had the advantage of modern equipment. A large percentage of her manufactured goods, furthermore, was produced by what amounted to home industries, in which whole families cooperated and the capital investment was practically nil. A fourth factor was low wages — not as low as in the rest of the Orient, to be sure, not even any lower than in the West, perhaps, if counted in terms of "net satisfaction," but so low that food prices had to be kept at a level which scarcely met the actual costs of agriculture.

So long as the people felt that they were all working together for the enrichment of the nation these wages were not complained of. Farmers' daughters were glad of the chance to work for a few years in a city textile mill to save up actual money toward their marriage. Country people seized opportunities for producing raw silk and welcomed industries in their villages which supplemented their meager earnings from the land. The old feudal loyalties persisted in many places for several generations and though wages were low, if the employer gave a little bonus on special occasions to show his good intentions, workers did not think of finding fault. They were as well off as they ever had been.

With the World War industrial boom, however, things began to change. Class distinctions became more marked. Some men developed millions almost overnight and expanded their buildings and equipment with abundant optimism. They also made large loans to Europe and China.[7] Others, however, knew no such prosperity, for though their salaries slowly rose, food and commodity prices far outstripped them. Strikes began to occur. Dockyard workers, mill operatives, newspaper printers, street-car motormen and conductors, letter carriers and many more occupational groups forced demands on their employers. Fisherfolk rioted because the price of rice was out of all proportion to the price of fish, and farmers formed cooperative unions. The whole populace, the greatest natural resource of the country, was in a state of agitation.

Then came the great earthquake of 1923. The Tokyo and Yokohama region, the very citadel of new Japan, tumbled into a chaos of smouldering ruins. A hundred and fifty thousand lives were taken, hundreds of thousands were homeless, without food, water or means of transportation. Property losses were estimated at almost three billion dollars. The local bank panics and failures which resulted were almost immediately followed and rendered more acute by the world-wide depression. All these economic and financial factors have contributed to the uneasiness of present-day Japan.

The civil affairs of Japan down through the World War era continued to be controlled by the Satcho clans, but as their profits mounted the new leaders of industry and finance came to wield greater power. During the period immediately following the war the army was not in favor. People began to complain of the burden of military expenditures, and demand limitation of them. In the course of three years about one hundred thousand men were dropped from the army, and almost four hundred million yen were deducted from military appropriations. Priests sold charms to ward off conscription; insurance companies sold policies against it, and the classes in military schools were very small. Young men and their fathers felt that in industry and commerce lay the future of both their families and their nation. There was a renaissance of interest in Western literature and learning. "Liberalism," "democracy" and "internationalism" were the words on every tongue and every editorial page. After the Washington Conference of 1922 this type of vocabulary lost a bit of its luster, but many civilian leaders, with characteristic Japanese taste, cherished it the more for that.

Their strongest critics were the conservative members of the military group, who after all three wars, the Sino-Japanese, the Russo-Japanese and the World War, had been incensed to find what they thought their rightful winnings pared down by stronger Western powers. The samurai had always held the merchant class in some contempt, and now their successors were inclined to feel that there was more of personal profit than of patriotism in the minds of those in control of the government. Many discontented factory workers were of the same opinion, and the army held its ground in spite of retrenchment. The manner in which it took charge during the earthquake of 1923, brought order out of confusion, rescued the injured, disposed of the dead, restored communication and transportation facilities, and in three weeks' time had erected barracks to shelter the homeless, increased greatly the esteem of the populace for the army.

Communist organizations also sprang up in opposition to the capitalistic government and even went so far as to attack the person of the prince regent in protest against the restriction of the people's liberties and the wanton spending of the nation's substance by the authorities while millions went ill-clothed, poorly fed and badly housed.

But the liberal attitude still prevailed. A universal manhood suffrage bill was passed in 1925 giving the vote to thirteen million men over twenty-five years of age. The government voted to refund its share of the Boxer indemnity to China,[8] made an effort to quell the public re-sentiment against the United States Exclusion Act and sponsored industrialization and colonization of its own territories as opposed to aggressive expansion.

When the depression struck, however, liberalism was crippled. The hardship of living, added to confusion in political thinking, provided favorable conditions for the growth of communist activities. Army leaders then called the capitalists incapable of managing the affairs of the country and defending its best interests. Several men of means and international sentiments were removed from public office by the expedient method of assassination. Army detachments guarding the South Manchuria Railroad took matters in Manchuria into their own hands and demanded the sending of extra troops to help put an end to local disturbances which threatened Japanese interests. Army leaders at home pushed farm-relief measures through the Diet and won the good feeling of a large part of the agricultural population. Such circumstances made possible a successful military coup and the creation of Manchukuo as an outlet for Japanese energies on the Asiatic mainland.[9]

But still the nation was uneasy. Each class had its own special form of uneasiness. The capitalists were uneasy because they were such a vulnerable minority. According to Fortune eight family concerns held more than half the financial capital of the country. Fifteen family concerns controlled almost three quarters of the nation's business. Ninety-three per cent of the remaining families lived on less than three hundred fifty dollars. The average annual income of this group was one hundred sixty-six dollars.[10] Under these conditions it was obvious that the public had to be handled with care. They had so little to live on that any added financial burden endangered social stability. Furthermore, the public had so few savings to invest that they could not be expected to buy government bonds. The capitalist-industrialists had to assume the responsibility not only of providing sufficient salaries for the people to prevent general discontent, but also of absorbing government bonds when taxes were not sufficient to balance the budget. With their remarkable business acumen and ability in organization they instituted a unified program for Japanese industries which enabled them to make profits while the factories of other nations were operating at a loss. Still their position was unenviable as long as the populace and the army continued to be uneasy too.

After the army had created Manchukuo the liberals had as much as said, "Well, now you have done it. Pray show us and the rest of the world that it was really worth while doing." But the Japanese army's genius has not been conspicuous in the sphere of colonial administration. Japanese colonies have generally been as much liabilities as assets, and Manchukuo as yet was no exception. It offered some markets and opportunities for capital investment but it also required very heavy expenditures for keeping it in order. For these the army had to obtain the approval of the moneyed interests ; regular taxes derived from liquor, incomes, customs, sugar, land and business profits were not sufficient for colonial expansion. Large manufacturers were not altogether averse to such expansion, for it kept their factories busy making general supplies and ammunition and thus helped to solve their problem of keeping the people employed and contented. But on the other hand the government paid for a large proportion of its orders with loans and taxes derived from the manufacturers themselves. The problems of the military were further complicated by the fact that the farmers' relief funds had had to be discontinued, and the farmers' ardor for the army had cooled.

To add to the army's uneasiness Finance Minister Takahashi in November, 1935, publicly declared that Japan was secure from challenges to war from any quarter and opposed the appropriations which the army demanded. When an impasse was reached on this issue, the government decided to dissolve the Diet and seek an expression of public opinion in a general election. The returns were announced on February 22 of the following year and indicated approval of the government as opposed to the military faction. But on February 26 a group of young army men in an excess of zeal attempted to murder in their beds the key men of the government and to occupy strategic government buildings. The emperor, they said, was being misguided by these advisers who preferred their own profits to the honor of the nation. Tokyo was under martial law for several months.

The people scarcely knew which way to turn. On the one hand were the great gentlemen of finance who, between goodwill tours to Europe or America, might be seen riding back and forth in limousines from their art collections and high-walled gardens to their air-conditioned offices and modernistic golf clubs. They paid salaries to millions of employees, it is true, and gave millions of yen to charity on occasion, but apparently were more deeply concerned with their foreign relations than with the social welfare of their own countrymen. On the other hand were the intense army patriots, aspiring to make Japan supreme in eastern Asia, who would impose enormous burdens on the people, but whose ranks, conscripted from all classes of society, were the most democratic organization in the country, willing to endure great hardships themselves and even give their lives for the principles they believed in. It was difficult to see in which direction lay the ultimate good of the nation. The only practicable course was compromise.

Earnest and continued efforts were made to bring the army, the bureaucrats and the capitalists to walk along together on the middle road. Two Cabinets met with failure and a third was finally organized after lengthy negotiations. The stumbling block to all of them was the clause in the Constitution requiring that the ministers of both the army and the navy be appointed from the list of active generals and admirals. The man [11] selected as Premier in June, 1937, was a prince descended from the old Fujiwara family. He had attended the Versailles Conference a year after graduating from law school, later had become President of the House of Peers and of the Radio Corporation of Japan. He was thought to be in favor of Asia for the Asiatics, but to have more interest in cultural than in military relations, and the liberal group began again to vision better days.

Affairs in China, however, very soon shattered their dreams. Anti-foreign feeling has always been prevalent in China. When China with her proud traditions was unable to throw off the domination of Western powers this antipathy broke out in the Boxer rebellion. It has cropped out at many places and on many occasions since. Formerly England was the usual target, but of late years Japan has succeeded to this position, and naturally enough, for Japan has accomplished what China has not been able to do, and has assumed the role of self-appointed mentor to her backward neighbor. By continued pressure brought to bear on Chinese authorities, in the summer of 1937 this anti-Japanese feeling was aggravated and fighting started in North China. It broke out with greater violence in Shanghai. Japan had greater cause than ever for uneasiness. Military victory was confidently expected, but the future was fraught with danger for all classes.

Under these conditions the people showed remarkable soberness and serenity. Their apparent readiness to cooperate with the government program, in spite of personal differences of opinion, was good evidence of the success with which the Department of Education had developed national unity. Individualism and personal liberty are luxuries. They may be indulged in where abundant space, wealth and leisure are available, but poor people and poor countries cannot afford them. Poor individuals wear mass-production clothes, and poor nations go in for mass regulation ; standardization is a great economy in more ways than one.

The elementary school is the first step in the standardization process. Children begin school at the age of six or seven, as full of their own little characteristic quirks as any children in the world, for Japanese babies all are pampered by their parents. By the time they come to the last year of their compulsory education, however, they are all buttoned into identical uniforms, with identical textbooks strapped in knapsacks on their shoulders and their heads crammed with identical ideas of Japanese history, rightful attitudes and dutiful conduct.

Elementary school students are taught to keep their senses keen and to find as much enjoyment as possible in the use of their own muscles. There is great emphasis on gymnastic exercises, hiking, climbing and swimming. Each elementary school has its own Olympic teams and contests. Pleasure in the perception of the world of nature is also encouraged ; children are taken out in sketching classes to train their eyes to beauty, and are taught to appreciate the music of water, wind and insects. Managers of factories and businesses employing elementary-school graduates often tell them, "He who is master of his mind is happy even if he has nothing."

The elementary schools are co-educational, but from that point on boys and girls go to separate schools. Boys who wish to enter middle school and girls who wish to continue with higher school have to pass with credit very rigid examinations. Not more than ten per cent of the children go beyond the compulsory level. For this, economic conditions are largely responsible.

This does not mean, however, that the salutary influence of the Department of Education ceases at this point, for it has a Bureau of Social Education whose function it is to guide the development of "sound thoughts" and prevent the spread of "dangerous thoughts" throughout the nation.

Realizing the importance of the press to the moral tone of the people, this medium of adult education is very carefully watched. It is forbidden to publish anything "subversive of public morals, provocative of disorder, disturbing army discipline, confusing the financial world or subverting the public mind." [12] Temporary bans are frequently issued on the mention of certain topics. Persons who live at a time like this in the ports where foreigners are continually arriving with disturbing rumors can appreciate fully the value of press control for orderly everyday life.

Though it does include a certain amount of indoctrination, Japanese education is eminently well-devised to meet the needs of Japanese life. For girls the aim is usually to produce "good wives and wise mothers," and for boys, to create dutiful and useful citizens. Standards of attainment in the technical schools and universities are very high, but most youths would rather ruin their eyesight and health than fail to pass an examination. This attitude is fostered ; everyone must live up to what is expected of him or be disgraced. Going to school is not a social pastime in Japan ; it is a serious business, preparing students for the keen competition and rigorous demands of the process of earning a living. While engineering schools cannot turn out graduates fast enough to fill all the places waiting for them at salaries far superior to those of other professions, less than fifty per cent of the graduates in other fields find employment the first year out, and they are grateful for a salary of sixty yen a month. The yen in Japan is supposed to have the buying power of the dollar in the United States, but in our money it is worth only about twenty-nine cents. Still a higher education commands such respect, especially among country people, that relatives band together in severe self-sacrifice in order to enable the brightest boy among them to attend a city university.

Nowadays the employment problem for men is complicated by the entrance of girls into business. Girls are now becoming bus conductors, dining-car waitresses and elevator operators, in addition to office girls, typists and secretaries. With the exodus of the motor transport corps to China girls are also appearing as taxi drivers.

A further problem associated with education and created by Western influence, as stated by a Tokyo university professor, is "a rational, practical re-interpretation of Japanese history." The masses do not worry about this problem ; they simply accept the glorious past and the world mission which the elementary school textbooks say are theirs. The intelligentsia are not so fortunate. In the religio-political theory of divine ancestorship they are confronted with a dilemma such as modern Christians face in the first chapter of Genesis. Though they cannot believe it literally, there is some emotional bond which makes them cling to it. They want a divine emperor just as sincerely as Christians want a personal God. The value of living depends on the Absolute ; unless this mortal put on immortality, all is dust and ashes. Faith is necessary to human dignity. The incentive must be preserved.

It was faith in the words of Amaterasu to her grandson, Ninigi, that made possible the transformation of Japan from an isolated and weak federation of feudal states into a world power. No other leader could command the untiring co-

operation and united loyalty which the Son of Heaven inspired. The divine ancestry theory has really worked in
practice and served the nation well. If the people begin
to lose faith in it, what can take its place? This question
is causing many minds great uneasiness.

Not only on the faith of Japan, however, does Western
culture put a strain. Her people's power of contentment
is also threatened by American mechanical devices and
Hollywood movies. Country people can seldom afford
trips to the big cities, and they are apt to think of city dwell-
ers as a race apart from themselves. But even if they never
come to know the comforts of air-conditioning in the summer or of central-heating in the winter, in their small home
industries they make articles for export to America, luxurious and convenient beyond anything which they themselves
possess. Commuters may, in the city, ride in spacious sub-
ways with blue plush seats and chromium wall-vases of fresh
flowers in the cars, but most of them have to return at night
by dirt roads too narrow for American automobiles to
homes where there are no comfortable chairs. Though
Tokyo businessmen have telephones in their offices, Tokyo
housewives have to walk perhaps several blocks to call their
friends from a pay station. While Osaka streets are alive
with cruising taxis, less than ten thousand pleasure cars in
all Japan are privately owned. While throughout the country every village post office has a radio around which local
inhabitants gather for education and entertainment,[13] only
the more fortunate families or shopkeepers have a radio of
their own. Those who have one turn it on very loud so that
neighbors can enjoy it. Mechanical refrigeration is not

especially desired or needed, for milk, meat and butter seldom find their way into Japanese kitchens ; tea and saké, the favorite beverages, are served warm. Though Japanese people seldom complain openly of lacking modern comforts, they must indulge privately in a certain amount of wishful thinking.

A popular escape from everyday repression and inhibition is offered in the cities by Hollywood movies. Japanese movies, like Japanese life, are notable for their economy. They employ neither large crowds of actors nor elaborate stage sets. They have little of the gaiety and glamour of Hollywood films and abound in close-ups of agonized faces. Their usual theme is the triumph of loyalty and duty over personal desire. When love themes are treated it is more often than not in a way to ridicule or discourage independent romantic adventures. But, real life in Japan is full of that sort of thing. Most marriages today are still arranged by parents for their children. Mates are chosen with an eye to family stability rather than to individual liking. Identifying themselves therefore with the light-hearted carefree lovers they see in American movies is a source of both satisfaction and uneasiness for Japanese young men and women. For them American movies in some ways afford at much less expense the escape which geisha provided for their fathers. They are able to defend their frequent attendance at American movies to their consciences and their elders by saying that talkies give excellent training in the use of spoken English.

Western music is also very popular among educated young Japanese. It, too, affords them great emotional satisfaction. They listen with closed eyes to Western symphonies and solos played on the radio or Victrola, and are familiar with the best of Western music. In contrast to the richness of Western music, Japanese music seems very thin and lacking in variety. In general it makes one feel silence and loneliness much more poignantly. Japanese musicians, no longer satisfied with it, are turning more and more to Western orchestras and instruments and creating compositions which combine occidental with oriental musical traditions.[14]

In the realm of art this tendency is noticeable too. Many painters still follow the classical schools in subject matter and technique but increasingly one sees at exhibitions the results of Western influence. Instead of the world of nature, the human figure takes on greater importance ; instead of water colors and black ink, oil paints are frequently used. Every Western art movement from the Old Masters down to Surrealism and Dada is reflected in contemporary Japanese painting. In sculpture and architecture and in applied design Western styles seem to give even greater satisfaction.

The field of Japanese culture most strongly affected by Western influence, however, is literature. Here there is to be found but little of either the old technique or the old spirit. It is sometimes critically said that Japanese progressives manage only to adopt the outward form of Western civilization, that they wear it like a derby on their Japanese heads. This is far from true of the literary men. The largest group of them, and the most constant, have championed English and American literature. They have made innumerable translations, and have created dramas and novels of their own based on the works they have translated. Another large and active group, interested chiefly in Russian literature, released a flood of psychological novels. French, German, Italian and Scandinavian writers have also had their eager followers in Japan, who not only wrote as they wrote, but also enjoyed living as they lived, in so far as the cafés and restaurants of various nationalities on Tokyo's Ginza [15] would permit.

The influence of these literary men on Japanese minds was very strong. They were read and reread and quoted ; they stirred up powerful currents of thought. Freedom is what they proclaimed — individual freedom of action and thought, freedom from encumbering Japanese traditions and social customs. Left to themselves they would have Westernized Japan very soon ; they were not the least nationalistic. The collapse of liberalism was profoundly disheartening to them. Those who continue to write fiction do so chiefly for newspaper serials and women's magazines and show little of either real life or true art. The greatest uneasiness in Japan may be that of men of letters.

Never completely satisfied with what they had, the Japanese seem always to have been ready to welcome new influences. Together with a careful treasuring of the old, they have shown a characteristic enthusiasm for unaccustomed exotic things. Buddhism from India, T'ang poetry, Chinese art of all ages, Portuguese shipping and Dutch learning, all were eagerly adopted. Buddhism, though practically extinct in the land of its origin, survives in its Japanese adaptation. The best of Chinese art, carefully preserved and reproduced by Japanese collectors, may be studied in their country better than on the continent. Japan ranks third among maritime nations. Her knowledge of Western culture and civilization is certainly greater than our knowledge of Oriental. Can she consolidate all her achievements and stabilize her position as a great world power? One must continue to watch the pageant of Japanese History.

OUTLINE CHART OF HISTORY OF JAPANESE CULTURE

PERIOD	GOVERNMENT	FOREIGN RELATIONS	RELIGION AND THOUGHT	ARTS AND CRAFTS	LITERATURE	SOCIAL AND ECONOMIC CONDITIONS	IN THE WEST
NEOLITHIC B.C. 3000		Migrations from the continent	Animism	Stone implements; Comb and cord design potteries		No private property; Scattered settlers; hunting, fishing	Bronze Age; Trojan War; Plato
SIDEROLITHIC B.C. 200	Clan system	Introduction of Pre-Han and Han culture from China via Korea	Fertility rituals and divination	Yayoi pottery (red); Paintings on household goods; Bronze swords and bells		Rice culture introduced from Korea; Slaves used for farming - division of labor	Roman supremacy in Mediterranean
IRON AGE A.D. 500	Clan system	Increasing migration from Korea; Yamato troops invited to assist warring Korean kingdoms establish settlement on Korean peninsula	Deities of the land - Shrines at Izumo, Ise, the; Conflict between native Shinto and immigrant Buddhism	Iron weapons and farming implements; Imported Buddhist art and artists; Metal mirrors of gilded; Haniwa (grave) pottery figures; Bronze mirrors; Weaving	Introduction of Chinese script; Records kept by Korean scribes	Leaders with iron axes and farm implements felling forests and extending cultivated areas; Growth of social distinctions	Gaul, Spain, Britain, Northern provinces; Christianity recognized
PROTOHISTORIC A.D. 600	Imperial clan versus Soga clan; Prince Regent Shotoku's attempt to centralize government; Kamatari, Tenji-Tenno and First Great Reform and land survey made; Nippon adopted as official name; Law-making activity based on Chinese	Korean nobles and Buddhist priests welcomed as teachers; Students sent to Chinese court; Adoption of Chinese calendar, system of measurement, medicine	17 article Constitution; Buddhism officially adopted; Onyodo (pseudo-science of Yin-Yang)	Temple building - Horyu-ji; Buddhist sculpture in wood and bronze; Embroidery; Korean music and dancing	History by Shotoku and Soga; Commentaries on native script; Development in use of Chinese script	Chinese court life introduced; Private ownership of lands theoretically abolished; Land distribution and tax system instituted; Peerage compiled	Constantinople envoys to China; Celts and Saxons in Britain
NARA A.D. 710	First permanent capital, modeled after Chinese and Yamato court under Chinese and Buddhist tutelage; Emperors in throne frustrated; War god; Shotoku Imperial clan; Accession of Emperor Kwammu (782); Removal of capital from Nara	Envoys exchanged with T'ang Court; India with temple and palace accessories	University established for study of Chinese literature, history, philosophy; Shomu's abdication of throne and devotion to Buddhism; Wealthy monastery of Buddhist priests	Palace roof tiles; Bronze casting; Silk weaving and dyeing; Casting of huge bronze statues; Wood-block printing; Dry lacquer sculpture	Kojiki and Nihongi (official histories); Kaifuso and Manyoshu (anthologies of poems); Adaptation of Chinese script; Sutra-copying	Social service work of Buddhists; almshouses, orphanages; bridge, road and harbor construction; Irrigation and land reclamation; Innovations concentrated in capital, outlying districts little affected; Smallpox epidemic	Arabian invasion of Gaul; Lowest ebb of culture
EARLY HEIAN 794	Establishment of Heian-Kyo (Kyoto); Subjugation of Aino; Gradual passing of imperial power into hands of Fujiwara regents; Changes in administration and commentaries on codes of law	Cessation of relations with China (consulship of Sugawara Michizane (895))	Court free from temple control; Tendai sect on Mt Hiei; Shingon sect on Koyasan; Michinao (died in exile) deified as God of letters; Persistence of Shinto	T'ang style sculpture; bulgy, stern, massive sculptures statues; Buddhist painting formularized; presentation of theology in mandaras	First dictionary; Vogue for Chinese poetry; Kokinshu and other official anthologies; Religious essays; Official histories; First monogatari	Lack of communication between capital and provinces, and between upper and lower classes; Growth of tax-free manors belonging to court officials and temples; Farmers' desertion of taxable lands, increasing vagrancy	Charlemagne; Christianity a unifying force to cement conquests; Vikings
LATE HEIAN 907	Fujiwara as regents, civil dictators and maternal relatives of emperors; Rule of retired sovereigns; Delegation of actual administration in struggle between emperors, retired emperors and Fujiwara	Taira Kiyomori's efforts to carry on trade with China	Esthetic Aside-worship, glorification of palace life; Rapprochement of Shinto and Buddhism	Calligraphy; Yamato-e, native style paintings; Painted wood sculptures; Jocho School; Buddhist paintings in use of gold, elegance, gentleness and grace; Golden Age of palace architecture	Court ladies' diaries, notes, novels, in colloquial Japanese; Sei Shonagon's Makura no Soshi; Murasaki Shikibu's Genji Monogatari; Development of Japanese script	Passing of real power into hands of provincial landlords; Growth of bands of armed defenders of feudal lords; Dependence of court on provincial troops for collection of taxes	Capture of Rome by Otto, king of Germans; Norman Conquest
KAMAKURA 1185	Military dictatorship initiated by Minamoto Yoritomo, carried on by Hojo regents	Sung political refugees welcomed; Kublai Khan's envoys (1274-81); Mongol invasions	Popular revival of Buddhism; Jodo, Zen and Nichiren sects; Revival of Shinto deities	Portrait sculpture in wood; Unkei; Metal work and swordmaking; Narrative scroll painting	Official anthologies, histories; Quasi-historical narratives; Biographies of famous priests	Efficient economic and justice for all classes; Courtiers supporting themselves	Crusades; Magna Charta; Cathedrals
DUAL DYNASTIES 1331	Collapse of Kamakura government; Assumption of Ashikaga Takauji; Simultaneous emperors at Kyoto and Yoshino (1336-92)	Flourishing piracy along China coast	Zen priests as political and trade advisers; History of the True Succession		Immediate..., miscellany by a hermit ex-courtier	Hojos and people bankrupted by defense against Mongols; Feudal disturbances	Hanseatic League; Gunpowder

Period	Political	Diplomatic / Foreign Relations	Social / Religious	Art / Architecture / Utensils	Drama / Literature	Economic	Western Contemporary Events
ASHIKAGA 1392	Ashikaga shoguns ruling in Kyoto. Imperial succession dispute settled by Toshimitsu. Feudalism and anarchy throughout the provinces	Diplomatic intercourse and official trade with China	Bushido, the Samurai's code based on Confucian loyalty, Zen stoicism, Shinto reverence for ancestors, social and economic conditions of the times. Cha-no-yu (tea aestheticism)	Importation of tea utensils and other Chinese works of art. Tea-house architecture characterized by landscape gardening and restrained aestheticism. Noh masks, netsuké, pottery, lacquer. Gold and silver Pavilions. Ink paintings; Sesshu	Noh dramas and Kyogen. Zen writings	Shogun enriched by overseas trade. Populace impoverished by epidemics and famines. Onin Civil War (1467-77); Kyoto in ruins, shogun powerless, court penniless, anarchy in provinces. Rise of trade guilds	Renaissance. Gutenberg's printing. Columbus. Reformation
WESTERN CONTACTS 1550	About 300 autonomous feudatories. Most powerful feudal chiefs contending for control of Kyoto. General Nobunaga's attempt at unification by force. Organization of feudal lords under leadership of Hideyoshi at Osaka. Supremacy of Iyeyasu after Sekigahara (1600)	Arrival of Portuguese traders and missionaries. Religious envoys to Rome (1582). Japanese carried off as slaves by Portuguese traders. Trade routes and spheres of influence through south Pacific. Arrival of Spaniards from Philippines and shipping with them to Mexico. Spain (Spaniards in Manila). Expedition to Korea (1592-8)	Introduction of Christianity by St. Francis Xavier. Growth of Jesuit influence in southwestern Japan. Destruction of Mt. Hiei temples by Nobunaga (1571). Rivalry between Franciscans and Jesuits. Zen influence in diplomacy. Loss of faith in spiritual and intellectual superiority of China	Castle building on heroic scale. Kyoto wall and screen painting. Kitoku and Sanraku. Intricate carving of wood panels and metals. Development of purely decorative and secular art. First movable type printing	Introduction of Jesuit literature and Aesop's Fables	Freedom and opportunity for individual initiative, enterprise, ability. Development of mercantile interests	Spaniards in North America. Elizabeth. Shakespeare
TOKUGAWA 1603	Centralized feudalism under Tokugawa. New political center at Tedo. Rigid regulations and strict supervision of all clans. Policy of isolation, internal and external peace. Decline of Tokugawa authority. Leadership assumed by southwestern feudal clans	Temporary trade agreement with Dutch, English and Spanish. Will Adams in Shogun's employ. Closed Door: prohibition against Japanese going abroad and expulsion of all foreigners. Foreign trade restricted to Dutch and Chinese at Nagasaki. Knowledge of Western imperialistic expansion obtained from the Dutch. Arrival of Perry (1853). Intercourse with West resumed. Extraterritoriality and control of tariffs granted (1858). First embassy to U.S. (1860)	Suppression of Christianity (1636). Official adoption of Neo-Confucianism. Neo-Shinto and growing nationalism. Zen materialism and urban... Interest in medicine and science learned from the Dutch. Decline of Buddhist influence	Artists from Hideyoshi's employ scattered to feudal castles throughout country under patronage of feudal lords. Ukiyo, epitome of period's era. Genroku Renaissance: Ukiyo-e, wood block prints, color prints. Lacquer and other applied arts. Erotic music for samisen and voice. Highly developed theatre	Realistic novels: Saikaku, etc. Drama: Chikamatsu. Haiku: Basho, etc. Historical studies. Philosophical, historical and economic writings	Agrarian foundation of Shogunate. Enforcement of peace and order. Persecution of Christians. Internal and external trade monopolized by Shogunate. Enormous increase of urban populace. Farmers' revolts against high taxes. Static population and dwindling natural resources	Galileo. Settlement of New World. Rembrandt. Bach. U.S.A. Napoleon. Steam engine. Industrial Revolution. Slavery abolished. Imperialistic expansion. Anaesthetics. Victoria
MEIJI 1868	Restoration of Imperial dignity. Satcho clans, the power behind throne. Tokyo (Tedo) made Imperial capital. Fallen feudal chiefs returned to emperor, regranted to occupants in return for taxes. Universal conscription for Imperial army. Granting of Constitution and first election (1890)	Members of students and envoys sent to U.S. and Europe. Western authorities retained as advisers. Trade treaty revision (1894). Sino-Japanese War (1894-5). Boxer Rebellion (1900). Russo-Japanese War (1904-5)	Enthusiasm for intensive study of Western civilization at home and abroad. Stress on science and physical education. Official revival of Shinto	Two simultaneous schools in all forms of art: Traditional school. Western influence. Commercialization of applied arts	Translation of Western works. Fiction and drama based on Western models	National system of compulsory education instituted (1872). Economic strains of samurai due to end of special privileges. Development of industries	Telegraph. Darwin. Electric light. Telephone
CONTEMPORARY 1912	Universal manhood suffrage (1925). Capitalist-bureaucratic leadership superseded by military	World War: Germany drives from Pacific. Expansion in China by negotiation. Racial equality denied by Paris Peace Conference. Growing apprehension of Russia and Communism. Hiao Treaty (1922). U.S. Exclusion Act (1924). Conciliatory attitude to China. Expansion in world markets. Armed invasion and political control. Chinese policies and activities	Buddhist adaptation of Christianity. Liberalism and internationalism, followed by reactionary... Emphasis on athletics and physical development	Manic development of symphony and Western forms. Excellent art catalogues and reproductions		World War prosperity. Increasing democracy and power of people. Strikes and communistic activities. Need for importing raw materials essential to manufacture. Tokyo-Yokohama earthquake (1923). Bank panics and world depression. Great expansion based on extraordinary organization and cooperation of people. Distress of farm population	Automobiles. Aeroplanes. World War. U.S.A. World Power. League of Nations. Radio. Communism. Fascism. Depression

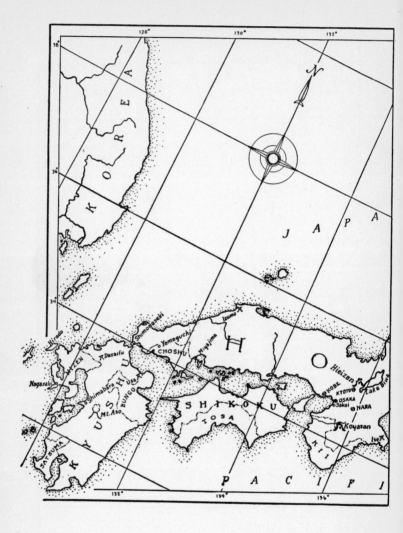

NOTES

[1] See : The Coming of Man from Asia in the Light of Recent Dis-
coveries, by Ales Hrdlicka, and The Antiquity of Man in America, by
N. C. Nelson, both of which are published in the 1935 Annual Report
of the Board of Regents, Smithsonian Institution; Prehistoric Finds
from the Island World of the Far East, by Ivar Schnell, in Bull. 4,
1932, Museum of Far Eastern Antiquities, Stockholm; North America,
Ethnology, etc., Encyclopædia Britannica, 14th ed., vol. 16, pp. 503-16.

[2] For recent Japanese studies related to the general subject of this chapter
see :
Tsuboi, Kumazo : Waga Kokumin Kokugo no Akebono, The Begin-
nings of the Japanese People, Their Language and Living, Tokyo,
Kyobunsha, 1927.
Kato, Genchi : Shinto no Shukyo Hattatsu Shiteki Kenkyu, A Study of
Shinto from an Evolutionistic Point of View, Tokyo, Chubunkan,
1935.
Historical Monograph Series, Kokushi Kenkyukai, comp., Tokyo,
Iwanami Shoten, 1932-5 :
Hamada, Kosaku : Nippon Genshi Bunka, Primitive Culture of Japan ;
Matsumoto, Nobohiro : Nippon Shinwa ni Tsuite, On Japanese
Mythology ;
Matsumoto, Shigehiko : Hikaku Gengo, Japanese History and Lin-
guistics ;
Umehara, Sueji : Jodai no Iseki to Sono Bunka, Early Sites and Relics
and the Culture They Represent ;
Yanagita, Kuniwo : Kokushi to Minzokugaku, Japanese History and
Ethnography.
The best discussion in English is to be found in the first three chapters
of Sir George Sansom's Japan, A Short Cultural History, New York,
Century, 1931, and An Outline of Recent Japanese Archeological
Research in Korea in Its Bearing upon Early Japanese History,
Trans., Asiatic Society of Japan, 1929, 2nd ser., vol. VI, pp. 5-19. See
also the chapters on the art of this early period in Tsuda's Handbook of
Japanese Art (below Chap. XII, note 11), and in Harada's A Glimpse
of Japanese Ideals (below Chap. VIII, note 12).

[3] These notes were incorporated in the official history of the Later Han,
25–220 A.D., repeated and slightly enlarged upon in the Wei records,
220–265 A.D. A translation of extracts from these ancient writings is
given in Early Japanese History, by W. G. Aston, Trans., Asiatic Society

of Japan, vol. XVI, part I. In this article Mr. Aston points out that Chinese writers say the Japanese are descended from Prince T'ai Peh of Wu, a Chinese colony having settled in Japan in 219 B.C. This theory of their origin was set forth again by Hayashi Doshun in his *Honcho Tsugan*, Complete Mirror of Japan, for further details of which see p. 271.

4 The total Ainu population now remains fairly stationary at about 17,500. The largest and most typical settlement is at Shiraoi, Hokkaido. They still live in a primitive fashion with bear hunts and bear festivals playing an important part in their life. Young Ainu, however, attend Japanese schools, serve in the Japanese army, and intermarry with Japanese, no longer learning the Ainu language or keeping up Ainu traditions. In addition to some income from tourist visitors, fishing, the production of fish oil and of fish meal for cattle feed and fertilizer is their chief source of livelihood. The best studies of the Ainu in English are by the Rev. John Batchelor, who spent many years among them. See his *Ainu and Their Folk Lore*, London, Religious Tract Society, 1901 ; *Ainu Life and Lore*, Tokyo, Kyobunkan, 1927.

5 One Japanese student of archeology indicated to the author that since most of these had already been rifled as early as the Nara period, the prohibition is not worrisome.

6 This tomb (Nintoku's) damaged in 1872 is the largest of its type in Japan. The total length of its "square-front" and "round-back" is about 1620 feet, the diameter of the "round-back" 816 feet. The entire mound is encircled by three moats. The author understood an archeologist in Tokyo to say that a bronze mirror in the Boston Museum of Fine Arts is from this tomb, but authorities at the museum did not corroborate this.

7 *Nihongi, Chronicles of Japan from the Earliest Times to A.D. 697*, tr. from the original Chinese and Japanese by W. G. Aston. Reissue of the original edition published by the Japan Society in 1896. 2 vols. in 1. New York, Dutton, 1924, p. 221.

8 Translated by Sir Ernest Satow in his article on Norito (Addresses to Shinto Deities). Trans., Asiatic Society of Japan, 1879, vol. VII, part I, p. 111.

9 Like Korean crown jewels, said to copy the tiger's tooth, which was used as a protecting symbol.

10 *Kojiki, Record of Ancient Matters*, tr. by Basil Hall Chamberlain. Second Ed. with annot. by W. G. Aston, Kobe, Thompson, 1932, p. 70.

11 A flourishing shrine to Susanowo still exists at Izumo ; according to popular tradition, marriages performed there are especially blessed.

12 *Kojiki* (see above note 10), pp. 112, 127, 131.

13 There is no historic evidence to indicate that he was other than legendary.

14 According to *Shinto Gobusho*, Five Important Shinto Scriptures, about as old as the *Kojiki*, contained in a series of publications known as *Kokushi Taikei, Standard Works of Japanese History*, comp. and ed. by Dr. Katsumi Kuroita.

15 The typical emotional reaction of a Japanese to this shrine was expressed by the soldier-priest-poet Saigyo (1118–90) in the lines :

Nani goto no	What sort of thing
O washi masu kawa	May be within,
Shirane domo	I do not know, but
Katajike nasa ni	Its awesome dignity
Namida kobururu	Brings tears trickling down.

CHAPTER II. THE DAWN OF HISTORY

1 See : *Lo-Lang : A Report on the Excavations of Lo-Lang, Wang-Han's Tomb in Lo-Lang Province an Ancient Chinese Colony in Korea*, by Harada and Tazawa, Tokyo, Toko-Shoin, 1935. Also *The Tomb of the Painted Basket of Lo-Lang*, Chosen, Koseki Kenkyu Kai, compiler.

2 *Nihongi* (see above Chap. I, note 7), vol. II, p. 72.

3 This peerage, *Shoji-roku*, is no longer extant, but much that it is supposed to have contained is embodied in a later one, *Shinsen Shoji-roku*, Revised Family Register comp. in 815. See p. 20.

4 *Nihongi* (see above Chap. I, note 7), vol. II, p. 66.

5 For fuller translations see *Nihongi*, pp. 129-133, or Brinkley : *A History of the Japanese People*, New York, Encyclopædia Britannica, 1915, pp. 140-2.

6 For illustrations see H. Minamoto, *An Illustrated History of Japanese Art*, tr. by H. G. Henderson, Kyoto, Hoshino, 1935. Also *The Craft of the Japanese Sculptor*, by Langdon Warner, New York, McFarlane, 1936.

7 The complete cycle of twelve is shown on the face of the Japanese clock, illustration p. 196.
The day was divided as follows :

Symbol	Japanese Hour Number	Our Corresponding Hours
Horse	9th	11 a.m. to 1 p.m.
Sheep	8th	1-3 p.m.
Monkey	7th	3-5 p.m.
Cock	6th	5-7 p.m.
Dog	5th	7-9 p.m.
Boar	4th	9-11 p.m.
Rat	9th	11 p.m. to 1 a.m.
Ox	8th	1-3 a.m.
Tiger	7th	3-5 a.m.
Rabbit	6th	5-7 a.m.
Dragon	5th	7-9 a.m.
Serpent	4th	9-11 a.m.

According to B. H. Chamberlain, *Things Japanese*, London, Murray, 1905, in the section on "Time," pp. 474-9, "Three preliminary strokes were always struck in order to warn people that the hour was about to be sounded. Hence, if the numbers one, two and three had been used to denote any of the actual hours confusion might have arisen . . . The hours were never all of exactly the same length except at the equinoxes. In summer those of the night were shorter, in winter those of the day. This was because sunrise and sunset were always called six o'clock throughout the year." According to Ernest W. Clement, *Japanese Calendars*, Trans., Asiatic Society of Japan, vol. XXX, 1902, part I, p. 3, Japanese time computations were based on multiples of 9 ($1 \times 9 = 9$, $2 \times 9 = 18$, $3 \times 9 = 27$, etc.), and the last figure of the product was used as the name of the hour.

[8] The Gregorian Calendar was officially adopted in Japan in the fifth year of Meiji (1873). Years, however, are still more frequently designated with respect to the beginning of a new imperial reign, rather than to the Christian Era. On postal cancellation stamps, for example, one finds 13 instead of 1938, the first year of the current period, Showa, having begun with the accession of Emperor Hirohito in 1926.

[9] *Nihongi* (see above Chap. I, note 7), vol. II, p. 139.

[10] Ibid., pp. 206-8.

CHAPTER III. NARA, THE FIRST CAPITAL

[1] Manyoshu, Lay No. 92, tr. by F. V. Dickins (see below note 6).

[2] An illustrated *English Catalogue of Treasures in the Imperial Repository, Shoso-in*, by Jiro Harada, was published by the Imperial Household Museum in Tokyo in 1932.

[3] This festival, called Tanabata, is still celebrated in Japan on July seventh. See *Children's Days in Japan*, Tokyo, Japanese Government Railways Tourist Library, vol. 12, 1936. For explanation of "day of the rat" see p. 25 and illustration p. 196. The cycle of twelve was sometimes applied to days as well as to months and hours.

[4] See Yosoburo Takekoshi, *The Economic Aspects of the History of the Civilization of Japan*, New York, Macmillan, 1930, 3 vols., vol. I, Chap. VI.

[5] For an excellent account of the introduction and development of writing in Japan see *An Historical Grammar of Japanese*, by G. B. Sansom, Oxford, Clarendon Press, 1928, pp. 1-68. Further discussion is also given in Chapter VI of this book, p. 46.

[6] For translations see F. V. Dickins' *Primitive and Mediæval Japanese Texts*, Oxford, Clarendon Press, 1906, and *Masterpieces of Japanese Poetry, Ancient and Modern*, tr. and annot. by Asataro Miyamori, Tokyo, Maruzen, 1936, 2 vols.

[7] The former interpretation is given by J. Ingram Bryan, *Literature of Japan*, New York, Holt, 1930, p. 42 ; the latter by Professor Tsunoda.

8   For the Japanese and for other translations see Miyamori (above note 6), vol. I, p. 110.

9   Lay No. 199, a condensation of Dickins' translation (see above note 6).

10 Lay No. 67.

11 Lay No. 121, literal translation.

12 Highly imaginary adventures of Kibi no Mabi in China are depicted in a scroll painting which in 1932 was added to the West's best collection of Japanese Art, in the Boston Museum of Fine Arts. Like the famous Ban Dainagon scroll it is attributed to Fujiwara Mitsunaga who painted during the early days of Kamakura (early thirteenth century). For illustrations see Kenji Toda, *Japanese Scroll Painting*, Chicago, University of Chicago Press, 1935.

13 For the development of katakana see p. 115.

CHAPTER IV. BUDDHIST PRIESTS AND THEIR NARA TEMPLES

1   See *Handbook of the Old Shrines and Temples and Their Treasures in Japan*, Bureau of Religions, Department of Education, Tokyo, Sanshusha, 1920.

2   These details from a document in the Shoso-in are to be found in Ishida Mosaku's *Shakyo yori Mitaru Nara Cho Bukyo no Kenkyu*, Study of Nara Period Buddhism based on Sutra manuscripts (with a summary in English), Tokyo, Toyo Bunko, 1930. For a translation and exposition of the Lotus Sutra (which is said to be to the Buddhist what the Gospel of St. John is to the Christian) see *The Lotus of the Wonderful Law, or The Lotus Gospel*, by W. E. Soothill, Oxford, Clarendon Press, 1930.

3   See J. J. Rein, *The Industries of Japan*, New York, Armstrong, 1889, chapter on Metal Industry, pp. 426-52, also pp. 160-1 of this book for swordmaking.

4   See *Textile Fabrics of 6th, 7th and 8th Centuries A.D. in the Imperial Household Collection*, Tokyo, Imperial Household Museum, 1929.

5   See K. Okakura, *Ideals of the East*, London, Murray, 1920, p. 118.

6   The Daibutsu (Great Buddha) was 53½ feet high and weighed over 500 tons. It was the world's largest metal statue, according to Sir Percival David, who gives a beautiful description of the Eye-Opening Ceremony in his article on the Shoso-in, Trans. and Proc., Japan Society of London, vol. XXVIII. As a result of fire and earthquake the statue has had to be repaired several times. The present head was cast in 1692.

7   The "three treasures" always associated with Buddhist temples are the sacred image, the sutras, and the priesthood.

8   This message was reported as the oracle of the deity Hachiman revealed at his shrine at Usa in Kyushu. See also p. 126.

⁹ English Catalogue of Treasures in the Imperial Repository, Shoso-in (see above Chap. III, note 2), p. 155.

¹⁰ See Medicine in Ancient Japan, by Keizo Dohi, The Young East (mag.) vol. II, no. 5, Oct. 1926.

CHAPTER V. THE IMPERIAL COURT

¹ Though of doubtful significance, it may be interesting to note that the active volcanoes of Japan were situated in these districts last to be controlled — Mt. Asama and Mt. Fuji in the northeast, and Mt. Aso in Kyushu. (Mt. Fuji has been inactive since 1707.)

² According to the Yin Yang philosophy of the Chinese Canon of Change.

³ The phœnix was an imperial emblem in China.

⁴ For details see R.A.B. Ponsonby-Fane, The Capital and Palaces of Heian, Trans. and Proc., Japan Society, London, vol. XXII, 1924–5.

⁵ See Matsuyo Takizawa, The Penetration of Money Economy in Japan, New York, Columbia University Press, 1927. Chapter II.

⁶ Posthumously Saicho was honored with the name Dengyo Daishi, Great Teacher or Propagator of the True Religion ; and Kukai, Kobo Daishi, Great Teacher or Propagator of the Law. Saicho on his return from China founded the Tendai sect ; Kukai, the Shingon. For details see Sir Charles Eliot, Japanese Buddhism, New York, Longmans, 1935 ; also, History of Japanese Religion, Masaharu Anesaki, London, Kegan Paul, 1930.

⁷ A commemorative volume published in 1933, Bunkashi Jo Yori Mitaru Kobo Daishi Den, Cultural History in Relation to Kobo Daishi, Tokyo, Shinkosha ; includes several controversial articles concerning Kukai.

⁸ See Sansom's Japan (above Chap. I, note 2), p. 223.

⁹ The Japanese title of this essay is Juju Shin Ron. It was written in 822.

¹⁰ The following translation is somewhat condensed from Sansom's Early Japanese Law and Administration reprinted from Trans., Asiatic Society of Japan, 1932.

¹¹ Shinsen Shoji-roku, Revised Family Register (see above Chap. II, note 3), published in vol. 4, Shinchu Kogaku Sosho, Newly Commentated Series, Tokyo, 1928.

¹² Sugawara Michizane (845–903), banished from court to the Dazaifu in Kyushu by Fujiwara rivals, but after his death deified as Tenjin-Sama, patron saint of literature.

¹³ See W. G. Aston, Shinto, New York, Longmans, 1905, pp. 97-132.

¹⁴ For history of the mirror, the bead and the sword see C. D. Holtom, Japanese Enthronement Ceremonies with an Account of the Imperial Regalia, Tokyo, Kyo Bun Kwan, 1928.

CHAPTER VI. THE POWER AND GLORY OF THE FUJIWARAS

1   Though Fujiwaras lost much power to the military clans in the twelfth century, seven hundred years later they still represented the court and the imperial heritage and had sufficient prestige to play an important part in the Restoration of 1868. Sanjo Sanetomi, a Fujiwara, then became premier; Prince Konoe who became premier in June, 1937, is also a Fujiwara.

2   These quotations and the following descriptions of Michinaga's palace and temple are from *Eiga Monogatari*, Tale of Splendor, by Akazome Emon, a court lady of the early eleventh century (not yet translated into English). The poem is quoted in *Two Tales of Historic Japan* (a comparative study of *Genji Monogatari* and *Heike Monogatari*), by Ryusaku Tsunoda, *Columbia University Quarterly*, June, 1935.

3   The original painting, Amida Raigo, is now in the Reihokwan Museum on Mt. Koya. It was attributed to the priest-painter Eshin Sozu (942–1017), but according to recent scholarship dates from somewhat later. For a reproduction see Minamoto (above Chap. II, note 6).

4   *The Pillow Book of Sei Shonagon* (see below note 7), p. 135.

5   From an unpublished paper on *Nenju Gyoja*, the Court Calendar, by Shunzo Sakamaki.

6   *The Tale of Genji*, a novel by Lady Murasaki, tr. by Arthur Waley, Boston, Houghton, 1935, 2 vols. The following is a slightly condensed quotation from vol. I, *Wreath of Cloud*, Chaps. VI and VII, pp. 479-80 and 497-8 respectively.

7   *The Pillow Book of Sei Shonagon*, tr. by Arthur Waley, Boston, Houghton, 1929, p. 37.

8   Ibid., p. 101.

9   Pronunciations of symbols are given in the following charts. There are only five vowel sounds in Japanese — father, gasoline, coo (u in many words is elided), end, hope. The usual arrangement of hiragana differs from that of katakana; it is based on a short Buddhist psalm which contains all the syllables. These tables should be read from top to bottom, beginning in the upper *right* hand corner.

n	wa	ra	ya	ma	ha	na	ta	sa	ka	a
	(w)i	ri	(y)i	mi	hi	ni	chi	shi	ki	i
	(w)u	ru	yu	mu	fu	nu	tsu	su	ku	u
	(w)e	re	(y)e	me	he	ne	te	se	ke	e
	wo	ro	yo	mo	ho	no	to	so	ko	o

katakana classification

(y)e	a	ya	ra	yo	chi	i
hi	sa	ma	mu	ta	ri	ro
mo	ki	ke	u	re	nu	ha
se	yu	fu	(y)i	so	ru	ni
su	me	ko	no	tsu	wo	ho
n	mi	e	o	ne	wa	he
	shi	te	ku	na	ka	to

hiragana arrangement

10 Taketori no Okina no Monogatari, written in the tenth century (author unknown), tr. by F. Victor Dickins, London, Trübner, 1888. A modern version of this story for children is called Kaguya Hime, The Moon Maiden.

11 In addition to Sei Shonagon's Makura Soshi, Pillow Book, and Murasaki Shikibu's Genji Monogatari, see Diaries of Court Ladies of Old Japan, tr. by Annie Shepley Omori and Kochi Doi, Tokyo, Kenkyusha, 1935. Some think that Tosa Nikki, Tosa Diary, tr. by Wm. Porter, London, Frowde, 1912, and Ochikubo Monogatari, Tale of Lady Ochikubo, tr. by Wilfrid Whitehouse, London, Kegan Paul, 1934, were also written by ladies.

12 See Toda (above Chap. III, note 12).

13 Eiga Monogatari (see above note 2).

CHAPTER VII. COURTIER GIVES PLACE TO PROVINCIAL SOLDIER

1 Used as introduction to Tale of Heike, a long narrative of the struggles between the Taira and Minamoto, parts of which are quoted on pp. 134-143 (see below note 6).

2 See A Biographical Approach to Shinto, by Ryusaku Tsunoda, in About Japan, New York, Japan Society, Nov., 1933.

3 Brinkley (see above Chap. II, note 5), p. 199.

4 Today soldiers and soldiers' families are especially frequent visitors to Hachiman shrines. Before going to Berlin for the Olympic games in 1936, athletes also paid their respects and prayed to Hachiman for victory.

5 Usually called Miyajima, Shrine Island.

6 The Tale of Heike, tr. by A. L. Sadler, Trans., Asiatic Society of Japan, vol. XLVI, part II, 1918, p. 13.

7   From *Hojoki*, written by Kamo Chomei in 1212. Tr. by W. G. Aston
    in his *History of Japanese Literature*, New York, Appleton, 1899, pp.
    145-56.

8   One of three scrolls of the *Tale of Heike* said to be by Sumiyoshi
    Keion is in the Boston Museum of Fine Arts. Its depiction of battle
    scenes, and especially of the burning of a palace, is superb. For illus-
    tration see (above Chap. III, note 12, Toda), p. 88, and also photo-
    gravure p. 107.

9   The thirteenth century witnessed a great revival of Buddhism in a
    popular form designed to appeal to common people. Four sects, espe-
    cially, began to flourish under the leadership of four very remarkable
    evangelists.

Sect (Shu)	Leader	His Dates
Jodo	Honen	1133–1212 (see p. 164)
Zen	Eisai	1141–1215 (see pp. 172-6)
Shin	Shinran	1173–1262
Nichiren	Nichiren	1222–1282 (see pp. 152-3)

10 Selected and condensed from T. A. S. J., vol. XLVI, part II, pp. 1-278,
    and vol. XLIX, part I, 1921, pp. 1-354 (see above note 6).

CHAPTER VIII. THE FIRST MILITARY DICTATORSHIP

1   See *Some Striking Personalities in Japanese History*, by Tan Hama-
    guchi, in the Trans. and Proc., Japan Society of London, vol. VI, part
    II, p. 256.

2   From *Tsuredzuregusa* (Sec. 184), by Yoshida no Kaneyoshi, tr. by Sir
    George Sansom in the Trans., Asiatic Society of Japan, vol. 39, 1911.

3   Emperor Go-Toba (1179–1239) ruled 1184-98.

4   See *Kyoto, Its History and Vicissitudes Since Its Foundation in 792 to
    1868*, by R. A. B. Ponsonby-Fane, Hong Kong, Rumford, 1931.

5   From translation of Nichiren's *Rissho Ankoku Ron*, The Establishment
    of Righteousness and the Security of the Country, by Arthur Lloyd,
    in his *Creed of Half Japan*, London, Murray, 1911, pp. 307-9.

6   See *Nichiren The Buddhist Prophet*, by Masaharu Anesaki, Cambridge,
    Harvard University Press, 1916.

7   See *The Book of Ser Marco Polo, the Venetian, Concerning the King-
    doms and Marvels of the East*, newly tr. and ed. with notes by Colonel
    Henry Yule, London, Murray, 3rd ed., 1921, vol. II, Book 3, Chap. 2,
    p. 253 et seq.

8   Letter given in full in James Murdoch's *A History of Japan*, London,
    Kegan Paul, 1926, 3 vols., vol. 1, p. 499. (What is now Vol. II was
    published first by the Japan Chronicle, Kobe, 1903).

9   Quoted by Murdoch, vol. 1, p. 499.

¹⁰ For details of sword-making see Rein (above Chap. IV, note 3).

¹¹ See *Bushido the Soul of Japan*, by Inazo Nitobe, Tokyo, Kenkyusha, 1935, p. 120.

¹² An incident from *Taikoki* as told by Dr. Jiro Harada at a forum on Japanese Culture, Lake Yamanaka, July, 1937. This story really belongs to the well-developed *Bushido* of the sixteenth century, but, though slightly anachronistic, is given here for its context. The treasures included two swords, a ceramic tea caddy, a blue glazed water jar, a tea bowl, a ceramic incense box named "plover," a painting of a hawk by a Chinese emperor. The incense box later came into the possession of Hideyoshi and is said to have mysteriously given warning whenever his life was in danger. The attitude of the samurai is further elucidated in the beautiful volume *A Glimpse of Japanese Ideals*, by Dr. Jiro Harada, Tokyo, Kokusai Bunka Shinkokai, 1937, Chap. IX.

¹³ For Jodo, see Eliot and Anesaki (above Chap. V, note 6), or *Honen The Buddhist Saint, His Life and Teaching*, by Coates and Ishizuka, Kyoto, Chion-in, 1925. Zen is described more fully in the next chapter.

¹⁴ This and the following story is told by Dr. Nitobe in his *Bushido* (note 11 above), p. 31.

CHAPTER IX. WANT AND CONFUSION

1 Translation of part of Kitabatake Chikafusa's *Jinnoshotoki*, given by W. G. Aston in his *History of Japanese Literature*, pp. 164-9. Aston calls this Jinko shotoki. Y. Kuno, in his *Japanese Expansion on the Asiatic Continent*, vol. 1, Berkeley, University of California Press, 1937, p. 352, calls it Shinko Shoto-Ki. This gives a suggestion of the difficulties involved in the Japanese language and literature.

2 *Tsuredzuregusa* (Sec. 120) (see above Chap. VIII, note 2).

3 The derivation of "maru" as applied to ships is still somewhat of a question, but the author is inclined to accept the interpretation that "maru" meant "darling" or "precious" and that it was applied to ships because they brought such highly prized treasures from China.

This record is given by Takekoshi (see above Chap. III, note 4), vol. I, p. 224, but he, perhaps wisely, makes no attempt to evaluate kwan mon in modern currency. The following estimate, though possibly far from accurate, is presented to give the reader some notion of the magnitude of the expenses recorded. According to *Dokushi-biyo*, Equipment Important to Reading History, by Tokyo Imperial University Bureau for Compiling Historical Materials, 1 koku of rice (approx. 5 bushels) in Ashikaga times was worth about 600 mon = .6 ryo. 2065 kwan mon at this rate would buy 3442 koku of rice. Today 1 koku is worth ¥30 (ryo and yen are synonymous). Thus, 2065 kwan mon in Ashikaga times may be estimated to be equivalent to ¥103,260, or about $35,000. The buying power of the yen in Japan, however, is about equivalent to that of the dollar in the United States.

4 Takekoshi (see above note 3), vol. I, p. 225. The gifts exchanged by
Yoshimitsu and the Ming Court are also listed in the same volume,
p. 216.

> 1,000 ryo of silver = about 4300 oz. of silver
> 15,000 kwan of copper (by method of estimate used in note 3
>   above) = 25,000 koku = ¥750,000 = about $250,000
> 1 hiki = 25 yards of cloth

5 Kwadensho, by Seami (1363–1444), tr. in part in Arthur Waley's introduction to his Nō Plays of Japan, New York, Knopf, 1922. See
also Japanese Noh Plays, vol. II, of Japanese Government Railways Tourist Library. For translations of 22 kyogen see Kyogen Comic Inter-
ludes of Japan by Dr. Shio Sakanishi, Boston, Marshall Jones, 1938.

6 Most Japanese are still extremely sentimental about O Cha no Yu, or
Tea Ceremony. See K. Okakura, The Book of Tea, Edinburgh, Foulis,
1919; Y. Fukukita, Cha no Yu, Tea Cult of Japan, Tokyo, Maruzen,
Japanese Government Railways Tourist Library, vol. I; also A. L.
Sadler Cha no Yu, the Japanese Tea Ceremony, London, Kegan Paul,
1933.

7 Emperor Go-Hanazono, 1419–71, reigned 1429–64.

8 A popular phrase from Ichijo Kaneyoshi's Shodan Chiyo, Woodcutter's
Remarks, written about 1480.

CHAPTER X.   CATHOLICS AND CASTLES

1 Murdoch (see above Chap. VIII, note 8), vol. II, p. 42.

2 For which see pp. 206-12.

3 On this site (supposedly) in Yamaguchi a monument to St. Francis
Xavier was recently erected.

4 Quoted by Murdoch, vol. II, p. 64, from the Letters of St. Francis
Xavier. See also H. H. Gowen, Five Foreigners in Japan, New York,
Revell, 1936.

5 Established in 1291 and still in existence as the only university in
Portugal.

6 Murdoch, vol. II, p. 155.

7 Ibid., p. 170.

8 See Japan As It Was And Is, by Richard Hildreth, Boston, 1855, p. 88.

9 See Toyotomi Hideyoshi, by Walter Dening, Tokyo, Kyo Bun Kwan,
1904.

10 A detailed account of Hideyoshi's invasion of Korea is given by W. G.
Aston in the Trans., Asiatic Society of Japan, vol. VI, part II, pp. 227-
245, vol. IX, pp. 87-93 and 213-22, vol. XI, pp. 117-25.

11 Murdoch, vol. II, p. 288.

12   This explanation is based on *Jokaku no Kenkyu, Study of Castle Strongholds,* by Nobu Orui, Tokyo, Rekishi Koza Series, 1915. For illustrations see *Castles in Japan,* Japanese Government Railways Tourist Library, vol. IX.

13   Quoted from *Taikoki,* by Fane (see above Chap. VIII, note 4), p. 261.

14   Murdoch, vol. II, p. 386.

CHAPTER XI.   PEACE AT ANY PRICE

1   By Brinkley. See his *History of the Japanese People* (above Chap. II, note 5), p. 527. "In the beginning of the 17th century," according to Takizawa (above Chap. V. note 5) p. 20, "the wealth of the entire country was calculated to be 28 million koku, of which 8 million was the possession of the Tokugawa Shogunate and 40,247 koku was reserved for the imperial court."

2   See James A. B. Scherer, *The Romance of Japan,* New York, Doubleday, 1928, p. 129.

3   Ibid., p. 173.

4   See *Yedo Castle,* by Thomas R. H. McClatchie, Trans., Asiatic Society of Japan, vol. VI, 1877.

5   See *The Maker of Modern Japan,* the life of Tokugawa Iyeyasu, by A. L. Sadler, London, Allen and Unwin, 1937, p. 167.

6   Scherer (note 2 above), p. 166. See also *Five Foreigners in Japan* (above Chap. X, note 4) and Wilson Crewdson, *The Dawn of Western Influence in Japan,* Trans., and Proc., Japan Society of London, vol. VI, part II.

7   Brinkley (note 1 above), p. 568.

8   Ibid., p. 577.

9   Ibid., p. 574.

10   See *Judo (Jujutsu),* Japanese Government Railways Tourist Library, vol. XVI.

11   For this and further details see *An Official Guide to Japan,* Japanese Government Railways, 1933, pp. 195-220.

12   Brinkley (note 1 above), p. 555.

CHAPTER XII.   THE GOLDEN AGE OF THE BOURGEOISIE

1   Takekoshi (see above Chap. IX, note 3), vol. II, p. 243.

2   Ibid., p. 252.

3   *Art, Life and Nature in Japan,* by Masaharu Anesaki, Boston, Marshall Jones, 1932, p. 150.

4   *History of Nations,* Henry Cabot Lodge, Editor, New York, Collier, 1916, vol. VII, p. 153.

5 Genroku literally means "good fortune."

6 In his novel, *Koshoku Ichidai Otoko*, "Middle-aged Gentleman of Passion," not yet available in English.

7 See *The Music and Musical Instruments of Japan*, by Sir F. T. Piggott, Yokohama, Kelly and Walsh, 1909, and also *Japanese Music*, and *Japanese Drama*, Japanese Government Railways Tourist Library, vol. XV and vol. XVI.

8 *The Autobiography of Fukuzawa Yukichi*, translated by Eiichi Kiyooka, Tokyo, Hokuseido, 1934, p. 4.

9 See *Masterpieces of Chikamatsu*, translated by Asataro Miyamori, New York, Dutton, 1926.

10 "Ukiyo" originally was Buddhist terminology for this "transient world" as opposed to the eternal realm. The sacrilegious use of it was typical of the Genroku Age in which all things sacred were travestied.

11 See *The Art of Japan*, by Louis V. Ledoux, New York, Japan Society, Inc., 1927, and *Handbook of Japanese Art*, by Noritake Tsuda, Tokyo, Sanseido, 1935, and *Japanese Art*, Encyclopædia Britannica, Inc., 1933.

12 *The Bamboo Broom, An Introduction to Japanese Haiku*, by Harold G. Henderson, Boston, Houghton, 1934, p. 25.

13 *History of Japanese Literature*, by W. G. Aston, New York, Appleton, 1899, p. 292.

14 *The Bamboo Broom* (see note 12 above), p. 35.

15 Each year during the climbing season, about six weeks in July and August, thousands of pilgrims, old and young, make their way to the top, chanting "sange, sange rokon shojo" (recognizing and admitting our faults, doing penance to purify our six senses) [the mind is included as a sense].

Chapter XIII. When Perry Came

1 Quotation from Murdoch, vol. III, p. 499. See also *Jan Compagnie in Japan, 1600–1817*, by C. R. Boxer, The Hague, Nijhoff, 1936.

2 Engelbert Kaempfer (1651–1716), a German medical doctor resident at Deshima 1690–92, in the employ of the Dutch East India Company, wrote the first complete history of Japan by a Westerner, an English translation of which, in two volumes, was published in 1792.

Carl Peter Thunberg (1743–1828), Swedish scientist and scholar resident at Deshima 1775–77.

Isaac Titsingh, statesman and gentleman, who impressed the Japanese by refusing to be searched by their officials, saying it was beneath his dignity; a bookhunter, interested in social customs, made two trips to Yedo during his stay in Japan (1779–84), and kept up correspondence with scholarly Japanese friends for years after he left the country.

Philip Franz von Siebold (1796–1886) resident at Nagasaki, 1823–30, forced to leave the country for having received from a Japanese official a map of Japan in exchange for a *Life of Napoleon*. He revisited it again in 1859, after its doors were opened. During his first period of residence his home was thronged with eager Japanese students who were required by him to write dissertations in Dutch on all sorts of Japanese subjects on which he wanted information. Based on these dissertations, Siebold published in Leyden in 1832 an encyclopædic work, *Nippon, Archiv zur Beschreibung von Japan un der dessen Neben und Schutzlandern*, with two volumes of illustrations (new edition by Japan Institute in Berlin in 1930).

3   Especially popular were the scientific treatises written in Chinese by the Jesuit Fathers and printed by them in China with no evidence of their Christian origin.

4   There is still preserved a print of the one Dutch wife and child who managed to visit Deshima. It is reproduced in Boxer (note 1 above), p. 92.

5   For these and a wealth of other details from native sources see *Tokugawa Japan* (Materials on Japanese Social and Economic History), ed. by Neil Skene Smith, Tokyo, Asiatic Society of Japan, 1937.

6   See *Tadataka Ino, The Japanese Land Surveyor*, by R. Otani, tr. by K. Sugimura, Tokyo, Iwanami, 1932.

7   See *Hiroshige and Japanese Landscapes*, Japanese Government Railways Tourist Library, vol. V.

8   Such a flag was first used as a symbol of the nation on the bow of the United States Navy's steamship, *Powhatan*, which carried the first official Japanese embassy to the United States in 1860. The standard proportions of the national flag were determined by official proclamation ten years later. The red disc is suggestive of both the rising sun and the mirror which Amaterasu charged her descendants to reverence. The populace first used rising sun flags on the occasion of the opening of the first railway from Tokyo to Yokohama in 1872.

9   For illustrations see *Japanese Architecture*, Japanese Government Railways Tourist Library, vol. 7, and *Folk Crafts in Japan*, by S. Yanagi, Tokyo, Society for International Cultural Relations, 1936.

10 *Onna Daigaku*, by Kaibara Ekken (1630–1714), a distinguished Confucianist. A complete translation is given by B. H. Chamberlain in his *Things Japanese*, London, Murray, 1905, pp. 502-8. "The five worst maladies that afflict the female mind (it says) are : indocility, discontent, slander, jealousy and silliness. Without any doubt these maladies infest seven or eight out of every ten women, and it is from these that arises the inferiority of women to men. A woman should cure them by self-inspection and self-reproach. The worst of them all and the parent of the other four is silliness."

11 Motoori Norinaga (1730–1801) was born near the sacred shrine of Isé and devoted most of his life to a study of Shinto and ancient litera-

ture. His *Kojiki-den*, Commentary on the *Kojiki*, comprises 44 volumes and occupied him for 32 years. It is remarkable for both its scholarship and its vigorous attack on Chinese ideas and institutions. Besides the *Kojiki-den*, which contains many of the seeds of the present discord in the Far East, Motoori wrote 54 other works on poetry, methods of study, abominable heresies, personal reminiscences, grammatical research, political reform, the prohibition of hari-kiri, etc. Undoubtedly disappointed in realizing after a lifetime of study that the *Kojiki* was rich in inconsistencies but devoid of moral value, Motoori commented that its very inconsistencies were proof of the authenticity of the document, for who would have gone out of his way to invent a story so ridiculous and improbable.

12 See *Narrative of the Expedition of an American Squadron to the China Seas and Japan, Performed in the Years 1852, 1853 and 1854 under the Command of Commodore M. C. Perry, United States Navy*, comp. from the original notes and journals of Commodore Perry and his officers, published by order of the Congress of the United States, Washington, 1856. Also, Edward Morley Barrows' *The Great Commodore*, New York, Bobbs Merrill, 1935.

13 See *The Complete Journal of Townsend Harris*, New York, Doubleday, 1930, p. 484.

CHAPTER XIV. THE SECOND GREAT CHANGE

1 Many of the details, concerning the foreign settlement, to be found in this chapter the author has drawn from M. Paske-Smith's *Western Barbarians in Japan and Formosa in Tokugawa Days*, Kobe, Thompson, 1930.

2 A favorite figure of Professor Tsunoda's, suggesting the part played by environment in making the Japanese genial, versatile and enduring.

3 (See Chap. XII, note 8). The following selections are somewhat condensed and do not represent the paragraph sequence of the original.

4 This is based on the fact that ryo and yen are synonymous and that the buying power of the yen in Japan is about equal to that of the dollar in the United States.

5 Heads of the Satsuma, Choshu, Tosa and Hizen clans.

6 W. W. McLaren, *Japanese Government Documents*, Trans., Asiatic Society of Japan, vol. XLII, part I, 1914, pp. 1-2.

7 Okubo as quoted by Scherer (see above Chap. XI, note 2), p. 231.

8 For description see Holtom (Chap. V, note 14 above).

9 These seventeen, Tokugawa adherents, were coerced by "Government" forces.

10 *Lectures on Japan*, by Inazo Nitobe, Tokyo, Kenkyusha, 1936, p. 91.

CHAPTER XV. ON THE WAY TO WORLD POWER

1   As expressed by Fukuzawa Yukichi.

2   *The Intercourse Between The United States and Japan*, Inazo Nitobe, Baltimore, Johns Hopkins Press, 1891, p. 180.   Other details told here of Japanese students in the United States and American advisers in Japan are also to be found in this book.

3   The majority of teachers in Japan today are men.

4   See *Grant in Peace, From Appomattox to Mount McGregor*, a Personal Memoir, by Adam Badeau, Hartford, Scranton, 1887.

    It is interesting to note that Grant went on to say, "A day of retribution is sure to come, these people are becoming strong, and China is sure to do so also.   When they do, a different policy will have to prevail from that imposed now."

5   For which see *Japan Manchoukuo Year Book*, Tokyo, 1937, pp. 298-344, also *Fortune*, September, 1936, pp. 135-7, 190-2.

6   See *McLaren* (above Chap. XIV, note 6), pp. 86-7.

7   See *Prince Ito*, by Kengi Hamada, Tokyo, Sanseido, 1936, and *Three Meiji Leaders — Ito, Togo, Nogi*, by James A. B. Scherer, Tokyo, Hokuseido, 1936.

8   Scherer (see above Chap. XI, note 2), p. 237.

9   This quotation and also the following one is from the *Encyclopædia Britannica*, vol. XII, p. 950.

CHAPTER XVI. UNEASY JAPAN

1   These designations "quaint," "amazing" and "presumptuous" are from the excellent leading article in *Fortune*, September, 1936, an issue devoted entirely to Japan, with the usual profusion of superior illustrations.

2   As far back as 1875 Japan, applying lessons learned from the West, had drawn Korea from her traditional isolation into the world of commerce, and had championed Korean independence from China.   As a result of the Russo-Japanese War, Korea had become a protectorate of Japan, but a very troublesome and expensive one it proved to be. In the summer of 1910 the following announcement was made : "An earnest and careful examination of the Korean problem has convinced the Japanese government that the regime of a protectorate can not be made to adapt itself to the actual condition of affairs in Korea, and that the responsibilities devolving upon Japan for due administration of the country can not be justly fulfilled without the complete annexation of Korea to the Empire."   Then Japanese troops were moved in, and the Korean dynasty was superseded by a Japanese Governor-General and his officials.

3   Known as "The Twenty-One Demands."

4   A cursory glance through the *New York Times Index* for this period reminds one of nation-wide strikes of railroad and marine workers which prevented the movement of raw materials and resulted in the closing of many mills and factories, the arrest of two hundred Reds in Chicago, Prohibition, bootlegging and the high cost of law enforcement, profiteering, Teapot Dome Oil Scandal, notification of Eugene Debs in Atlanta penitentiary of his nomination for the presidency of the United States, White Slave traffic, bank bandits and holdups, and an increasing number of divorces.

5   Local telephone service costs 200 yen a year, gasoline over half a yen per gallon, Ford license plates 400 yen, meat and butter almost a yen a pound, bread 20-30 sen a loaf, milk (sold in bottles containing less than ½ pint) 10 sen. (Sen = .01 yen.)

6   Japan, in 1937, according to Japanese Chamber of Commerce figures, imported raw cotton valued at ¥849,749,034, rayon pulp valued at ¥80,370,768, exported cotton textiles valued at ¥573,064,772, rayon textiles valued at ¥154,860,384.

7   Short term temporary loans of large sums were made to the Bank of England and to Russia ; some investments were made in other European countries. Large sums were also lent to China for development projects.

8   According to agreements reached between China and Japan in May, 1925, Japan proposed to establish :

    1.   A cultural research institute and library at Peking.
    2.   A natural science research institute at Shanghai.
    3.   Fellowships and scholarships for Chinese students abroad.

Work was begun on these projects in 1926. The institute at Shanghai initiated studies of medicinal herbs, fish of the Yangtze, bacilli, local and epidemic diseases, and carried on a geological survey. Needless to say, this whole project was "temporarily discontinued" in 1931.

9   See *Japan Manchoukuo Year Book* (Chap. XV, note 5 above), pp. 674-80.

10   *Fortune*, September, 1936, p. 80. Reproduced by permission of the editors.

11   Prince Fumimaro Konoe, 1891–

12   Cf. *Japan Manchoukuo Year Book*, Chap. XIV, Press and Publications, and *Fortune* article, September 1936, "No Left Turn."

13   As in England, broadcasting is financed by public subscription rather than by advertisers. The charge on every radio owner is 50 sen a month.

14   An outstanding leader in this is Michio Miyagi, a blind composer and koto player. See *Japanese Music*, Japanese Government Railways Tourist Library, vol. XV. Of contemporary painters, Yokoyama Taikan is dean. His landscape masterpieces are done in black ink wash. Wood-

block print landscapes, especially popular with Westerners, are being made by the able artist Hiroshi Yoshida.

15 Ginza — so called from the Tokugawa Silver Mint — now the street of Tokyo's most fashionable shops and restaurants.

Perhaps the most remarkable of these literary men was Dr. Shoyo Tsubouchi, who translated Shakespeare's complete works into Japanese, and was the pioneer of a New Theater movement in Japan. There is a museum of the theater in his honor at Waseda University. Other eminent authors of contemporary Japan whose works have been translated into Western languages are : Koyo Ozaki, Soseki Natsumé, Toyohiko Kagawa. There are also English translations of collections of poems by three contemporary women : Akiko Yosano, Takeko Kiyo, and one who calls herself "White Lotus."

GLOSSARY AND DICTIONARY OF JAPANESE PROPER NAMES

Ainu — Aborigines of Japan.

Akechi Mitsuharu (d. 1582) — A soldier in the service of Nobunaga.

Amaterasu — Sun Goddess, ancestress of the imperial family.

Amida Buddha — Buddha of the Western Paradise; a deity of mercy.

Ashikaga — A district about 100 miles north of Tokyo; the ancestral estate of the Ashikaga shoguns.

Ashikaga Takauji (1305–1358) — First Ashikaga shogun (1338–1358).

Asuka — A region south of Kyoto, site of ancient capital.

Bakufu — Camp administration; government with headquarters at Kamakura, 1185–1333.

bashi — Bridge.

Basho (1644–1694) — Japan's greatest poet; leader of haiku movement.

be — A sort of craft guild (early Japan).

Biwa, Lake — Largest lake in Japan, close to Kyoto.

bodhisattva — Buddhist saint.

Bungo — Province in northeastern Kyushu.

bushido — The warriors' code.

Chikafusa (Kitabatake Chikafusa), (1293–1354) — Leader of the Southern Dynasty and author of political treatise.

Chikamatsu (Monzaemon Chikamatsu), (1653–1724) — The most celebrated Japanese dramatist.

Chion-in — Headquarters of the Jodo sect in Kyoto; built in 1211.

cho — 2.45 acres.

Choshu — District in southwestern Japan, which belonged successively to Ouchi and Mori clans.

Chu Hsi (A.D. 1130–1200) — A Chinese philosopher on whose teachings official education in Japan was based during the Tokugawa period.

Daibutsu — Great statue of Buddha.

Daigo — Emperor, 897–930.

daimyo — Lit. "Great Name," a feudal lord.

Daruma — Indian Buddhist priest (of the sixth century) and saint.

Dazaifu — Government headquarters in Kyushu (Nara and Heian periods).

Deshima — Island off Nagasaki; center of Dutch trade.

Dokyo (d. 772) — Buddhist priest consort of Empress Koken; aspired to become emperor.

e — A painting, drawing, picture.

Eisai (1141–1215) — Famous Zen priest, architect.

Eitoku (Kano Eitoku) (1548–1590) — Official painter in service of Nobunaga.

eta — The most despised class of Japanese society, traditionally engaged in occupations having to do with the handling of dead bodies.

Fubito (Fujiwara Fubito) (659–720) — Son of Kamatari; minister during four reigns, father-in-law of Emperor Shomu.

Fugen — Bodhisattva of all-pervading wisdom, usually shown mounted on an elephant.

Fujisan, Mt. Fuji — Japan's sacred and highest mountain (12,467 ft.).

Fujiwara — District in central Japan given to Kamatari, from which Fujiwara family name is derived.

Fukuzawa, Yukichi (1835–1901)— Educational leader, founder of Keio University, Tokyo.

Gempei—Era of the Genji and Heike.

Genji (or Minamoto)— Military clan, derived from imperial princes during ninth and tenth centuries.

Genji, Prince — Fictitious hero of Japan's most famous novel by Lady Murasaki (c. 1000).

Genroku — Name of period of great commercial prosperity (1688–1703).

Genryaku — Name of period 1184–1185.

Ginkaku-ji — Silver pavilion built in Kyoto in 1473 by Ashikaga shogun, Yoshimasa.

Ginza — Silver mint, name of fashionable street in Tokyo.

giri — Duty.

Go-Daigo — Emperor (1319–1338).

Gyogi (670–749)— Buddhist priest.

Hachiman — Shinto god of war ; tutelary deity of Minamotos.

haiku — Seventeen syllable poem.

Hakodate — Principal seaport of Hokkaido.

Han (206 B.C.–220 A.D.)— Ruling dynasty in China.

Hayashi — Family of Tokugawa Education Ministers, wrote Honcho Tsugan c. 1650.

Heian — Peace and ease ; name of period 794–858.

Heian-kyo — Capital of peace and ease ; i.e. Kyoto, founded 795.

Heike (or Taira)— Clan descended from great-grandson of Emperor Kwammu.

Hideyori (1593–1615)— Son of Toyotomi Hideyoshi.

Hideyoshi (Toyotomi Hideyoshi), (1536–1598)— "The Taiko," military ruler of late 16th century.

Hieizan, Mt. Hiei — Mountain northeast of Kyoto, famous temple center.

hiki — A unit for measuring cloth — about 25 yards.

Hirado — Island off northwest coast of Kyushu ; Portuguese and English trading center.

hiragana — Phonetic symbols in running script.

Hiroshige (1797–1858)— Color print artist.

Hizen — Province in Kyushu.

Hojo — Branch of the Taira clan which ruled Japan 1199–1333.

Hojo-ji — Temple built c. 1000 by Fujiwara Michinaga in conjunction with his palace.

Hojo Tokimasa (1138–1215)— Father of Masa, wife of Yoritomo.

Hokkaido — Large northern island of Japan.

Horyu-ji — Buddhist temple founded by Prince Shotoku, early seventh century.

Isé — Province in central Japan where Sun Goddess is enshrined.

Ito (Hirobumi, Prince), (1841–1906)— Leader in Restoration movement and author of Constitution.

Itsukushima — Island of Inland Sea, better known as Miyajima.

Iyeyasu (1542–1616)— First Tokugawa Shogun, appointed 1603 ; had son appointed shogun in 1605.

Izumo — Province in northwestern Japan where Susanoo was enshrined.

ji — Temple.

Jimmu — Traditionally first emperor of Japan, 660–585 B.C.

Jingu, Empress — Traditionally first empress of Japan, 170–269 A.D., and conqueror of Korea.

Jocho (d. 1057)— Buddhist priest sculptor.

Jodo — Name of Buddhist sect founded by Honen, thirteenth century. To Jodoists, repetition of the name, Amida, was sufficient for salvation.

kabuki — Popular type drama.

Kai — One of the eastern provinces of Japan.

Kaifuso — Anthology of Chinese poetry of Nara period.

Kamakura — Headquarters of first shogunate, 1192–1333.

Kamatari (614–669) — Founder of the Fujiwara clan.

kami — Superiors or gods of the land.

kana — Phonetic symbols.

karuta — Playing cards.

kastera — Sponge cake.

katakana — Phonetic symbols in block script.

ke — Family, clan.

Kebiishi — Law-enforcing agency of the Heian period.

Kenzan (1663–1743) — Kyoto artist, designer in applied arts.

Kibi no Mabi (693–775) — Minister and scholar.

Kii — Peninsular province in central Japan.

Kinkaku-ji — Golden pavilion built in Kyoto by Ashikaga Yoshimitsu, 1397.

Kiyomori (Taira Kiyomori), (1118–1181) — Ruler 1159–1181.

Kojiki — Earliest history of Japan, 712.

Koken — Empress of Japan 749–759; reascended throne six years later as Empress Shotoku.

koku — Dry measure used for rice, about five bushels.

Komyo, Empress (701–760) — Wife of Emperor Shomu.

Korin (Ogata Korin), (1661–1716) — Artist.

koto — The classical stringed instrument.

Koyasan, Mt. Koya — Temple center of Shingon sect, founded by Kukai 816.

Kukai (745–835) — Founder of Mt. Koya, center of Shingon sect; posthumously known as Kobo Daishi.

Kwammu — Emperor of Japan (782–805).

kwan mon — Unit of weight — 1000 mon, 1 mon (or monme) = .12 oz. (troy); pertaining to currency, usually copper.

Kwanto — Half of Japan east of Lake Biwa.

kyogen — Lit. "foolish words"; short, humorous folk plays; used for comic relief on programs of Noh.

Kyoto — Capital founded by Emperor Kwammu, 795.

Kyushu — Southern island of Japan.

Lolang — Chinese colony in northern Korea in late Han period.

Loochoo (or Ryukyu) Islands — Islands scattered between Kyushu and Formosa.

Manyoshu — "Collection of 10,000 Leaves"; anthology of Japanese poems, Nara period.

Masa (Hojo Masa), (1157–1225) — Wife of Yoritomo.

Meiji — Reign of Enlightenment (1868–1912).

Michinaga (966–1027) — Fujiwara who brought family to zenith of its power.

Minamoto — See Genji.

Mito — City about fifty miles east of Tokyo.

Mitsukuni (1628–1700) — Head of Mito branch of Tokugawa family; initiated great historical work.

miyako — Capital.

Momokawa (Fujiwara Momokawa) (722–779) — Minister during two reigns; arranged succession of Emperor Kwammu.

monogatari — Narrative, tale.

Moronobu (Hishikawa Moronobu), (1688–1703) — Painter.

Motoori (Motoori Norinaga), (1730–1801) — Famous man of letters.

Murasaki, Lady — Author of Tale of Genji, c. 1000.

Musashi — Province in eastern Japan, especially Musashi Plain, the broadest in Japan.

Muso (1275–1351) — Zen priest and poet.

Nagasaki — Chief port of Kyushu, center of Dutch learning.

Naka, Prince — Associated with Kamatari and First Great Change; became Emperor Tenji (662–671).

Nara — First permanent capital of Japan, established 710.

Netsuké — Carved pendant.

Nichiren (1222–1282) — Nationalistic evangelist, founder of Buddhist sect.

Nihongi — Ancient chronicles of Japan, 720.

Nikko — Mountain shrine to Tokugawa Iyeyasu.

Ninigi — Grandson of Sun Goddess.

ninjo — Sentiment.

Nippon (or Nihon) — Ni (or hi) = sun, pon (or hon) = root, source. Nippon has recently been made the official pronunciation.

Nobunaga (Oda Nobunaga), (1534–1582) — Hero-general.

noh — Classical drama.

Nyorai — Saviour; name applied to certain Buddhist deities.

o-cha-no-yu — Lit. tea's hot water; tea ceremony.

Ogata — Kyoto scholar and schoolmaster, middle nineteenth century.

Onin Civil War — 1467–77 around Kyoto.

onyo-do — The way of Yin and Yang; a Chinese pseudo-scientific philosophy of natural phenomena used for divination.

Osaka — Castle town and seaport, central Japan.

Ouchi — Clan with capital in Yamaguchi, southwestern Japan, middle sixteenth century.

Owari — Province of eastern Japan.

pan — Bread.

roju — Members of Tokugawa shogun's council.

ryo — Old name for yen; standard of currency, varying in value in different periods.

Ryo no Gige — Commentary on law code, published 833.

Sado — Island in Japan Sea, frequent place of exile; contains gold and silver mines.

Saicho (767–822) — Founder of Hieizan temple center; posthumously Dengyo Daishi.

Saigo Takamori (1827–1877) — Army leader and hero of Satsuma clan.

Saikaku (d. 1693) — Realistic novelist.

Sakai — Seaport of central Japan, now part of Osaka.

saké — Rice wine; alcoholic content about 17%.

samisen — Three-stringed musical instrument usually associated with popular type music.

samurai — A feudal warrior and retainer.

san, zan, sen, yama — Various pronunciations of the symbol for "mountain."

Sanraku (Kano Sanraku), (1559–1635) — Official painter in service of Hideyoshi.

Satcho — Combination of Satsuma and Choshu clans (abb.).

Satsuma — District of S.W. Kyushu belonging to Shimazu family.

Seami (1363–1444) — Noh writer and actor.

Sei, Lady — Author of "Pillow Book," notes on Fujiwara court, c. 1000.

Sei-i Tai Shogun — Great Barbarian-subduing General.

Seika (Fujiwara Seika) (1561–1619) — Founder of school of Chu Hsi philosophy in Japan.

Sekigahara — Village near Lake Biwa, site of Iyeyasu's conclusive victory in October, 1600.

Sesshu (1420–1506) — Famous Zen painter.

shibumi — Lit. astringent taste; refined æsthetician.

Shikoku — One of the four main islands of Japan.

Shimoda — Port where first United States consulate was established in Japan, southeast of Izu Peninsula.

shinchu — An alloy very closely resembling gold in appearance.

Shingon — Buddhist sect founded in Japan in 806 by Kukai, with center at Mt. Koya.

Shinto — Way of the Gods ; national religion of Japan.

shogun — General.

Shomu, Emperor, 724–748 — Devout Buddhist.

Shoso-in — Storehouse belonging to Todai temple with treasures preserved from 756.

Shotoku, Prince — Regent (572–621). "Father of Japanese Culture."

shu — Sect or denomination.

Shuko (1422–1502) — Importer and connoisseur for Ashikaga Yoshimasa ; first master of tea ceremony.

Soga — Clan which usurped imperial power in 7th century.

Sui — Ruling dynasty in China (A.D. 589–618).

Suiko, Empress (593–628) — For whom Prince Shotoku was regent.

Susanowo — Impetuous Male, brother of Sun Goddess.

sutra — Buddhist scripture.

Taiho — Code of laws promulgated in 701.

Taiko — Lit. Great Lord (title of Hideyoshi), from which is derived our colloquial, tycoon, industrial magnate.

Taikwa — Great Change ; name for period 645–649.

Taira — See Heike.

tairo — Chief officials of the Tokugawa shogunate.

Tamura Maro (or Saka-no-Uye) (758–811) — First Sei-i Tai Shogun, Great Barbarian-subduing General.

T'ang — Ruling dynasty in China (618–907).

tanka — Thirty-one-syllable poem.

Temmu — Emperor 673–686.

tempura — Fish (usually shrimp) or vegetable covered with batter and fried in deep vegetable oil.

Tenji, Emperor (662–671) — See Naka.

Tenjin-Sama — God of letters.

Tenno — Son of Heaven, Emperor.

Tenryu-ji — Zen temple west of Kyoto, built by Muso, 1342.

Todai-ji — Buddhist temple erected at Nara in 728.

Tosa — Province in S.W. Japan.

tripitaka — Buddhist Bible.

T'sin — Chinese dynasty (255–202 B.C.).

ukiyo — Buddhist terminology, "fleeting or transient world" ; in Genroku travesty, "floating world," the gay pleasure-quarters.

Unkei (d. 1223) — great sculptor.

Uraga — Fishing village near Kamakura where Perry landed.

Usa — Place in Kyushu where shrine to Hachiman has been in existence since early eighth century — probably longer.

Vairocana — Buddhist deity identified with Sun Goddess ; the deity represented by the Nara Daibutsu.

Wa — Ancient Chinese name for Japan.

Yamaguchi — City in S.W. Japan.

Yamato — District in central Japan ; original settlement of imperial clan.

Yamato-e — Native Japanese style of painting.

yang — In Chinese philosophy the active, light elements of the universe.

Yayoi — A type of Stone Age pottery.

Yedo — Castle town and capital of Tokugawas ; since 1868, Tokyo.

yen — Standard of currency, corresponding in buying power in Japan to dollar in U. S. At par worth $.50.

yin — In Chinese philosophy the passive, dark elements of the universe.

Yoritomo (Minamoto) (1147–99) — First Military Dictator of Japan.

Yoshimasa (1435–1490) — Eighth Ashikaga Shogun.

Yoshimitsu (1358–1408) — Third Ashikaga Shogun.

Yoshinaka (Minamoto) (1154–1184) — A hero in the *Tale of Heike*.

Yoshino — Mountainous district in central Japan, famous for cherry blossoms, capital of southern court.

Yoshitsune (Minamoto) (1159– 1189) — Younger brother of Yoritomo.

za — Trade guild (mediæval Japan).

Zen — Buddhist sect; emphasis on meditation and practical accomplishment.

Zojo-ji — Temple in Tokyo built by Tokugawas.

INDEX